THE ROUGH GUIDE TO
Led Zeppelin

by
Nigel Williamson

ROUGH
GUIDES

Credits

The Rough Guide to Led Zeppelin

Design and layout: bounford.com
Editor: Andrew Heritage
Picture Research: Andrew Heritage
Index: Margaret Binns
This edition was prepared by Heritage Editorial and
bounford.com for Rough Guides Ltd.

Rough Guides Reference

Series editor: Mark Ellingham
Director: Andrew Lockett
Editors: Peter Buckley, Duncan Clark, Tracy Hopkins,
Sean Mahoney, Matt Milton, Joe Staines, Ruth Tidball

Picture Credits

Redferns: 3, 9, 10, 16, 27, 28, 31, 34, 38, 40, 44, 50, 52, 54, 59, 62, 69, 73, 76, 79, 83, 87, 89, 94, 97, 100,
103, 108, 112, 113, 119, 123, 124, 128, 131, 133, 135, 140, 153, 244, 245, 249, 251

Corbis: 46, 51, 82, 92, 143, 146

Private collections: 48, 56, 63 (Malcolm Strachan); 102, 103

Publishing Information

This first edition published August 2007 by
Rough Guides Ltd, 80 Strand, London WC2R 0RL
345 Hudson St, 4th Floor, New York 10014, USA
Email: mail@roughguides.com

Distributed by the Penguin Group:
Penguin Books Ltd, 80 Strand, London WC2R 0RL
Penguin Putnam, Inc., 375 Hudson Street, NY 10014, USA
Penguin Group (Australia), 250 Camberwell Road, Camberwell, Victoria M4P 27E, Australia
Penguin Books Canada Ltd, 10 Alcorn Avenue, Toronto, Ontario, Canada M4V 1E4
Penguin Group (New Zealand), 67 Apollo Drive, Mairangi Bay, Auckland 1310, New Zealand

Printed in Italy by Lego Print S.p.A

© Nigel Williamson, 2007
288 pages; includes index

A catalogue record for this book is available from the British Library

ISBN 13: 978-1-84353-841-7
ISBN 10: 1-84353-841-5
1 3 5 7 9 8 6 4 2

Contents

Contents cont.

Introduction

The rock world in 1968 was an amazing place. The Beatles had just released the *White Album* and the Stones had come storming back with *Beggar's Banquet*. Jimi Hendrix was at his explosive peak, The Who were soon to release *Tommy*, and Cream were the heaviest group around.

It was unsurprising, then, that few took much notice of a new group called Led Zeppelin, fronted by a session guitarist who had played on records by Lulu and Tom Jones and a singer nobody had heard of from an obscure band called Hobstweedle.

In fact, although they couldn't have known it at the time, Led Zeppelin's timing was perfect. Within two years, The Beatles had split, the Stones had retreated into tax exile, Hendrix was dead, Cream were no more and Pete Townshend was agonizing over how to follow The Who's groundbreaking rock opera. Zeppelin stepped into the breach, and remained the mightiest band in the world until 1980, when they called it a day following the death of John Bonham.

I confess that as a teenage rock fan I was one of those who initially ignored them. In 1969, I was 15 and fighting daily battles with the authorities at my local grammar school over my shoulder-length hair. Every Saturday afternoon a bunch of us would meet in Bromley High Street, Kent to sit in the soundproofed booths of W.H.Smith's, listening to new LPs that we didn't have the money to buy. The staff were indulgent and would usually allow you to hear both sides of an album and, if it wasn't too busy, maybe one side of a second album, too. When we'd pushed our luck too far and been thrown out, we'd drink coffee and share a packet of ten Senior Service at Lyon's Tea Shop in the market square or, if one of us had enough cash to score a quid deal that week, we'd retire to the municipal library gardens for a badly-rolled joint.

One Saturday in late March 1969, I was scuffling around Bromley High Street as usual with a bunch of school friends when a student from the local Technical College handed us a flyer advertising a show that evening featuring Led Zeppelin. I was already an enthusiastic attender at gigs at the college and had seen various bands there, including Jethro Tull. But I had no interest in seeing Zeppelin. I'd read about them in *Melody Maker* and concluded – stupidly, as it turned out – that they were simply a hyped-up new version of the old Yardbirds, whom I regarded with studied adolescent disdain as little more than a pop group who didn't qualify as a serious part of the "underground rock" scene. My best friend

Pete Badham, however, took a more enlightened view and reckoned they were well worth his pocket money. Several decades later he was able to write in *Led Zeppelin: The Concert File* that he had "felt privileged to be in at the start of something special". I didn't get to see them until almost two years later at the Royal Albert Hall, after I'd recognized the folly of my youthful snobbery, and I've been kicking myself ever since over that missed opportunity to see one of the earliest gigs by one of the greatest bands of all time, in a venue that probably held no more than 300 people.

In the years since, I've interviewed Jimmy Page several times and Robert Plant on numerous occasions. It's always dangerous for rock journalists to claim they've become "friends" with the stars they write about but I like to think that Plant has become just that. The first time I met him more than a decade ago, he arrived two hours late and apologized profusely. He than added, with a twinkle in his eye, that when Zep were in their pomp, I'd have been kept waiting not for two hours but for two weeks. I took to him immediately and we further bonded over a mutual love of African and Arabic music and a passion for gardening that, on one famously non-rock'n'roll occasion, found us swapping tips on the propagation of strawberry plants, much to the bemusement of those around us. Several years later, I was highly flattered when a taped interview I'd done with him was released as a bonus disc with some copies of his most recent album, *The Mighty Rearranger*.

In making some of the most visceral rock music ever heard, both live and on record, Led Zeppelin acquired mythological status – in the truest sense of the word. At a distance of 30 years and more, it has become almost impossible to tell which of the outrageous stories about them are true, which have grown in the telling and which are total fiction. This book attempts to unravel the myths from the truth, as well as analyzing the band's music and providing a guide to the solo careers of its individual surviving members. It's a story that – like Zeppelin's unforgettable music – has it all. We shall never see their like again.

Nigel Williamson
May 2007

Acknowledgements

Grateful acknowledgements to all the books, films, interviews and websites quoted herein. This book also draws on interviews by the author with Jimmy Page and with Robert Plant, who was kind enough to give the project his personal blessing. With additional thanks to Mark Ellingham and Andrew Lockett at Rough Guides, my editor Andrew Heritage and to Allan Jones at *Uncut*, who has regularly commissioned me to write about the band over the past ten years.

Finally, a special thank you as always to Magali, Adam and Piers. I only hope you enjoyed listening to a diet of non-stop Zep during the months I was writing the book…

About The Author

Nigel Williamson is a former news editor of *The Times* and a respected rock writer and journalist, whose work has appeared in many papers and magazines, including *Uncut*. His books include *Journey Through the Past: The Stories Behind the Classic Songs of Neil Young* (2002); *The Rough Guide to Bob Dylan* (2004) and *The Rough Guide to The Blues* (2007).

Part One:
The Story

Pre-Flight
1944–1968

"The four musicians that eventually came together as Led Zeppelin were a gift from on high..."

Jimmy Page, 2005

Pre-Flight
1944–1968

In rock'n'roll mythology, many of the great groups have a fateful moment when the principal players meet by chance or accident, recognize in a moment glowing with poetic resonance that they share a common destiny, and resolve to unite forces to take on the world. The famous encounter between John Lennon and Paul McCartney at a church fête in Woolton, Liverpool in 1957, or Mick Jagger and Keith Richards bumping into each other on a platform at Dartford railway station four years later come to mind. But the genesis of Led Zeppelin wasn't quite like that.

From Surrey To North Of The Watford Gap

The first meeting between **Jimmy Page** and **Robert Plant** was almost comical – according to Plant, Page and the band's larger-than-life manager, Peter Grant, mistook the singer for a roadie. What's more, unlike The Beatles or The Rolling Stones, whose members broadly shared a common social, cultural and geographical background, the two men came from very different sides of the street. Page hailed from the metropolitan suburbs of **Surrey**, within easy reach of swinging London. At 24, he was already a pop star, an urbane, seasoned session-man who had played on dozens of Top Ten hits and secured legendary status as the guitarist with **The Yardbirds**. Plant was from the stolid, unfashionable part of the **West Midlands** known as the "Black Country". At 19, he was still a gauche newcomer, with only a couple of failed solo singles to his name, associations with a few unsuccessful bands, and was contemplating the unwelcome prospect of having to quit music for a job in an accountant's office to support his pregnant wife and their imminent child.

The same disparities of background and experience existed between bassist **John Paul Jones** and drummer **John Bonham**, soon to unite as the band's crunching rhythm section. Jones was a sophisticated, in-demand session-player and arranger, whose credits included working with the Stones, and who moved in the same hip London music industry circles as Page. Bonham was a mate of Plant's from the Black Country with a rough-and-ready style, who balanced playing in a string of failed groups with working on a building site as a hod-carrier; his philosophy of drumming was simply to hammer away until the skins broke and his hands bled. As Plant recalled in 2005: "It was very obvious that Jimmy and Jonesy had a far more lateral collection of thoughts and ambitions and knowledge of what was going on than me and Bonzo. We were just wide boys from the sticks". It was out of these polar opposites that the loudest, heaviest and, many would say, greatest rock'n'roll band the world has ever known was forged.

In fact, Plant was far from first choice as the lead singer for the new group that The Yardbirds' guitarist Page and manager, **Peter Grant**, was putting together. "I don't think he'd played much down in the south of England, so consequently I hadn't heard of him", Page candidly admitted some years later. Top of his wish list had been the likes of **Stevie Winwood**, **Steve Marriott** and then **Terry Reid**. The latter turned the gig down but suggested instead his West Midlands mate, Plant. Hence, on 20 July 1968, Page, Grant and Yardbirds' bassist **Chris Dreja** found themselves travelling to Birmingham to see Plant singing at the local teacher training college with the unpromising band name Hobbstweedle.

The gig, by everyone's account, was not very good; Page reckons there were only about a dozen people in the audience. Nor did the band's covers of songs by Love, Buffalo Springfield and Moby Grape and Hobbstweedle's own fey, *Lord Of The Rings*-influenced fairy-ringed fancies fit the vision Page had in mind for the new group at all.

Yet Page heard something in Plant's voice that thrilled him, and he invited Plant to spend a few days at the plushly-renovated Victorian boathouse that was his home on the River Thames at **Pangbourne** in Berkshire, 30 miles upstream from central London, with the intention of exploring if there was sufficient common ground for them to work together. The would-be singer arrived at the guitarist's pop star home clutching a bunch of his favourite LPs and just enough money for his train fare back home if it all went horribly wrong. Fortunately, as they played each other their favourite albums and bounced around ideas, they discovered a musical bond. It was in that record-playing session that Led Zeppelin was, in effect, born.

Yet we are getting ahead of our story because each of the four members of Led Zeppelin came from very different backgrounds and brought such contrasting experiences to the group. Some serious pre-history is necessary.

Jimmy Page: Beat Boomer Baby

James Patrick Page was born on 8 January 1944 in Heston, Middlesex into a respectable, middle-class family. His father was a clerk in a wartime aircraft works and his mother a doctor's secretary. An only child, many of his earliest memories are of long holidays spent at a great-uncle's farm near Northampton, where

Page went fishing and chased butterflies. When the weather kept him inside, his stamp collection occupied much of his time, and there was no early indication of any musical talent. There wasn't even a family piano.

In 1952, his father took a step up in the world to became an industrial personnel officer and the family moved to a comfortable house in Miles Road, Epsom, a prosperous and leafy country town in Surrey. Music didn't enter his life in a serious way until four years later when he heard **Elvis Presley**'s 'Baby Let's Play House'. Yet while most of his contemporaries (including a young Robert Plant) were attracted by the voice and Presley's image, Page was far more interested in the musical accompaniment. In particular, he was drawn to the sound of the guitarist Scotty Moore.

A few months later, on his 13th birthday, his parents bought him a Spanish acoustic guitar with steel strings. His mother recalls sending him to a guitar teacher in Kingston for half a dozen lessons, but the tuition was rudimentary, and essentially Page set about teaching himself. A school friend showed him how to tune his guitar and he bought himself a copy of **Bert Weedon**'s indispensable *Play In A Day*.

Weedon had made his name as the featured soloist in Mantovani's orchestra and went on to become the improbable progenitor of British rock'n'roll guitar. Around the same time as Page was poring over *Play In A Day* and forcing his fingers to form the unfamiliar chord positions, George Harrison, Eric Clapton, Jeff Beck, Brian May, Pete Townshend and a number of others who were later to become household names were teaching themselves by following the same instruction book. "I always thought the good thing about guitar was that they didn't teach it at school", Page later observed. "Teaching myself to play was the first and most important part of my education".

British guitar hero Bert Weedon's enormously influential basic playing manual remains in print today

Unlike Robert Plant's parents, who were appalled by their son's attraction to rock'n'roll and told him it was "the Devil's music", Page's mother and father were supportive of his ambitions, and his father acted as guarantor when he bought his first electric guitar on a hire-purchase agreement – a cheap copy of a Fender Stratocaster called a Grazioso.

At school, Page was a good hurdler, a decent artist and bright enough to pass all his exams, but once the guitar took over, he swiftly lost interest in everything else and he left school in 1961, against his parents' wishes. However, although he was by now seriously proficient on the guitar and playing in local bands around Epsom, a professional music career still seemed a distant and unrealizable dream, so he applied for a job as a laboratory assistant.

Before he had a chance to take up the job, he was spotted at Epsom's Ebisham Hall playing

The Story

with a local rock'n'roll outfit called Red-E-Lewis and The Redcats by a singer and would-be manager called Chris Tidmarsh. Better known as **Neil Christian**, he was impressed enough with Page's ability to offer him a job in his backing group, The Crusaders. He even called upon Page's parents to reassure them that pop music wasn't as risky a venture as they might fear, and assured them that it offered plenty of exciting opportunities for a young musician as highly talented as their son. Christian was polite and persuasive, the flattery helped no end, and parental approval was duly given. At the age of 17, Page became a professional guitar player.

The Crusaders played rudimentary versions of Chuck Berry and Bo Diddley songs, but in their lead guitarist, who took the stage name Nelson Storm, it was clear they had a potential star in the making. Soon Page was making £20 a week – at the time probably double the average working wage – and he bought himself an orange Gretsch Country Gentleman guitar and a foot pedal, making him one of the first guitarists in London with such a gadget. Both his expertise and his equipment contributed to a fast-growing reputation; among those who came to check him out were **Jeff Beck** and future Led Zeppelin bass player, John Paul Jones: "I can remember people saying, 'You've got to go hear Neil Christian and The Crusaders, they've got this unbelievable young guitarist'", Jones recalls. "I'd heard of Pagey before I'd heard of Clapton or Beck".

His time in The Crusaders was cut short when, one night in late 1961 at a gig in Sheffield, the tyro guitarist collapsed. Always slightly built (Beck describes him as resembling "a shrimp" at this time), it seemed he lacked the constitution for life on the road and its accompanying regime of bad food and little sleep. Glandular fever was diagnosed, and the guitarist reluctantly returned to his parents' home in Epsom. When he had recovered, they persuaded him to enrol at art college in Sutton, Surrey.

Page was a talented artist. He insists that he was serious about his studies, and for a time wanted to become a painter. But a brush and easel were never going to take the place of a guitar and amp and art school, as for so many British musicians of his generation, provided the convenient means to a quite different end. First, it kept his parents happy. Secondly, he received a government grant. And thirdly, and most importantly of all, the student life gave him plenty of free time to practise the guitar.

His parents could hardly have been more supportive, turning over the downstairs front room of the family home to their only son as a music den. Among the visitors who played with him there was Jeff Beck, introduced by his sister Annetta, who knew Page as a fellow art student. "It was a lot of fun", Page's mother later recalled, "the jam sessions forced Jim's father and myself to develop an opinion about so-called heavy rock music. I found that I have a thing for it".

Incorporating The Blues

Page stayed 18 months or so at college before he began to feel the urge again to play somewhere bigger than his parents' front room. During his time at art school, he had been turning up at London's Marquee club to watch **Blues Incorporated**. Led by **Alexis Korner** and **Cyril Davies,** they were the first serious British blues band and a major influence on a generation of young musicians, including Mick Jagger, Brian Jones, Charlie Watts, Jack Bruce and Ginger Baker, all of whom played

Korner (right) and Cyril Davies at The Crawdaddy, Richmond, with a young Charlie Watts on drums

with them at one time or another. Page had also been asked to join when he was in The Crusaders, an invitation he declined, although he occasionally joined them in jam sessions. It was on one such evening that he met **Eric Clapton** for the first time. "He came up to me and said 'You play like Matt Murphy, Memphis Slim's guitarist", Page recalled. He was impressed by Clapton's sharp ear for he admitted that he had, indeed, "been following Murphy quite heavily".

When Blues Incorporated fell apart, Korner soon transferred his allegiance to the rival Flamingo Club. But as Page re-emerged onto the London gigging scene, he continued to turn up at the Marquee's blues nights to jam during the interval spot and also played at those other shrines of the early London R&B scene, **The Crawdaddy Club** in Richmond and **Eel Pie Island.** Suddenly, it seemed there were legions of like-minded musicians – young white British guys raised in the lace-curtained gentility of the Home Counties and obsessed with the music of black sharecroppers from the Mississippi Delta. "Most of us had the same upbringing", Page recollects. "We'd been locked away with our blues records and then we came out with something really new to offer Britain. It just exploded from there".

That explosion was taking place, simultaneously, all over the country. In London it produced **The Rolling Stones** and The Yardbirds. In Newcastle, it gave birth to The Animals. **The Spencer Davis Group** would soon emerge in Birmingham, and the ripples crossed the

The Story

Irish Sea to Belfast, where **Van Morrison** was putting together a band called Them.

Yet although Page would eventually join The Yardbirds, he was not to be part of the first wave of British R&B groups who would go on to conquer America in the wake of The Beatles. Instead, a potentially far more lucrative offer came along when he was invited to join the elite crew of top London session musicians. The initial invitation came from tape operator **Glyn Johns** and one of Page's first sessions found him playing on 'Diamonds' by Jet Harris and Tony Meehan, who had just left The Shadows. The single went to Number One and his art school days were over. "I was missing lectures, taking days off and I finally had to make a choice", he later remembered. "I was really enjoying the work. Many of the sessions were really good and I was allowed to do the solos, which I found to be really constructive work. So it was down to painting or playing. It wasn't too difficult a decision".

'Diamonds' was followed by a session with Carter Lewis and The Southerners and Page was briefly persuaded to join them, before he realized that studio work was far more lucrative. As he seemed able to play in any style and imitate almost any other guitarist, demand for his skills was high, particularly as at the time the supply was severely limited. Indeed, just about the only other serious guitarist on the London session scene was **Big Jim Sullivan**, and as the British Beat Boom got into full swing, it became de rigeur that if you needed a guitarist, you booked Big Jim or "Little Jimmy", as Page inevitably became known.

Eminence grise: Page (cravatted, centre) with (left to right) pop babe Lulu, Yardbird Keith Relf, producer Mickie Most, and Herman's Hermits Derek Leckenby and the famously dentally-challenged Peter Noone

Soon he was playing on early recordings by the likes of Them, The Kinks and The Who as top producers such as **Shel Talmy** and **Mickie Most** preferred Page's known virtuosity to gambling on the unknown talent of the groups' resident guitar players. Sometimes they were up to the task, which is why Page was only required to play rhythm guitar behind Pete Townshend's lead on The

Jimmy Page's Top Twenty '60s Sessions

From the tens (if not hundreds) of recordings in the 1960s to which Page contributed as a hired session-man, these are among the more famous hits that "Little Jimmy" played on.

'DIAMONDS' Jet Harris and Tony Meehan, 1963 (UK Number One)

'TWIST AND SHOUT' Brian Poole & The Tremeloes, 1963

'THE CRYING GAME' Dave Berry, 1964 (Page played acoustic, while Big Jim Sullivan played fuzz guitar parts)

'YOU REALLY GOT ME' The Kinks, 1964 (UK Number One)

'TERRY' Twinkle, 1964

'WALK TALL' Val Doonican, 1964

'AS TEARS GO BY' Marianne Faithfull, 1964

'SHOUT' Lulu & The Luvvers, 1964

'TOBACCO ROAD' The Nashville Teens, 1964

'HERE COMES THE NIGHT' Them, 1965

'IT'S NOT UNUSUAL' Tom Jones, 1965 (UK Number One)

'I CAN'T EXPLAIN' The Who, 1965

'DIGGIN' MY POTATOES' Heinz, 1965 (a myth also exists that Page played on Heinz's 1965 hit 'Just Like Eddie')

'I'M NOT SAYIN'' Nico, 1965

'THE PIED PIPER' Crispian St. Peters, 1966

'TIME DRAGS BY' Cliff Richard, 1966

'SUNSHINE SUPERMAN' Donovan, 1966

'OUT OF TIME' Chris Farlowe, 1966 (UK Number One)

'(WITH) A LITTLE HELP FROM MY FRIENDS' Joe Cocker, 1968 (UK Number One)

'LITTLE ARROWS' Leapy Lee, 1968

Page also played on an early version of The Rolling Stones, 1965 'Heart of Stone', but only on a demo tape, not the final release. Other lesser known bands he sessioned with include Carter-Lewis and The Southerners, The Lancastrians, The Primitives, The Factotums, Les Fleurs De Lys and The Fifth Avenue.

Who's 'I Can't Explain'. On other occasions, such as **Them**'s first session, not only the guitarist but the entire band were replaced by session players. "The group went in thinking they were going to record and all of a sudden they find these other people playing on their records", Page recalled of the first Them sessions, "it's a miracle they didn't replace Van Morrison as well".

One American authority has asserted that Page played on "anywhere between 50 to 90 per cent of the records released in Britain in the 1963–65 era". It's a ridiculous exaggeration – but perhaps not that ridiculous. Page was in huge demand, playing up to a dozen sessions per week. For a while, he didn't seem to care what he played on, as long as he was paid well enough; alongside his hipper clients, he provided the guitar parts for the likes of Burt Bacharach, P.J. Proby, Herman's Hermits and **Cliff Richard**. His guitar can be heard on a number of TV jingles from the time and he admits to having been paid to record cheap muzak for supermarkets (see box above)

Eventually, he grew tired of prostituting his talents and later referred to his sessioning period with some embarrassment as "grovelling around". Stepping from the anonymous shadows of uncredited accompanist to take the spotlight, in 1965 he recorded his first – and only – solo single, 'She Just Satisfies'. Released on Fontana, it found the guitarist singing and playing every instrument except the drums, while the B-side included backing vocals from his girlfriend of the time, the American singer-songwriter Jackie de Shannon. The record failed to bother the chart compilers, and Page swiftly decided that singing and a solo career were not for him.

From A.L.O. To The Yardbirds

Producing, however, was a different story. Sometime early in 1965, **Andrew Loog Oldham,** who in addition to managing The Rolling Stones had by now set up his own label, Immediate, contacted him and asked him to produce Eric Clapton for a British blues series he was planning. Together they cut four tracks, 'Telephone Blues', 'I'm Your Witchdoctor', 'Sittin' On Top Of The World' (a Howlin' Wolf song later to become a **Cream** favourite) and 'Double Crossing Time'. Around the same time he was also sounded out about replacing Clapton in The Yardbirds. But the money he was making playing sessions (at the time he could be heard on no less than three records in the British Top Ten), was too good to give up for an uncertain life in a beat group and he was still wary following his collapse on the road with Neil Christian and The Crusaders. He recommended instead his friend Jeff Beck, who was probably second on the group's shopping list in any case.

Page also recorded several more tracks with Clapton. Little more than blues jams taped in the front room of Page's parents' home, they were never intended for release but appeared on two compilations called *Blues Anytime*, released by Immediate in 1968, much to Clapton's chagrin. Although Page denied all blame for their release, it led to a rupture in their friendship that was never really healed.

The relationship between Page and Beck, however, continued to flourish. Page was present in the studio when The Yardbirds recorded

Andrew Loog Oldham, not satisfied with simply managing and producing The Rolling Stones, wanted to create an "Immediate" R'n'B empire

'Heart Full of Soul', the follow-up single to their breakthrough hit 'For Your Love' and lent him his fuzz box to play on the track. A group of Indian musicians had also been booked for the session and Page ended up buying a sitar from them, making him probably the first British rock guitarist to experiment with the instrument, ahead of **George Harrison**. In May 1966, the two guitarists recorded an instrumental called 'Beck's Bolero' in London's IBC Studios on which they were backed by The Who's drummer Keith Moon, bass player John Paul Jones and keyboardist Nicky Hopkins. Despite the title, and the fact that it subsequently appeared as the B-side of Beck's first solo single, 'Hi Ho Silver Lining', the track was largely written and produced by Page, who enjoyed the experience so much that there was talk of the two guitarists forming a group. Names that were thrown around as possible members included **John Entwistle** on bass (rather than Jones at this stage) and either The Small Faces' Steve Marriott or The Spencer Davis Group's Stevie Winwood on vocals.

In the event the plans came to nothing, but it was clear that Page was growing increasingly frustrated and felt his own creativity was being stifled as a guitar-for-hire session man. At the second time of asking, in June 1966, he agreed to join The Yardbirds.

Initially, he deputized on bass for Paul Samwell-Smith, who had quit suddenly and went on to become an acclaimed producer. But the understanding was always that once the band's other guitarist, Chris Dreja, had learnt the bass parts, Page would switch to guitar, giving The Yardbirds a dream-like double-lead attack.

Sadly, the Beck-Page incarnation of The Yardbirds never delivered on its huge promise and was to last a mere four months. In October 1966, just two dates into an American tour, the increasingly erratic Beck walked out. The band decided not to replace him and continued as a quartet. Page did his best to steer The Yardbirds in a musically credible direction, developing at least some of the elements that he would subsequently explore further in Led Zeppelin. But his efforts were derailed by producer Mickie Most, whose relentless pursuit of hit singles, and contempt for the album format, led to such miserable covers as 'Ha Ha Said The Clown' (on which Keith Relf was actually the only Yardbird to appear) and meant that the interesting ideas Page had for The Yardbirds' 1967 LP *Little Games* were left sadly under-developed.

By early 1968, it was clear the group was staggering towards a messy end and the group's final gig came in July that year at an end-of-term dance at Luton Technical College. Together with Dreja, Page began putting together a new line-up and attempted to recruit singer Terry Reid and drummer **B.J. Wilson**. Both declined and Dreja also left the scene to take up a career in photography. Enter fellow session-man John Paul Jones, a wild and untamed Midlands drummer named John Bonham and a young little-known singer from West Bromwich called Robert Plant....

Robert Plant: The Blues Had A Baby...

Robert Anthony Plant – later 'Percy' to his friends – was born on 20 August 1948 in West Bromwich, Staffordshire. His father was a civil engineer and the family soon moved to an affluent new home in the upscale Hayley Green area of the quiet Worcestershire town of **Kidderminster**, famous mostly for its manufacture of high quality carpets. Plant was by all accounts a bright child who devoured books and at eleven he earned a place at the King Edward VI Grammar School in nearby Stourbridge, although by then he had already fallen in love with rock'n'roll and decided he wanted to be Elvis. By the age of 13 he was spending hours in front of his bedroom mirror perfecting Presley's hip wiggle and pelvic gyrations as he sang 'Hound Dog' in an uncertain, quavering voice that was just beginning to break.

His passion for rock'n'roll horrified his strait-laced, middle-class parents who, he claims, denounced the new sounds coming out of Memphis, New Orleans and other American cities as "the Devil's music". One of his favourite stories has them cutting the plug off his record player after he had spun Chris Kenner's 'I Like It Like That' 17 times in one hour. As his school studies fell by the wayside, Plant put his enquiring mind to work researching the roots of early rock'n'roll and soon discovered the **Delta blues** and the electrified sounds emanating from Chicago on labels such as Chess and Vee-Jay.

By 14 or 15, he was hanging out not with his fellow Grammar School pupils but with a more bohemian crowd from the near-by Stourbridge Art School and, using his pay-packet from a Saturday job in Woolworth's to buy the first LP release of **Robert Johnson**'s legendary sessions, recorded a quarter of a century earlier. He also began singing with a school group called Andy Long and His Original Jaymen. Despite stern parental disapproval, by 1963, Plant's father was driving his 15-year-old son every week to the Seven Stars Blues Club in Stourbridge, on the grounds that this at least allowed him to keep an eye on the bad company their son was keeping. At the club, Plant happily jammed – on washboard and kazoo – with the Delta Blues Band, murdering songs by the likes of Johnson, **Muddy Waters** and **Howlin' Wolf**. Grammar School could no longer hold him, and that summer he left, although he couldn't quite shed the shackles of parental expectation at such a young age and began training as a chartered accountant. Almost immediately, he knew he had made a terrible mistake and that autumn enrolled at a local technical college to get some A-levels.

Yet whatever way he looked at it, school, accountancy and college were all distractions from his desired path, as he rebounded from one failed West Midlands band to another – many of them named after his favourite blues songs, such as the Crawling King Snakes (with a certain John Bonham on drums) and Black Snake Moan. He also tried various sartorial fashions, becoming a full-on Mod after seeing The Small Faces and The Who play a concert in Birmingham.

When, in late 1966, one of his unsuccessful bands The Tennessee Teens transmuted into Listen and were signed by CBS, he made his recorded debut as a singer on their first and only single, a cover of The Young Rascals' 'You Better Run'. When it flopped, the band were swiftly dropped and despatched back to West Midlands oblivion, but CBS persevered with Plant for two solo singles, 'Our Song' (backed with 'Laughing Crying Laughing') and 'Long Time Coming' (coupled with 'I've Got A Secret'), both released in 1967. Listen to these teenage efforts today and, while the material is obviously unsuitable, it is just possible to make out the first rumblings of the potent singer he was to become. To Plant's embarrassment, CBS marketed him as a middle-of-the-road balladeer, like a blonde surrogate of **Tom Jones** or another **Long John Baldry**, a one-time respected British blues singer, who had just had a Number One hit with the schmaltzy 'Let The Heartaches Begin'.

Away from stilted poses of record company promo shots, other photos of Plant at the time – including one taken at a "legalize pot'" protest – reveal a dope-smoking hippie in velvet kaftan and love beads. Desperate as he was to succeed, ultimately it was to his relief that both singles flopped hopelessly.

...And They Called The Baby Rock'n'Roll

By this time, he had left home amid considerable family rancour: his parents simply couldn't understand how he could throw away a comfortable future as a chartered accountant for the dubious life of an unsuccessful pop singer, and told him so in no uncertain terms. After a period sleeping on friends' sofas (including John Bonham's), he moved into a multi-occupancy house in Walsall, full of first-generation immigrants, accompanied by his Anglo-Indian girlfriend Maureen, whom he had met at a Georgie Fame concert in 1966. The couple were to marry in 1968, less than three months after Plant's 20th birthday.

After his failed solo career, Plant was forced to support the pregnant Maureen by taking a day job as a navvy on a road-laying gang (he later claimed that he had been personally responsible for spreading "half the asphalt on West Bromwich High Street"). But when he took off his work clothes of an evening and donned his velvet flares and flower-patterned lace shirt, he spent his nights singing with **Band Of Joy**. The group's first line-up was little more than a soul covers band, but when Plant was unceremoniously sacked by a manager who told him he couldn't sing, his response was to form a rival band with the same name and take them in a more psychedelic direction, indulging his new passion for the West Coast sound of bands such as Buffalo Springfield, Moby

Grape, Jefferson Airplane and Love. With Bonham on drums, Kevin Gammond on guitar, Chris Brown on keyboards and Paul Lockie on bass, the second Band Of Joy very nearly made it, too, expanding their circle of gigs beyond the West Midlands to London clubs such as **UFO** and **The Speakeasy**, supporting Fairport Convention and Ten Years After and joining American singer-songwriter **Tim Rose** on a tour bill that also included Terry Reid.

Full of optimism, the band recorded some demos at Regent Studios in London in early 1968, but a recording contract remained elusive. One of the tracks, 'Adriatic Sea View', would eventually surface in 1989 when Plant donated it to a fund-raising cassette compilation for a community project at Kidderminster College, run by former Band Of Joy guitarist Gammond, who would also reunite with Plant in the late 1990s in his low-key pub band, the

A glum-looking Band of Joy, with Plant second from left and Bonham over his shoulder, pretending that winter in Holland Park is the "Summer of Love" in the Golden Gate Park

Priory Of Brion. Covers of Tim Rose's 'Hey Joe' and Buffalo Springfield's 'For What It's Worth' from the same session finally emerged on Plant's 2003 two-disc career retrospective, *Sixty Six To Timbuktu*.

Yet by the spring of 1968 it was clear the Band Of Joy were going nowhere. The final straw came when the engine dropped out of their van onto the road while on the way to a gig in York. The father of bass player Paul Lockey was summoned to rescue them and, faced with a bill of several hundred pounds for a tow-away and a new engine, the band threw in the towel.

Musical history might have been very different if Plant had joined a band from Wolverhampton called **Slade,** led by his friend Noddy Holder, who had once roadied for one of Plant's bands. But his recruitment was vetoed at the last minute – depending on which story you believe, either because Holder didn't want to share the microphone or because the rest of the then proto-skinhead group thought the golden-maned future golden god of cock-rock was an arrogant hippie poseur. Conceivably, both accounts are true, and it's hard to imagine Plant as a shaven-headed skin in cherry-red DMs and red braces chanting 'Cum On Feel The Noize'.

For a while he worked on an *ad hoc* basis as a duo with British blues veteran Alexis Korner, who had been impressed with him at a Band Of Joy gig at The Speakeasy. They even recorded a few tracks for a never-released album, including 'Operator', which

J.R.R. Tolkein/ Summer Of Love

Three books formed part of the inventory of every hippie's ruck-sack: Aldous Huxley's *Doors of Perception,* recounting his use of LSD; Hermann Hesse's *Steppenwolf* concerning an hallucinatory voyage to self-aware-ness; and Oxford medi-evalist J.R.R Tolkien's *The Lord Of The Rings.* This elaborate descrip-tion of an arcane world where humble hobbits voyage through Middle Earth to confront the ultimate evil, aided and abetted by magicians, elves, dwarves, dark riders and orcs, provided an ideal fantasy realm for habitual dope and acid users. It sparked off a fantasy sub-movement in "progres-sive" rock, not just with Plant's band Hobstweedle, but influencing bands such as Caravan and Yes. Despite Page's disdain for Hobstweedle, his own taste for the occult soon combined with Plant's for Tolkeinesque imagery to form a golden thread through Zeppelin's work, in songs such as 'The Battle of Evermore', 'Houses Of The Holy' and, ulti-mately, 'Stairway To Heaven'. Page commissioned artwork of The Hermit (above) for the gatefold of *Led Zeppelin IV* which could have sprung directly from the pages of Tolkien.

later turned up on a Korner LP and Plant's own *Sixty Six To Timbuktu*.

The sense of drift was deepened when he failed an audition for Denny Cordell's Regal Zonophone label, after a strong recommendation from Tony Secunda, who managed another Midlands band, **The Move**, with whom Plant was on friendly terms. Cordell, who at the time was preoccupied with masterminding **Joe Cocker**'s career, apparently had "reservations" about Plant's sense of timing as a singer. After this disappointment, he seriously considered going back to a desk and taking his chartered accountancy exams, having promised himself (and Maureen, who was by now pregnant) that if he hadn't made it by the time he was 20, he would settle down in a "proper job". In all probability he didn't really mean it, but things were looking desperate when in the summer of 1968, he abandoned the Mississippi Delta for Middle Earth and joined the appallingly-monickered Hobbstweedle, named in honour of J.R.R.Tolkien's *The Lord of The Rings*.

Then a telegram from Peter Grant arrived, suggesting that he might care to audition for The Yardbirds. Suspecting a practical joke, Plant ripped it up. Fortunately, the persistent Grant sent a second message in which he invited himself, Jimmy Page and Chris Dreja up to Birmingham to see Hobbstweedle – or rather, to see the band's lead singer. The job in the chartered accountant's office could wait, and Plant still has that second telegram framed on his wall.

John Paul Jones: Born To Play

Born John Baldwin on 3 January 1946 in Sidcup, Kent, the future Led Zeppelin bass player came from a musical family. His parents worked as a musical comedy and variety duo, but his father Joe Baldwin also had a more serious side as a pianist and arranger for a number of big bands in the 1940s and 1950s, including perennial favourites of the BBC's Light Programme, Ambrose and his Orchestra.

By the time young John had been packed off to Christ College boarding school, he was already an accomplished piano player and could read music expertly. He was soon playing the pipe organ in the school chapel as if he had been born to it and at the age of fourteen he became choirmaster at his local church. At the same time, his teenage musical curiosity soon led to a passion for the jazz keyboards of the likes of **Fats Waller** and **Jimmy Smith**. Keen to play a second instrument, he toyed briefly with the saxophone, at the suggestion of his father, but after hearing the instrumental 'You Can't Sit Down' by the Chicago-based Phil Upchurch Combo, he resolved to become a bassist, his trained musical brain having decided that it was the bass part that gave a song its shape and direction.

After experimenting by restringing the family's ancient ukulele to resemble a bass, he cajoled his father into acting as guarantor on the hire purchase of a solid-body electric bass guitar, which he then amplified via a suitably adapted television set. By late 1960, as he approached his 15th birthday, he was leading an intriguing musical double life, playing organ at Sunday evensong and bass guitar with a beat combo at the church youth club straight afterwards. His first paid engagement came in a band which included his father on piano. Further bookings followed at fêtes, weddings, army bases, hunt balls and even Masonic lodges around north-west Kent and London's south-eastern suburbs. One summer, there was even a residency at a yacht club in Cowes on the Isle of Wight. Meanwhile, away from playing with his father, Jones pursued his rock'n'roll ambitions with a band called The Deltas and, in early 1963, he gatecrashed an audition in the upstairs room of a Soho pub for a new band being assembled to back two former members of The Shadows – Jet Harris and Tony Meehan – on whose Number One hit single, 'Diamonds', a certain session guitarist called Jimmy Page had already played.

Jones got the job and, armed with a new Fender Jazz bass and Vox amplifier, spent the next year touring with Harris and Meehan, adopting the stage name John Paul Jones, inspired by a 1959 film about the American War of Independence naval hero on suggestion of the duo's manager – not, as is widely reported in several of the many books about Led Zeppelin, at the behest of Rolling Stones' manager Andrew Loog Oldham, who attempted to launch him on a solo career.

Oldham produced Jones' only solo single, 'Baja', released on Pye in early 1964, a bouncy, beat-group instrumental typical of the period which found him playing six-string bass with overdubbed orchestration. The B-side was called 'A Foggy Day In Vietnam' and didn't feature Jones at all but "The Andrew Loog Oldham Orchestra", and it seems likely that members of The Rolling Stones played on the track. Yet like Jimmy Page's lone solo single, 'Baja"s only useful purpose was to make it evident that the talented but undemonstrative Jones was not cut out to be a solo star.

Instead, he drifted into studio session work, first for **Tony Meehan**, who by 1964 had become a staff producer at Decca, and then for the likes of Oldham and Mickie Most. "Organ was originally my favourite instrument", he has said of the period. "But for session playing, I found it much easier to carry a bass guitar to work than a Hammond".

Getting Groovy

Paradoxically, the man who was to become Led Zeppelin's "straight one" was reputedly a bit of a raver in his early years. **David Bowie** claims that it was an 18-year-old Jones who persuaded him to smoke marijuana for the first time. "Pop music was all pills in those days", Jones later admitted. He also reportedly gatecrashed a coming-of-age party at 11 Downing Street thrown for Caroline Maudling, the daughter of the Conservative Chancellor of the Exchequer, Reginald Maudling.

The Story

Heavily influenced by the thick, fat bass lines he was hearing on Tamla Motown records, Jones went on to play bass (and often keyboards, too) on records by The Rolling Stones, Herman's Hermits, Donovan, Jeff Beck, Cat Stevens, Rod Stewart, Shirley Bassey, Dusty Springfield, Lulu, the Walker Brothers and countless others – many of them far too embarrassing to mention in polite musical company. "You would do The Rolling Stones, the Everly Brothers, French rock'n'roll sessions, German ones, Engelbert Humperdinck and Tom Jones – and all in the same day quite often", he recalled many years later.

His breakthrough into arranging came on **Donovan**'s 1966 hit 'Sunshine Superman', although it came about by accident. "I happened to be on the session as a bass player but the arranger they'd picked really didn't know anything", he later recalled. "I got the rhythm section together and we went from there. Arranging and general studio direction were much better than just sitting there and being told what to do". His next assignment was arranging for **Herman's Hermits** (and helping them to sell more records in America during the course of 1966 than The Beatles). Before long he'd landed an even more prestigious gig when he was asked to help out The Rolling Stones on 'She's A Rainbow', creating the elaborately baroque arrangement that is one of the highlights of their 1967 album *Their*

Mickie Most's ambitious Yardbirds album *Little Games* failed to hit the spot (despite the great psychedelia-meets-super-hero-comic design)

Satanic Majesties Request.

On many of his sessions for producers such as Most and Oldham, he would bump into Jimmy Page. The two were hardly close friends but there was already developing a strong mutual respect, reinforced when Jones came up with the orchestral arrangement and played the cello on the title track of The Yardbirds' 1967 album *Little Games* and contributed to the band's misconceived single, 'Ten Little Indians'.

Jones was also invited by Page to play on 'Beck's Bolero', a 1966 track which also featured The Who's drummer **Keith Moon**. He was only wheeled in after first choice John Entwistle failed to show up, but the track worked so well that it became an early template for the sound of the new band that Page would eventually form two years later – and which, of course, would feature Jones on bass and keyboards.

It was after working in the studio with Page on Donovan's 1968 hit single 'Hurdy Gurdy Man', that Jones rang the guitarist to enquire about a new band he was putting together out of the ashes of The Yardbirds. His wife had pointed out to him a news item in *Disc & Music Echo* which reported that Page was recruiting musicians, and Jones wondered whether he might need a bass player. Session work was beginning to pall for him, just as it had for Page.

"John Paul Jones was an incredible arranger and musician and he didn't need me for a job", Page subsequently recalled. "It was just that he

The Story

John Paul Jones' Top Ten '60s Sessions

As a bass player, keyboardist and arranger, John Paul Jones, like Jimmy Page, was involved in literally hundreds of sessions in the mid-1960s. These ten are just the tip of the iceberg but display the sheer diversity of his talents. How many of them he ever put on the stereo when he got home for his personal listening pleasure is another matter...

'SUNSHINE SUPERMAN' *Donovan, 1966*

'NO MILK TODAY' *Herman's Hermits, 1966*

'A GROOVY KIND OF LOVE' *Wayne Fontana and The Mindbenders, 1966*

'THE THIRD DEGREE' *Marc Bolan, 1966*

'HI HO SILVER LINING' *Jeff Beck, 1967*

'TEN LITTLE INDIANS' *The Yardbirds, 1967*

'THE BOAT THAT I ROW' *Lulu, 1967*

'MATTHEW AND SON' *Cat Stevens, 1967*

'DELILAH' *Tom Jones, 1968 (UK Number Two)*

John Bonham: Keeping The Beat

John Henry Bonham was born on 31 May 1948 in Redditch, about ten miles south of Birmingham in the green and pleasant rolling pastures of Worcestershire. The son of a carpenter and the oldest of three children, his future calling was evident from an early age as he bashed pots and pans and any other household object from which he could coax a rhythm. "I'd wanted to be a drummer since I was about five years old", he later recalled. "Later I played a bit of acoustic guitar but it was always drums, first and foremost. I felt nothing for any other instrument".

At the age of ten, his mother bought him a snare drum (he'd already attempted to make his own with a coffee tin and a piece of loose wire) and, by the age of 15, his father had bought him his first full kit, a second-hand job on which most of the metal had rusted. His drive was evident to all; it was simply that nobody knew where it was going to take him. "He will either end up as a dustman or a millionaire", one of his school reports concluded.

Bonham himself had no doubts about his direction: "As soon as I left school, I decided I was definitely going to be a drummer. I was very determined", he told a percussion magazine in the 1970s. By 1964, he was drumming with his first band, Terry Webb and The Spiders, dressed in a uniform of purple jackets with velveteen lapels and a bootlace tie, topped

felt the need to express himself, and he thought that we might be able to do it together. He had a proper music training and he had quite brilliant ideas". Jones confirms his disenchantment with his lucrative life as a session player. "I was becoming a vegetable and I wasn't saying anything musically", he explained many years later. "I was churning this stuff out, and making a ton of money, doing 20–30 arrangements a month for everybody – and going crazy". Page told Jones he was going to see an unknown singer Terry Reid had told him about, and promised to call him when he'd checked them both out.

off with Elvis Presley-style greased-back hair. A highlight of their repertoire was a version of **Little Richard**'s 'Good Golly Miss Molly', the drum pattern from which was later reborn as 'Rock And Roll' on *Led Zeppelin IV*.

A brief sojourn in another group, The Nicky James Movement, came to an abrupt end when the combo's hire-purchased equipment was repossessed at a gig. Next, he replaced future Move drummer Bev Bevan in The Senators, with whom Bonham reputedly recorded a 1964 single called 'She's A Mod' – presumably with the grease now washed out of his hair. A spell with Pat Wayne and The Beachcombers followed before he joined a group called A Way of Life and then Locomotive, who were not named after Bonham's relentless rhythmic style, although they might well have been. Then, at 18, his promiscuous drumming career almost came to a premature end when he married **Pat Phillips**, a girl he had met at a dance near his family's home in Kidderminster and with whom he would soon have a son, **Jason**. "I swore to Pat that I'd give up drumming when we got married", he later said. "But every night I'd come home and sit down at the drums and just play. I'd be miserable if I didn't".

Home by this stage was a 15-foot caravan trailer, and the Bonhams were so broke that he had to give up smoking to meet the rent on even this humble residence. On the grounds that he could hardly earn any less money making music than he was casual labouring as a hod-carrier on a building site, he eventually decided to give drumming one last go. If it didn't work out, he again promised Pat he would find another career.

Bonham contacted Robert Plant, whom he knew from the small-town scene around Kidderminster, and asked if his band, The Crawling King Snakes, could use a drummer. As it happened, they had just lost their regular sticksman, but Plant and his colleagues were at first far from certain. "Bonzo", as he was almost universally known, already had a reputation as the loudest drummer around. His muscles bulging from carrying hod-loads of bricks and with his bass drum reportedly lined with aluminium to make it sound like a cannon, he'd been evicted from The Beachcombers for drowning out the rest of the band, and some of the more timid club owners around Birmingham had made it clear that they wouldn't book any band in which Bonham hammered. He hit his kit with such force that he could wreck more sticks and skins in a single night than a less aggressive drummer might break in a lifetime. "I was always breaking drumheads when I first started playing", he admitted. "Later on I learned how to play louder but without hitting the drums so hard. It all has to do with the swing of the stick". When his sticks broke, he would play with his bare hands – a technique he continued to use for the rest of his life. "You get an absolutely true drum sound because there's no wood involved", he enthused. "It hurts your hands at first but then the skin hardens. I think I can hit a drum harder with my hands than sticks".

The cash-strapped, struggling Crawling King Snakes were also concerned that he didn't have a car. "It was a long way to go and pick him up for a gig, and we never knew whether we'd have the petrol money to get over there", Plant admitted. In the end Bonham was invited to join but within months the petrol money was proving too much of an issue and he went back to playing with one of his former bands, A Way Of Life. Nevertheless, the Plant-Bonham axis had been established, and it was soon back in action in late 1967 in Band Of Joy, whose live sets became notable not only for Plant's gyrating but for Bonham's crashingly belligerent solos, much inspired by **Ginger Baker**'s extended solo on 'Toad' on Cream's 1966 debut album, *Fresh Cream* (which also remained an evergreen number in Cream's live set). However, Plant's claim that he had to stand alongside the drummer one night at London's Speakeasy while he treated punters to a 45-minute drum solo is probably a slight exaggeration.

For a moment, it looked as if Band Of Joy were on the verge of making it. But when a record deal failed to materialize and the group found themselves splitting nightly fees of £60–£70 five ways, Bonham accepted an invitation to join the touring band of American singer-songwriter Tim Rose. By now, it seems Baker had created a vogue for loud drumming, and suddenly in the summer of 1968, for the first time in his life, Bonham found himself in demand. He was earning the best money of his career to date with Rose, and there were offers on the table to join established hit-maker Chris Farlowe and to back Joe Cocker, who was on the verge of a major breakthrough with his extraordinary reinterpretation of The Beatles' '(With) A Little Help From My Friends'.

But the Midlands mafia has always stuck together, and Robert Plant hadn't forgotten his old mate. When Jimmy Page invited him to join The Yardbirds in late July 1968 and proposed that Procul Harum's B.J. Wilson might make a suitable drummer, an emboldened Plant told his new colleague that he had a much better idea and asked him not to take any decision until he had seen Bonham play. "We needed a drummer who was a good timekeeper and who really laid it down", he later recalled. "And the only suitable candidate I knew was my old mate Bonzo".

Zeppelin Forefathers: The Yardbirds

Despite a line-up that at different times boasted the holy trinity of British rock guitarists in Eric Clapton, Jeff Beck and Jimmy Page, The Yardbirds' career was characterized by underachievement and disappointment. Even the handful of pop hits they enjoyed never really reflected their true potential. In the end, the group itself seemed uncertain whether it wanted to be a blues combo, a pop group or a rock band and although their use of fuzz tone, feedback and distortion was genuinely innovative, the musical virtuosity of the band's various guitarists failed to compensate for their lack of a strong in-house songwriter. With the benefit of hindsight, it was the links the group forged between British R&B, pop experimentalism, early psychedelia and prototype heavy metal that made The Yardbirds significant in rock history. Yet at the time, it simply gave the impression that the band lacked direction and

focus and ultimately left their audience dazed and confused.

Formed at Kingston Art School in 1963 as the Metropolitan Blues Quartet by singer Keith Relf, lead guitarist "Top" Topham, rhythm guitarist Chris Dreja, bass player Paul Samwell-Smith and drummer Jim McCarty, the band first achieved notice on the British blues

The British Blues Scene

The late and modest Alexis Korner would have, quite honourably, accepted the credit for inventing the British blues scene, and consequently the British "Beat Boom". But he wasn't alone. In addition to selling rarely-seen blues records off a market stall in West London in the late 1950s, he linked up with a range of like-minded souls such as Cyril Davies, and seasoned jazz/blues performers such as George Melly, Chris Barber, Humphrey Lyttleton *et al*, and created an electric arc which fused around the time of the American Folk Blues Festival tours of 1963–66. Between them, they made it possible for not only young London-based aficionados like Mick Jagger, Brian Jones, Keith Richards, Clapton and Beck to actually see and hear black American blues veterans such as Sonny Boy Williamson, Muddy Waters and Howlin' Wolf for the first time in the flesh – but they also took it to the provinces. Plant claims he stole Sonny Boy Williamson's mouth harp when he saw him in Birmingham. The impact all of this was enormous, and within Britain a new purist blues movement started, notably under the aegis of John Mayall's Bluesbreakers, Korner's Blues Incorporated and Graham Bond's Organization. Each of these godfathers, turned on to the possibilities of electric blues,

saw talents such as Jagger, Jack Bruce, Eric Clapton and Jeff Beck, Ginger Baker, Rod Stewart, and Jimmy Page pass through their ranks, learning their chops on the way. Meanwhile bands like the Stones began to create their own unique interpretations of American R&B. It is no accident that the Stones insisted on recording at Chicago's Chess Studios on their 1964 tour of the States, whilst at the same time awakening young America's eyes to the wealth of powerful black musical heritage it had been ignoring.

Thus, the "British invasion". And it is no accident that, on this side of the Atlantic, bands like The Who, The Kinks and The Small Faces began to turn out hymns to teenage angst in a distinctively British streetwise style – they had learned their tricks from American songwriters liked Chuck Berry and Jimy Reed. And soon, they would be joined by another new generation who would take R&B into a new place, the Supergroup, exemplified by Cream: Clapton ("is God"), Jack Bruce and Ginger Baker, who could play covers of radically, but lovingly, reinterpreted Robert Johnson and Howlin' Wolf songs alongside original compositions like 'White Room', 'Sunshine Of Your Love', 'Politician' and 'Badge'. The stage was set for the next wave of British innovation.

scene when they took over from The Rolling Stones as the house band at The Crawdaddy Club in Richmond, by which time they had become known as The Yardbirds. Like the Stones, their repertoire mixed the Chicago blues of Howlin' Wolf, Muddy Waters, Sonny Boy Williamson and Jimmy Reed with the more commercial rock'n'roll sounds of **Chuck Berry** and **Bo Diddley**.

In October 1963, shortly after they had taken over the Crawdaddy residency, Topham was replaced by Eric Clapton, who substantially raised the group's musical prowess. They were still raw, however, when at the end of 1963, they backed Sonny Boy Williamson on a tour of Britain and Germany. "Those English kids want to play the blues so bad – and they play the blues so bad", the great bluesman was reported as saying.

Under the management of Crawdaddy impresario **Giorgio Gomelsky**, the following year the group signed to EMI's Columbia label and made its album debut in late 1964 with *Five Live Yardbirds*, recorded at London's Marquee Club. The group might have seen itself as an authentic R&B combo, but from the outset the group came under pressure from EMI to record a hit single. It eventually came via 'For Your Love', written by Graham Gouldman. Clapton, a true blues purist, was appalled and by the time of the single's release in early 1965, had departed in disgust, to be replaced by Jeff Beck.

'For Your Love' made Number Three in Britain and Number Six in America, and was

R&B Art Schools

It was a peculiarity of the time that many of the British "Beat Boom" bands of the 1960s had their origins in art colleges. Sean Egan, author of *The Rough Guide to The Rolling Stones*, has suggested that this might be because under the then generous grant system, students could practise their guitar playing at the taxpayers' expense, whilst knocking out the odd artwork to justify their existence. The roster of art school attendees of the period, in addition to Jimmy Page, is amazing: John Lennon, Keith Richards, Eric Clapton, Eric Burdon, Jeff Beck, Ray Davies, Pete Townshend and, later on, David Bowie and Bryan Ferry of Roxy Music.

It is instructive, however, to look at other stalwarts of the 1960s scene in terms of their tutelage: Joe Cocker (welder), Robert Plant (accountant), Mick Jagger (London School of Economics), Steve Marriott (busker), Van Morrison (window cleaner) and Jess Conrad (milkman) an observation that speaks volumes about how a shared interest in blues and R&B broke class barriers and established common bonds.

followed by a further big hit with another Gouldman composition, 'Heart Full Of Soul'. By the end of the year, the double A-sided 'Evil Hearted You/Still I'm Sad' had made it a trio of Top Ten hits.

Even better was to come with the psychedelic-tinged 'Shapes Of Things', which reached Number Three in Britain and Number 11 in America early in 1966; this was followed by an album, 1966's *Yardbirds*,

The Story

widely known as "Roger The Engineer" and released in America in slightly different form as *Over Under Sideways Down*. It was the only album the band ever recorded of all-original material and bounced somewhat erratically between blues-rock, guitar rave-ups and proto-psychedelic experimentalism. By the time it was released, in July 1966, however, the band had a new line-up, with Page having replaced departing bassist **Paul Samwell-Smith**. For a few gigs Page played bass, while Chris Dreja learned the instrument. Page, the consummate session player, apparently needed no instruction. "They were stuck, so of course I said 'well, I'll play.' I offered to play bass for them even though I'd never played a bass guitar before in my life", he recalls. "Then they suggested that I stay on in the group and I did. Session work had become so predictable and boring".

Beck remembers it slightly differently. "We had to talk to him and bribe him with lots of money to come into the group", he says. Whatever the exact circumstances, once Dreja had learned the bass parts, Page switched back to his natural instrument, giving The Yardbirds a unique twin guitar line-up to die for.

Yet for various reasons, the Beck-Page teaming only ever offered tantalizing glimpses of its potential, most notably on the single 'Happenings Ten Years Time Ago'. It proved too experimental to chart, but was one of the finest recordings The Yardbirds ever made. It also featured Page's future Led Zeppelin colleague John Paul Jones on bass.

The one other recorded monument of the Beck-Page era Yardbirds was 'Stroll On', a variation on 'Train Kept A-Rollin'', recorded for Michelangelo Antonioni's 1967 film *Blow Up*. The group's appearance in the film was not planned but came about when they filled in at short notice for The In-Crowd, who had initially been contracted but were unable to attend on the scheduled filming date (although interestingly, Antonioni had originally wanted the Exploding Plastic Inevitable, Andy Warhol's multi-media event featuring **The Velvet Underground** for the scene, but flying them over from New York was too expensive). The Yardbirds' performance in the cult movie was chiefly memorable for Beck smashing his guitar, but by the time the film came out in 1967 and the group appeared at the Cannes Film Festival to promote it, Beck was long gone.

Beck was not replaced, and The Yardbirds remained as a quartet for the remainder of their career. After a tour of Australia and Singapore, Page took time off to go back-packing in India. On his return, it was increasingly evident that the weight of the band rested on his shoulders and, left to his own devices, his growing experimentalism as a guitarist and pioneering the use of fuzz tone, wah-wah pedal and even such unusual techniques as scraping a violin bow across his guitar strings would surely have taken The Yardbirds in a new and interesting direction. But with the failure to chart of their last single, 'Happenings Ten Years Time Ago', EMI was agitating for a return to their former hit-making ways.

The Story

Jeff Beck

The synergy between Beck and Page was explosive in every way. The two guitarists may have been close friends, but there was also a distinct rivalry between them and – according to Dreja – when Page joined, "Jeff felt, justifiably, that his space was being invaded". In August 1966, during a tour of America, Beck suffered some sort of breakdown (or a "freak-out" in the parlance of the time) and The Yardbirds completed the trek with Page as sole lead guitarist. Beck was back the following month for a dozen UK dates supporting The Rolling Stones, on which they reportedly played up a storm, but on a further American tour in October, Beck was sacked after just two dates. His band-mates felt his unreliability and volatility had left them no option. "One time in the dressing room Beck had his guitar up over his head, about to bring it down on Keith Relf, but instead smashed it to the floor", Page recalled of one particularly fraught night back stage. "Keith looked at him with total astonishment and Jeff said, 'What did you make me do that for?'"

Jeff Beck was born in Surrey on 24 June 1944. He showed early talent as a pianist, but gave the instrument up when he made his own guitar. He attended art school, but dropped out to join an R&B band, The Tridents, and from there was recruited to replace Eric Clapton in The Yardbirds. His fast, inventive and jagged guitar interpretations added a distinctive edge to the often slavishly imitative or soft-mouthed riffs and patterns of many of the British "Beat Boom" R&B school, and although never noted as a composer in his own right, his covers of a wide range of tracks, from the Chicago bluesmasters to Bob Dylan, are always distinc-tive. His slide guitar version of Presley's 'All Shook Up' remains an exemplar of idiosyncratic reinterpretation.

When Beck was told that he was being fired from The Yardbirds, he expected his friend Page to quit with him in sympathy, turning to Page and asking if he was leaving with him. "No, I'm going to stay behind", his colleague answered uneasily, knowing full well that Beck would regard this as an act of betrayal. "Jeff and I were very close but this strange professional jealousy came between us and I don't understand why", Page confessed years later. The official announcement of his departure cited "persistent ill health". He went on to play in a number of proto-groups, alongside such alumni as Rod Stewart, Ronnie Wood and Nicky Hopkins, and was near the top of the list as a replacement when Mick Taylor retired hurt from The Rolling Stones in 1974. A gifted one-off, Beck nevertheless seemed consistently to miss opportunities, although an interesting Zeppology footnote was his alliance with the Vanilla Fudge rhythm section, Carmine Appice and Tim Bogert, in an attempt (delayed by his injury in a car crash) to hit the "Supergroup" high ground in the early 1970s. Over the last 30 years his reappearances have been warmly received by the public and his peers alike, not least with his appearance alongside Plant on the first Honeydrippers release in 1984.

Some 26 years after his untimely ejection from The Yardbirds, Beck was reunited with his old colleagues when the band were inducted into The Rock And Roll Hall of Fame in 1992. At the ceremony he quipped: "I suppose I should say 'Thank you', but they fired me, so fuck 'em!"

Their answer, it seemed to them, was to draft in hitmeister producer Mickie Most, a ludicrous notion that was a disaster waiting to happen. Page knew Most well, and had worked as a session guitarist on many of his successes for artists such as Herman's Hermits and Lulu. But recruiting the master of three-minute throwaway pop songs to produce a serious rock band just as psychedelia was dawning and the world was preparing to enter 1967's "Summer of Love" was hopelessly misconceived. With their deeply-ingrained musical pedigree, The Yardbirds should have been up there in the vanguard of the new wave of progressive rock groups alongside bands such as Cream, **The Jimi Hendrix Experience** and **Traffic**. Instead, while George Martin was helping The Beatles craft the masterful *Sgt. Pepper's Lonely Hearts Club Band*, Most's instincts were to treat The Yardbirds as a lightweight pop group. His decision to have them cover Manfred Mann's 'Ha Ha Said The Clown' was particularly crass and inept (particularly as Manfred Mann's original was an ironic pop-chart one-off, not a classic worthy of a cover version). Worse, Most's brazen attempts at commercialism didn't even work. 'Ha Ha Said The Clown' predictably flopped and an equally weak cover of Harry Nilsson's 'Ten Little Indians' (described by Page as "an extremely silly song with a truly awful brass arrangement") deservedly suffered the same fate.

The Most-produced 1967 album *Little Games* fared no better and, after staggering to Number 80 in the *Billlboard* chart in America, it was not even released in the UK. "On half

Mickie Most's new, improved, Yardbirds all set for an appearance on BBC's *Top Of The Pops* in 1965

the tracks we didn't even hear the playbacks", Page complains today. "Some of them were first takes. We'd spend time on the singles, but Mickie Most thought that albums were nothing, just something to stick out after a hit single". Jim McCarty complained the album was "recorded just like a Herman's Hermits LP". Yet, despite Most's inappropriate and lightweight production, the album has its moments, and contains several pointers to the style Page would develop more fully with Led Zeppelin, not only in his electric guitar work but also on the acoustic 'White Mountain', which reveals the influence of such folk stylists as **Bert Jansch** and **Davey Graham**, and was originally titled 'Arabic Number'. Some later reissues of the album are bolstered by the inclusion of a live BBC session that includes the original template of the Zeppelin classic 'Dazed And Confused' and 'Think About It', the B-side to the group's final single 'Goodnight Sweet Josephine', which contains some of Page's most explosive pre-Zeppelin playing.

The group spent most of 1967 on the road, often in a blizzard of drink and drug abuse, with singer Keith Relf regularly out of it on stage and frequently singing in the wrong places. They were at last making some decent money – largely because an aggressive human dynamo called Peter Grant (see pages 40–41) had, in January 1967, taken over their management from Simon Napier-Bell – but by the start of 1968 it was becoming increasingly plain that The Yardbirds were no longer serious contenders. A planned live album recorded in **New York City** in March 1968 was shelved at the band's request, only to be released as *Live Yardbirds! Featuring Jimmy Page* by their US label Epic three years later when Led Zeppelin hit big. The album was swiftly withdrawn after Page's lawyers slapped an injunction on it. "A total embarrassment, recorded on jet lag and by a guy who had never recorded a rock band in his life',' was the guitarist's merciless judgement.

The Yardbirds played their final gig in Luton in July 1968, but Relf and McCarty had decided to quit long before that during the preceding tour of America. Indeed, the news leaked back to *Melody Maker* in Britain which, in early June, ran an item which reported: "Break-up of The Yardbirds is expected on their return from America ... lead guitarist Jimmy Page is to reform the group with a new lead singer and drummer". The group had divided into factions. Relf and McCarty were keen to move in a more folk-rock direction, and started the short-lived Together, before enjoying greater success with **Renaissance**. Page and Dreja favoured a louder, more dynamic and heavier approach, albeit with acoustic elements. Light and shade.

Grant negotiated with the departing duo for Page and Dreja to retain the rights to The Yardbirds name and on 8 July 1968 EMI Records issued a press release stating: "The band will be reformed under the same name by Page and Dreja, who seek two new members."

In the event, their first choices were unavailable, and they were turned down by singer Terry Reid and Procul Harum drummer B.J.Wilson. A still enthusiastic Dreja stayed around long enough to be part of the scouting mission with Page and Grant to Birmingham to check out Robert Plant but, after a change of heart, he baled out soon after. "I wasn't interested in becoming a jobbing musician with strangers, and made a conscious decision to go into freelance photography", he explained.

While Page recruited a new line-up that would fit his own musical vision, he kept his hand in playing a few sessions, including one by a Sheffield gas-fitter called Joe Cocker on his cover of The Beatles' '(With) A Little Help From My Friends'. By the time the track reached Number One in the British charts in November 1968, Page's reinvented band was in place – but they were no longer known as The Yardbirds – or even The New Yardbirds.

The Balloon
Goes Up
1968–1969

"I had it in my mind exactly what I wanted to try and get together. Then it was just a matter of searching around for the right personnel to pull it off".

Jimmy Page

The Balloon Goes Up
1968–1969

As The Yardbirds moved inexorably towards their use-by date in mid-July 1968, Jimmy Page was busy reviving a plan he had originally hatched back in 1966. The cast of The New Yardbirds existed, somewhere, and Page had done his research. In addition, he had some clear ideas about what he wanted to achieve: not so much a phoenix rising from the ashes, more a brand new band with a brand new sound. But there was a lot of work to do to get the venture off the ground.

Who To Choose?

After The Yardbirds played their final gig in July 1968, Jimmy Page was depressed and disillusioned. As **Ritchie Yorke** put it in his 1974 book, *Led Zeppelin: The Defintive Biography*, the guitarist was at a crossroads: "He could return to session work. He could go back to art. Or he could lunge ahead and create a new band from the still-engrossing embers of The Yardbirds' fiery career". His indecision did not last long. Although he did a few sessions to keep his hand in and to maintain the cash flow, there was never any real doubt that forming a new band was the only real thing on his mind.

Page's first intention was to reform The Yardbirds and with Chris Dreja still at the time part of the set-up, a reconstituted band would at least have had one member of the original line-up to justify the continued use of the name. Asked about the new band by *Go* maga-

zine he reasoned that he was going to keep the old name because "people have associated a type of sound with the name. It's a heavy beat sound and I want to keep that".

But his mind also went back to a session that he had organized in May 1966 at London's IBC Studios involving John Paul Jones on bass, **Nicky Hopkins** on piano, The Who's Keith Moon on drums and Page and Jeff Beck on guitars. The session produced a track called 'Beck's Bolero' and Page enjoyed it so much that there was talk of forming a group built around a dual guitar attack with Beck and The Who's rhythm section of Moon and John Entwistle (Jones at this stage was not prepared to give up his lucrative position as a session player and arranger).

Talk turned swiftly to a singer. "The first choice was Steve Winwood, but he was too committed to Traffic", Page later recalled. "Next we thought of **Steve Marriott** of the Small Faces.

Seminal British R&B band Small Faces: (from left) Ronnie Lane, Steve Marriott, Ian Mclagan and Kenney Jones. Lead singer and guitarist Marriott was a contender for the LZ singing role. 1965's 'You Need Loving' indicates why

He was approached and seemed full of glee about it. A message came back from the business side, though, which said "How would you like to play the guitar with ten broken fingers? You will be if you don't stay away from Steve". The Small Faces at the time were managed by **Don Arden**, who had once famously dangled rival manager Robert Stigwood over a second-floor balcony and threatened to throw him head first on to the pavement below, so Page knew the threat was no joke. So the plan ground

to a halt. Nevertheless, it seems that the Led Zeppelin name had its origins in these discussions (see page 46).

Moon, it seems, was not serious about changing bands and more concerned about making a point to his colleagues in **The Who**. Without a singer or a drummer, Page gave up and joined Beck in The Yardbirds instead. "The idea just sort of fell apart", he later said. "Instead of being more positive about it and looking for another singer, we just let it slip by. The Who began a tour and The Yardbirds began a tour and that was it".

Yet Page did not forget the idea or the experience and when in the summer of 1968 he began to think about his dream line-up for the new group he still planned to call The Yardbirds, he resolved this time to find his singer before recruiting any other musicians. Winwood and Marriott were unavailable for pretty much the same reasons as before, and so the first choice soon became Terry Reid, whose soulful voice Page knew from his days singing with Peter Jay and The Jaywalkers. Reid had recently gone solo and, encouragingly, was signed to RAK, run by Mickie Most and Yardbirds' manager Peter Grant. But Reid felt his solo career was about to take off and was also doubtful that The Yardbirds could be re-established as a commercially-viable entity; he declined.

Sadly, his solo career never quite ignited, although almost 40 years on, he remains remarkably good-humoured about turning down the opportunity to join what was to become the biggest rock band in the world and gamely insists that he has no regrets. Instead, he suggested Page should check out his friend Robert Plant.

Plant Comes On Board

Page was unfamiliar with the name and it's a cruel but justifiable judgement that Reid's recommendation was probably his greatest contribution to rock history. It's perfectly possible that Plant's cause was also pleaded by others, including noted musical matchmaker Alexis Korner, with whom Plant had formed an *ad hoc* duo, and by Tony Secunda, the manager of Procul Harum and The Move, who had tried to get Plant a solo deal after Band of Joy had split up and claims that he mentioned him as a likely lad to Peter Grant. But even if there were other supporters, there's little doubt that it was Reid's endorsement which on 20 July 1968 sent Page, Grant and the still-keen Dreja heading up the M1 to see Plant's band Hobbstweedle play at a god-forsaken teacher training college in Birmingham in front of a crowd which **Richard Cole** – wickedly but by all accounts accurately – described as "barely big enough to fill a Volkswagen van".

The handful who were in the audience that night had no idea that they were witnessing history in the making and, frankly, neither did Jimmy Page. Firstly, he hated the material, which he'd heard before, when The Yardbirds had shared shows in America with West Coast bands such as **Moby Grape** and **Love**. He was unimpressed enough with the American originals and he didn't need to hear a West Midlands band covering them. "It was stuff that I personally didn't like very much", he later admitted. Secondly, although he was impressed by the voice ("Robert was all right... he was singing really well"), he then began to fret over why, if Plant was that good, he hadn't already been snapped up by someone else. "Why isn't this guy a star?" Page wondered to himself, according to Richard Cole. "Something's got to be wrong with him. Maybe he has one of those obnoxious personalities and no one can get along with him". There was also opposition from Chris Dreja, who told Page that he didn't think much of Plant's voice at all.

Yet, despite such misgivings, Page recognized that Plant's voice "had an exceptional and very distinctive quality", a view reinforced when he listened to a demo Plant had given him from his Band of Joy days. He invited the singer down to his home in Pangbourne for a few days so that they could get to know each other better.

Plant was acutely aware that he was on trial. "It certainly wasn't a foregone conclusion that I was going to be the singer", he admitted to this writer in an interview in 2005. "But we had a glorious first meeting and an exchanging of ideas. You can smell when people have travelled and had their doors opened a little wider than most and you could feel that was the deal with Jimmy. His ability to absorb things and the way he carried the whole plan

The Story

was far more cerebral than anything I'd come across before and so I was very impressed. And when it came to the music, we realized we were dealing from the same pack of cards".

Page, however, had a far clearer idea of the musical card game they were playing than Plant. During that same 2005 interview, the singer was asked if at this stage there was a musical vision behind their planning. "I don't think we had a clue", he replied. "We'd never played together before and so you fall back on your roots to see how it works and that's what we did". Asked the same question, Page gave a rather different answer: "I certainly had a good idea of the sort of direction I wanted us to go in", he answered. "It went back to the band I was going to form with Jeff Beck, in which we wanted a Steve Marriott or Steve Winwood-type vocalist. That was the call. And the person we accessed at that point for Zeppelin was Terry Reid. If you're familiar with his vocal style on an album like *River*, that's the way I was thinking. And having a really dynamic drummer was always going to be very important within the framework of it, because it was going to be a trio instrumentally with the fourth member being the singer and using the voice as an instrument. I knew the material I wanted us to do, as well. I had a game plan for it. Most definitely".

Sometime in the week following the Hobbstweedle gig, Plant made his way down to Page's house in Berkshire with a pile of his favourite albums and the musical bonding began. His tastes were eclectic and the influ-

Back To Mine

When Robert Plant made his way down to Jimmy Page's houseboat at Pangbourne on the River Thames in late July 1968, it was still far from certain that he was going to be invited to become the lead singer with The New Yardbirds, as the group was initially to be known. The deal was struck when they played each other their favourite records and discovered shared musical tastes. As far as we can reconstruct it at almost 40 years distance, based on Page and Plant's own recollections this is the soundtrack they bonded over. Several of the items were to have a considerable influence on the first Led Zeppelin album...

BABE I'M GONNA LEAVE YOU *Joan Baez*

HOWLIN' WOLF (aka The Rockin' Chair album) *Howlin' Wolf*

5000 SPIRITS OR THE LAYERS OF THE ONION *The Incredible String Band.*

KING OF THE DELTA BLUES SINGERS *Robert Johnson*

SHE SAID YEAH *Larry Williams*

JUSTINE *Don and Dewey*

AS LONG AS I HAVE YOU *Garnett Mimms*

A MAN AND THE BLUES *Buddy Guy*

LOVE ME *Elvis Presley*

'YOU SHOOK ME' *Muddy Waters*

'IN-A-GADDA-DA-VIDA' *Iron Butterfly*

'NO MONEY DOWN' *Chuck Berry*

LITTLE WALTER *Little Walter*

ences on his singing style unusual, ranging from raw and earthy Delta blues to British folk music, via West Coast 1960s rock. Page didn't think much of the latter, but his own tastes also ran from Howlin' Wolf and Robert Johnson to English folk guitarists such as Bert Jansch and Davey Graham.

One day during his stay, Plant started leafing through Page's record collection. "I pulled out a pile to play and somehow or other they happened to be the same ones that Jimmy had put aside to play to me when he returned, just to see whether I liked them", Plant recalled. "When he saw that I'd picked them out too we just giggled at each other for a bit. We found we had exactly the same tastes in music".

The listening session would have a profound effect on the shape of the first Led Zeppelin album, most notably in the decision to cover the traditional 'Babe I'm Gonna Leave You'. Both were enamoured with **Joan Baez**'s version of the song and their retooling of the song became an early model of Zeppelin's ability to combine acoustic and electric moods as Page explained to Plant his notion of a new kind of "heavy music" with quieter touches and dynamic contrasts of light and shade and a band in which the singer and guitarist worked in unison and played off each other. "Jimmy wasn't dominating or anything as I might have expected", Page recalled. "I could suggest things and the two of us rearranged 'Babe I'm Gonna Leave You'. It was good to hit it off like that".

Drumming Up A Rhythm Section

Plant got the gig and before he left he put in a word for his old friend, John Bonham. At this stage, several other names were under consideration for what was still going to be called The Yardbirds. Page and Chris Dreja, who was still very much involved, had drawn up a shortlist and Grant set about contacting the suggested names to see who was available and interested. Dreja was so sure that the drummer was going to be **Paul Francis**, whom both he and Page knew from their session work, that he even gave an interview in which he stated that the new line-up consisted of Page, Plant, himself and Francis. Somewhat jumping the gun, he went on to claim: "Now we're starting to get things together with the new group, we're very keen to get on the road. Our first set of new shows will be starting in September in Scandinavia, where we have a tour arranged. After this it'll be down to work in England. We've done a fair amount of rehearsing, with some new songs and also plenty of old Yardbirds hits". The announcement of dates in Scandinavia was true enough, but at this stage no rehearsals of any kind had taken place – with or without Francis.

Page's own first choice as a drummer was B.J. Wilson of Procul Harum but, in addition to Francis, others on the list included Clem Cattini, who had played sessions for The Yardbirds, and **Aynsley Dunbar**, at the time leading his own band Aynsley Dunbar's Retaliation, the name of which was perhaps an ironic reference to his having lost out to **Mitch Mitchell** as the drummer with The Jimi Hendrix Experience on the toss of a coin.

The manner in which Mitchell was chosen is indicative of how little importance was paid to drummers at the time: the prevailing thinking was that they were there to keep the beat and little else. Page thought differently and was looking for a drummer whose chemistry could contribute to the overall sound. "You know, you can get four really good musicians but it doesn't mean they're going to play as a band", he told this writer in 2005. "The thing about Zeppelin was that we always played as a band".

Page was intrigued by what Plant told him about Bonham, who at the time was touring with **Tim Rose**. The notion of the loudest drummer in the West Midlands backing a folk singer seemed to fit Page's own vision of a new style of rock music, heavy but with dynamic contrasts between electric and acoustic elements. A hyped up and

overexcited Plant, meanwhile, on his way back home from Pangbourne and now fully enrolled as a Yardbird, hitched to Oxford, where Rose was playing a gig that night, to tell Bonham his news and urge him to audition for the group.

The drummer, however, was unimpressed. Plant explained, "Bonzo said, 'Well, I'm all right here, aren't I?' He'd never earned before the sort of bread he was getting from Tim Rose so I had to try and persuade him. I had nothing to convince him, really, except a name that got lost in American pop history – The Yardbirds".

When Rose's tour arrived in London a few days later on 31 July 1968, Page, Dreja and Grant went to see his band at The Country Club in Hampstead. The guitarist was immediately convinced that Plant had been right. "Although I had in mind the need for a very powerful drummer, I must say I wasn't ready for John Bonham. When I saw what a thrasher Bonzo was, I knew he'd be incredible", Page subsequently recalled. "He was playing 'Hey Joe' as an acoustic number and I could see the whole thing fitting together. He was into exactly the same sort of stuff that I was and he was beyond the realms of anything I could have possibly imagined".

Despite writing 'Hey Joe', Tim Rose was one of a number of successful 1960s performers who got swept away by the tsunami of heavy rockers in the 1970s

Bonham became the second former member of the Band of Joy to be invited to Page's Pangbourne home, and was offered an invitation the guitarist hoped couldn't be refused. But the drummer was still reluctant. After years of struggle, he now suddenly found himself in the previously unimagined position of being able to play the field. "Joe Cocker was interested and so was Chris Farlowe, along with Robert and Jimmy", he later recalled. "It was baffling. I had so much to consider. It wasn't just a question of who had the best prospects, but also which music was going to be the right kind of stuff. Farlowe was fairly well established and I knew that Cocker was going to make it. When I first got offered the gig, I thought that The Yardbirds were **finished**. In Britain they had been forgotten".

Uncontactable by phone, Page and Grant pursued Bonham with a series of increasingly frantic telegrams, several of them delivered to his favourite pub, The Three Men In A Boat in Walsall. Eventually Bonham relented. "I knew that Jimmy was a good guitarist and Robert was a good singer so even if we didn't have any success, at least it would be a pleasure to play in a good group", Bonham said later. "I already knew what music Robert liked and Jimmy told me what he was into and I decided I liked their music ideas better than Cocker or Farlowe". However, his insistence that musical considerations swayed him did not prevent him seeking further reassurance about his income, given that he had a young family to support. "There were all sorts of negotiations about retainers and Bonzo was very keen to get an extra £25 a week to drive the Transit van", Plant remembers. "His wife Pat wasn't happy at all with us going down there and hanging out with those guys. It was like going to the far side of the moon".

Peter Grant also confirmed the attempted van driving scam, adding that "it was remarkable how naïve Robert and Bonzo were". Plant does not disagree. "Me and Bonzo were 20 years old and we were definitely the boys from the black stuff", he cheerfully admitted in 2005. "I don't think we were in awe. We were just really pleased to be offered some kind of security. We thought we were on to something. But we'd never seen a manager before – let alone Peter Grant".

Clearing The Nest

By the time Bonham finally signed on, other changes that would profoundly affect the line-up were under way. Some time between Page's invitation to Bonham and his acceptance, Chris Dreja retired – or was eased out of the picture. In theory, as an original Yardbird, Dreja was the senior member of the new band. In practice, of course, it was very much Page who was calling the shots. With Plant on board, he came to see setbacks to Dreja's continued presence. Apart from a bit of harmonica, Plant did not play an instrument, meaning that the group would in effect be a power trio fronted by a singer. Although Dreja was versatile enough as a bassist and guitarist, Page began to think

Peter Grant: The Pilot

At a party in Los Angeles in 1973, Peter Grant introduced himself to Bob Dylan as the manager of Led Zeppelin. "I don't come to you with my problems, do I?" was Dylan's only reply. His terse response was a reference to the band's already legendary reputation for on-the-road debauchery on an industrial scale but, rather than tearing his hair out over his band's behaviour, Grant not only indulged Zeppelin's excesses but gave the impression that he rather enjoyed the mayhem and was not averse to joining in on occasions. It would then fall to him as manager to apologize for the carnage, placate the hotel management, square

The Yardbirds reinvented, post-Mickie Most, with the energetic Grant (second from left) sporting an interesting moustache. Apparently unembarrassed by this, the band (left to right Jim McCarty, Chris Dreja, Keith Relf and Jimmy Page), sort out cravats for the next show

the local police and pay for the damage by peeling off prodigious quantities of crisp, new $100 bills.

Born on 5 April 1935 in South Norwood, Surrey, Grant was a tough wheeler-dealer whom you messed with at your peril and whose fame as a manager has probably only been exceeded by Colonel Tom Parker and Brian Epstein. His early life was poverty-stricken and, after being evacuated during the second World War, he left school at the age of 13 to work in a sheet metal factory. His first steps into show business came as a stagehand at the now long-demolished Empire Theatre in Croydon and, by the mid-1950s, he was a doorman and bouncer at the Two I's coffee bar in Soho, famous as the cradle that spawned such early British rockers as Cliff Richard, Adam Faith and Tommy Steele.

A spell as a professional wrestler under the name Prince Mario Alassio led to a new career as a bit-part actor and film stuntman and, in the late 1950s and early 1960s, he appeared in minor roles in such films as *A Night to Remember, The Guns of Navarone* and *Cleopatra*. His size led to a regular gig as Robert Morley's double in a number of films, and he also appeared in such popular television series as ITV's *The Saint* and BBC's *Dixon of Dock Green*. To supplement his income, he ploughed the money from his acting career into his own transport business, ferrying such groups as The Shadows on package tours of the British Isles. In 1963, he was hired by promoter Don Arden as a tour manager, working for visiting US artists such as Bo Diddley, The Everly Brothers, Little Richard, Chuck Berry and Eddie Cochran. Using his prowess as a wrestler to good effect, on one occasion in Rome he laid out six Italian policemen intent on beating the shit out of Little Richard. Within a year he had started his own management company, and had taken charge of the careers of The Nashville Teens, The New Vaudeville Band, Jeff Beck and Terry Reid, running his management company from the same office at 155 Oxford Street in London's West End as his friend and partner, the record producer Mickie Most.

In January 1967, he began a long association with Jimmy Page when, on Most's recommendation, The Yardbirds' manager Simon Napier-Bell asked Grant to take over the group. Unlike many managers, Grant liked to travel with his charges, using his intimidating physical presence to ensure that promoters paid his band on time – and in full. Although he made The Yardbirds more money than they had ever earned before, he couldn't keep the band together, and when they fell apart in July 1968, he set about helping Page to put together Led Zeppelin. "I always had the most respect and admiration for Jimmy", Grant later told author Ritchie Yorke. "I felt that I was closer to him than any of the other members of The Yardbirds, and I had immense faith in his talent and ability. I just wanted to do whatever he felt was best for him at the time".

In effect, Grant became Led Zeppelin's fifth member and was integral to the group's commercial success. He began by negotiating a lucrative five-year recording contract with Atlantic Records, and set up the band's publishing company Superhype; he also encouraged Zeppelin to concentrate on albums and live shows and to ignore the singles market and television appearances, all of which only served to enhance the group's mystique. He was also instrumental in1974 in establishing Zeppelin's own record company Swan Song, going on to manage several of the acts signed to the label, including Bad Company and Maggie Bell, although he turned down an invitation to manage Queen – an undoubted misjudgement in terms of money, if not sound in terms of taste.

Always happier when he could be on the road with his band rather than being stuck behind a desk, stories of his tenacious and often belligerent defence of Led Zeppelin's interests are legendary.

His methods may have been unconventional but his stewardship was key in effecting a shift in the balance of financial power within the music industry in favour of the artists. Zeppelin not only made more money than any band in rock history, but Grant ensured that they retained most of it too. Taking on the American promoters who for years had grown fat on 50% of concert takings, Grant insisted on a preposterous 90% for the band. As Zeppelin had become the biggest draw in America, the grumbling promoters had little choice but reluctantly to agree.

Away from Zeppelin's on-the-road madness, Grant was a contented country man, living deep in rural Sussex with his wife and two children in a moated house. When they divorced, Grant raised the kids alone and moved to genteel Eastbourne. Eventually, the years of pressure and hard living took their toll. When the group split following John Bonham's death in 1980, Grant seemed at a loss and was fighting heroin addiction. His long association with Jimmy Page ended in 1983, and he disappeared into virtual retirement. It was "a period of blackness", but he never got involved in rock management again. He suffered a fatal heart attack on 21 November 1995.

"The man who made it all possible ... he never likes to be in group pictures, he doesn't like playing soccer with us, but what a manager – what a member of the group".

Robert Plant, Earls Court, May 1975

he needed someone who could also play keyboards. Given the conflict that had dogged The Yardbirds, he further wondered whether a clean break with the past might be beneficial. Inevitably, his thoughts turned to his conversation with John Paul Jones, who came with no such baggage and in addition to his bass playing was an arranger and an excellent keyboardist. Page contacted him and Jones came on board in place of Dreja.

Whether Page and Grant were legally in a position to sack Dreja is debatable. The ex-Yardbird has always insisted that he backed out of his own accord, but it is equally clear that Page actively encouraged him to do so. Whether he jumped or was given a helping nudge overboard, as Keith Shadwick put it, Dreja's involvement was "allowed to wither". He turned to a new career in photography and remained on good terms with the band, taking the photograph that appeared on the back jacket of their debut album.

Page also toyed briefly with the idea of a second, rhythm guitarist and according to some sources, sounded out Top Topham, who had been The Yardbirds' original axeman in 1963 before Eric Clapton's arrival. If so, it was another idea that was allowed to wither. By early August, Page was convinced that he was close to finalizing his ideal line-up and a press statement on 5 August 1968 announced that Plant and Jones were now members of the group. Bonham's signature followed a few days later. The New Yardbirds were in place.

With a tour of Scandinavia due to start in the first week of September, the new band had to get up to speed in double-quick time. Fortunately, when **The New Yardbirds**, as they were still called, assembled in mid-August in a tiny basement rehearsal room in Gerrard Street in London's Chinatown, according to all four participants it was evident almost from the first note that it was going to work.

Jones had met Bonham and jammed with him when he had visited Page's home prior to agreeing to join, but for the bassist and Plant it was their first encounter. "We all met in this little room to see if we could stand each other", Jones recounts. "Robert had heard I was a session man and he was wondering who was going to turn up. I think he was half-expecting some old bloke with a pipe. Then Jimmy said, "well, we're all here, what are we going to play?"

After a few blank looks, Page asked his new colleagues if they knew The Yardbirds' staple 'Train Kept A-Rollin'. They didn't, but he told them it was "a 12-bar with a riff on G" and with that most rudimentary of instructions, they were away. "He counted it out and the room just exploded", according to Jones. "There were lots of silly grins and 'Oh yeah man, this is it'. It was pretty bloody obvious from the first number that it was going to work".

'As Long As I Have You', a Garnett Mimms song which Plant had sung in Band Of Joy, was next up. 'I Can't Quit You Baby', rearranged by Page and Plant from the Joan

Baez version followed, and then Howlin' Wolf's 'Smokestack Lightnin'' (another old Yardbirds warhorse) and then 'Dazed and Confused'.

An effusive Plant later claimed: "I've never been so turned on in all my life. Although we were all steeped in blues and R&B, we found in that first hour-and-a-half that we had our own identity. I could feel that something was happening within myself and to everyone else in the room. It felt like we'd found something that we had to really be careful of because we might lose it. The power of it was remarkable". Almost 40 years later he was still enthusing: "The rehearsals were really good. Bonzo opened up more and more, and Jimmy had the swagger and the musicality. It was very exciting for me to be in the middle of that. I'd never experienced that in my life before".

Page concluded: "At the end of it, we knew that it was really happening, really electrifying". Even the fact that Plant and Bonham were penniless and when they left the rehearsal had to ask the guitarist for money for food and drink could not take the shine off the elation they were all feeling.

Lift-Off

The combination of two established musicians and two of raw and untried potential had proved so explosive at the first exploratory rehearsal that they could hardly wait to reconvene, this time over several days at Page's home in Pangbourne. A further and unexpected opportunity to get to know each other better musically presented itself at the end of August in the improbable forum of a **P.J. Proby** session, which Jones was committed to arranging. Responsible for booking a band, he invited both Page and Bonham and even Plant turned up to bang a tambourine.

By the time they departed for the brief Scandinavian tour which was the last contractual obligation of the old Yardbirds, they had worked up a repertoire not too different form the set Page had played with that band in America earlier in the year, with a number of key additions that already looked forward to the material that would appear on the first Led Zeppelin album.

The band's first gig at the Gladsaxe Teen Club in **Copenhagen**, Denmark took place on the afternoon of Saturday 7 September 1968, and was followed that evening by a second gig at the Brondby Pop Club in the same city. Still billed as The Yardbirds (or rather, The Yard Birds as the Danish promoter apparently believed they were called), the following day they played two more gigs, supported by a troupe of topless go-go dancers called The Ladybirds, before they travelled to Norway and Sweden for further gigs.

The set throughout the tour opened with 'Train Kept A-Rollin' and also included 'Dazed and Confused' – on which Page used a violin bow on his guitar – blues standards 'You Shook Me' and 'I Can't Quit You Baby', 'Communication Breakdown', 'How Many More Times' (built around a Howlin' Wolf number), and the Page/Plant rearrangement of

The Balloon Goes Up

Plant earns his chops in teen clubland in Copenhagen, while Jimmy merely plays them. The fact that topless go-go dancers were sometimes on the same bill means that both had to work very hard to make an impression

'Babe I'm Gonna Leave You'. It also included a number of covers, such as Plant's longtime favourite 'As Long As I Have You' by Garnett Mimms, Ben E. King's 'We're Gonna Groove', which featured a long organ introduction by Jones and, somewhat surprisingly, 'Flames' by Elmer Gantry's Velvet Opera. This obscure British psychedelic band had emerged in the summer of 1967 briefly to become John Peel favourites and achieved a certain notoriety

when their second single 'Mary Jane' was banned by the BBC when it was pointed out that the title was a slang term for marijuana.

The band knew that they could – and would – play better, but the tour had gone well enough and Page and Plant had found a real chemistry as the singer's primeval wail fed off the guitarist's lead lines. "I wasn't trying to scat sing but I found the voice was imitating the guitar", Plant recalls. However, he also confesses: "In Scandinavia we were pretty green. It was very early days and we were tiptoeing with each other. We didn't have half the recklessness that for me became the whole joy of Led Zeppelin. It was a tentative start."

Page felt that Bonham was overplaying and gently reprimanded him, telling the drummer: "You've got to keep it a bit more simple than that". When his words had little effect, Peter Grant stepped in with a characteristically more blunt approach. "Behave yourself Bonham or you'll disappear", the burly manager told him.

What's In A Name?

Nevertheless, when they returned to Britain on 18 September, they felt confidently ready to get straight into the studio and begin recording their **debut album**. They also had to deal with the issue of the band's name. The Scandinavian shows had been contracted to The Yardbirds before the split, and so there had been some logic to using the old name. On their return, Page admitted to *Melody Maker's* Chris Welch, the band's first significant press champion, that he was "not sure whether to call them The Yardbirds or not" and also considered such variations as 'The New Yardbirds' and 'The Yardbirds featuring Jimmy Page'. In the course of the same interview, he noted: "The new chaps are only about 19 and full of enthusiasm. It was getting a bit of a trial in the old group" and described the music as "blues, basically" and "more or less" similar in style to what The Yardbrids had been playing on their final American tour.

But if Page was happy to continue using The Yardbirds name, "the new chaps" were less keen, and argued that they needed to differentiate themselves once and for all from the former band. There was also a potential legal problem. Although Relf and McCarty had signed over rights to The Yardbirds name to Page and Dreja back in early July, once the latter had withdrawn, ownership of the name became debatable. Dreja owned a piece of the name via his stake in the company Yardbirds Ltd., which had been formed in 1965 well before Page's arrival. Without his approval, the new line-up would probably have lost any court action if it had called itself The Yardbirds for, unlike Relf and McCarty, the bass player had not signed over his rights. Indeed, he took the exact opposite course of action and instructed his solicitors to write to Peter Grant asking the new line-up to desist from using the old name.

Whether it was Dreja's legal threat or the persuasion of his colleagues, Page took the point. "We dropped the name because we felt it was working under false pretences", the guitarist told *Melody Maker* a couple of years later. "The thing had gone beyond where The Yardbirds had left off", Plant added. "There was no point in calling it The Yardbirds". After rejecting such names as **Mad Dogs** and **Whoppee Cushion** (how history might have been so very different...), they settled upon Lead Zeppelin – the name that had come up two years earlier for the putative Beck-Page supergroup – with a suitable amendment to the spelling by Peter Grant.

The Story

Why 'Led Zeppelin'?

The origin of The New Yardbirds' new name seems to have first emerged in Page's discussions with Keith Moon and John Entwhistle of The Who in 1966. However, memories differ.

The name was originally coined back in 1966 when Page was in dicussion with Jeff Beck, and The Who's Keith Moon and John Entwhistle about forming a band. The group was to remain stillborn and there is some dispute as to who first came up with Lead (*sic*) Zeppelin. Entwistle, to his dying day, insisted that he was the one who had come up with the name when he commented that such a line-up was "so heavy it will go down like a Lead Zeppelin". Moon claimed it was his coinage, a claim supported by both Page and Jones, who say that two years later when The New Yardbirds decided a change of name was required, the permission of The Who's drummer was sought. A third explanation is that the name was a joint effort and emerged out of some witty banter and repartee between the two members of The Who. Whatever the exact origins of the Led Zeppelin name, the putative Page-Beck-Hopkins-Moon-Entwistle line-up was never realized.

Graf von Zeppelin, the airship man, whose descendent would later object to the use of his name by the band (see page 73)

Two years later, with the dream of a new band becoming a reality, Page says they considered Mad Dogs, but preferred the old idea of Led Zeppelin, comparing it to "the Iron Butterfly light-and-heavy connotation. Richard Cole asked Keith Moon for his permission when we decided to use the name." Nevertheless, Page also pointed out that "the name wasn't as important as whether or not the music was going to be accepted. We could have called ourselves the Vegetables or the Potatoes".

Nevertheless, when it was adopted for The New Yardbirds, the name seemed to fit with the zeitgeist: UFO was the hippest London venue, and although Jefferson Airplane had been around since 1965, Blind Faith's only album was soon to be released with a naked girl brandishing a jet airliner on the cover. Which did, incidentally, sink like a lead balloon. Things were in the air, and the imagery associated with Graf von Zeppelin's doomed flying machine was fully exploited on the band's first three albums.

Blind Faith's naughty album cover failed to take off in the USA

On 27 September, a week after their return from Scandinavia, the band went in to **Olympic Studios** in Barnes, West London to begin recording their debut album, still booked in under the name The Yardbirds. Sessions continued throughout the first week of October and, with Glyn Johns engineering, the entire album was completed in just 30 hours studio time. "We had begun developing the arrangements on the Scandinavian tour and I knew what sound I was looking for", said Page, who produced the album. "It just came together incredibly quickly". He added that he knew it was only 30 hours because he had paid the studio bill – a princely sum of just £1,782. The album was "pretty much a recording of the first show, which was why it had so many covers on it. That's all we had ready to play at the time", according to Jones. In fact, despite the fact that the entire record was done and dusted so quickly, in addition to the nine tracks that made the album, the band recorded at least five further numbers, including 'Tribute To Bert Burns (Baby Come On Home)', dedicated to the songwriter and producer who had worked with The Drifters, Ben E. King and The Isley Brothers who had died in 1967; 'Flames', by Elmer Gantry's Velvet Opera (perhaps they were dissuaded from releasing this by the that fact The Joe Loss Orchestra had also recorded a version); the Garnett Mimms/Band of Joy staple 'As Long As I Have You'; 'Fresh Garbage', a cover of a song by **Spirit,** one of the West Coast bands Plant so revered but about whom

Page was distinctly unenthusiastic; and a version of The Yardbirds' 'Train Kept A-Rollin", the very first song they had played at the inaugural rehearsal.

Of the additional tracks, only 'Tribute To Bert Burns' has ever been officially released, appearing under the title 'Baby Come On Home' on both the 1993 *Led Zeppelin* boxed set and the 10-CD *Complete Studio Recordings* set issued the same year, which goes to show that this set is not really complete.

Slow Ascent In The Home Country

As soon as they had the album in the can, the new band played its first British dates amid continued confusion over what they were actually called. The exact date and venue of their debut UK performance also remains disputed and unverified. This lack of basic information is less surprising than at first it might seem: with no album out and the old Yardbirds regarded as a spent force, the new band was seen as no big deal and on some of their initial dates they were paid as little as £75 a night. Hence the untried Page/Plant/Jones/Bonham line-up was pretty much allowed to road-test their new show away from the glare of the media – and almost everyone else, come to that. "We couldn't get work in Britain", Grant later complained. "It seemed to be a laugh to people that we were getting the group together and working the way we were".

The Story

According to Dave Lewis and Simon Pallett's book, *Led Zeppelin: The Concert File,* the first UK appearance of the new band may have come at the **Mayfair Ballroom,** Newcastle on 4 October. Certainly the concert was listed in the local paper as "The Yardbirds featuring Jimmy Page", but no review appeared and whether the gig ever took place, nobody seems to know or remember. Another contender was **Guildford Technical College,** now the University of Surrey, at least if you believe the plaque which Jimmy Page unveiled there in 2003 which reads: "THIS PLAQUE IS TO COMMEMORATE THE DEBUT PERFORMANCE OF LED ZEPPELIN, UNIVERSITY HALL, OCTOBER 15, 1968." In fact, it seems certain that their appearance there came ten days later on 25 October, and was therefore made somewhat less historic by the fact that by then the band had appeared at London's legendary Marquee Club on 18 October (billed perversely as "The British debut of The Yardbirds") and the following night at Liverpool University (where the gig was billed as "the last-ever appearance of The Yardbirds"). The first gig at which they were officially billed as Led Zeppelin took place a week later on 26

WITH a swing towards heavy music in recent months, Led Zeppelin, formerly the Yardbirds, have the potential to become important in this field. Guitarist Jimmy Page, John Paul Jones (bass) and John Bonham (drs) provide a powerful and often imaginative backing for Robert Plant's vocals. Plant and Page particularly appear to have a good rapport going and this could emerge as a prominent feature of Led Zeppelin. They may well be successful in the U.S.—TONY WILSON.

The *Melody Maker* announcement of the new band's formation was the first in a number of brilliant PR releases masterminded by Peter Grant. He moved the whole idea of promoting a band way beyond the traditional chart- or singles-based paradigm

October in the improbable surroundings of **Bristol Boxing Club.**

The new group received a significant snub when Led Zeppelin were touted for a slot in *The Rolling Stones Rock'n'Roll Circus* television spectacular in December 1968, but were personally vetoed by Mick Jagger, who took one listen to the band's tape and opted for **Jethro Tull** instead. It was just another example of the prejudice towards the new band about which both Page and Peter Grant bitterly complained. Perhaps this early slight also contributed to what would become an ongoing rivalry throughout the 1970s when Zeppelin and the Stones vied with each other for the title "the biggest rock'n'roll band in the world" (see page 93)

More memorable, at least for Robert Plant, was a gig at The Roundhouse on 9 November, at which "The Yardbirds now known as Led Zeppelin" (as they were this time billed) were supported by one of his heroes, **John Lee Hooker.** It was the perfect wedding present for a 20-year-old self-confessed blues nut: earlier that same day he had married his eight-months pregnant girlfriend, **Maureen,** although his joy nearly turned to despair when his car broke

Turn the volume down!

Quite what Led Zeppelin were about produced an element of confusion in the UK music press, not least concerning their apparent disdain for singles material, and love of volume. Among the first reviews was one by Tony Wilson in Melody Maker on 14 December 1968. It began by misspelling the name "Led Zepplin", but went on to admire Plant's singing, bemoaned equipment problems and continued "there seemed to be a tendency for too much volume, which inevitably defeats musical definition". 'Days of Confusion' (sic) was picked out as a good example of Plant's vocal interplay with Page's guitar, and the latter's use of a violin bow was noted as producing an "unusual effect". Bonham's style was acknowledged, but was maybe too forceful. The review ended with "generally there appears to be a need for Led Zeppelin to cut down on volume a bit".

down *en route* between the registry office and the venue and he almost missed the gig. Yet further evidence of Led Zeppelin's early inability to land prestige gigs in Britain came with an appearance at the utterly unsuitable Bridge Place Country Club near Canterbury, Kent on 13 December, although the band might have been amused by a concert flyer which tweely announced: "Ladies may come unescorted if they wish". At this early stage, Led Zeppelin's lock-up-your-daughters reputation had clearly still to reach the county they call "the garden of England".

While Led Zeppelin honed their live chops around Britain's university campuses and country clubs, Peter Grant was even busier on their behalf behind the scenes, setting up a record deal and organizing their first American tour. After first establishing Superhype Inc. to oversee the band's publishing, at the end of October he flew to America to finalize a deal with Atlantic Records – not for The Yardbirds, as he had originally planned and anticipated, but for a new and fabulous beast now called **Led Zeppelin**.

Grant had already struck a handshake deal with Atlantic for the band under its old name in early August. But this time he had not only a new name to sell but a copy of Led Zeppelin's already-completed debut album to play to Atlantic founder **Ahmet Ertegun** and his right-hand man, **Jerry Wexler**. To make an album without first signing a record deal was an unusual way of working, particularly at the time, but Page had been adamant that he wanted to finance the making of the LP himself and to present it to the record company on a take-it-or-leave-it basis. The more usual practice of accepting a record company advance to fund making the record would have conceded to the label's A&R department a say in the material, the sound and the production – and, as the guitarist put it, he wanted "artistic control in a vice-like grip". In particular, Page was determined that the new band was to be purely **album-led** and was adamant that there was to be no repeat of the ludicrous, and at times farcical, search for hit singles that had tarnished The Yardbirds' reputation at the hands of Mickie Most.

Page's bow

The notion that Jimmy Page was the first to play the guitar with a violin bow has always been challenged by fans of The Creation, a London-based mod band of the 1960s who then joined the psychedelic revolution. The band's guitarist Eddie Phillips, who once famously described their music as "red with purple flashes" and allegedly turned down an invitation from Pete Townshend to join The Who, used a violin bow on his guitar on the band's 1966 single 'Making Time' to create a venomous wall of sound.

Page refutes any suggestion that he copied the technique from Phillips and claims that it was suggested to him by a session violinist around at the same time. He used it on stage with The Yardbirds on 'I'm A Man' and 'I'm Confused' (later to become 'Dazed and Confused') and in the

studio on the 1967 album *Little Games*, on the tracks 'Glimpses' and 'Tinker, Tailor, Soldier, Sailor'.

He developed it with Led Zeppelin, using it in conjunction with an Echoplex to throw out a wall of reverberating sound, used to particularly devastating effect on 'Dazed and Confused', a showpiece of the band's set from their first gigs through until 1975. The bow was also used in early shows on 'How Many More Times'. After 'Dazed and Confused' was dropped, Page continued to use the violin bow on stage during guitar solos on 'Achilles' Last Stand' and 'In The Evening'.

In an odd coda to the Page-versus-Phillips saga, The Creation's second guitarist Kenny Pickett became Zeppelin's roadie on their first tour of America in early 1969.

Zeppelin's case was no doubt helped by the fact that Atlantic had just lost its biggest British signing in Cream, who had disbanded and were playing their farewell concerts even as the negotiations were taking place. But one listen to the tapes was more than enough to convince the astute Ertegun that, as Keith Shadwick rather cleverly puts it, here was a band that had that "elusive combination of musical quality and sheer raw excitement that would translate to consumer reaction".

According to Grant, there was still some jockeying when Atlantic said they wanted **Tom Dowd** to remix the record but, after Page had met Dowd and persuaded him that technically he knew what he was doing, the point was not pushed and Led Zeppelin were allowed to establish the unusual if not unique precedent that they would enjoy total control of their own recordings without label interference. By the time the negotiations had finished, the forceful Grant had turned his original handshake deal into a written five-year contract, a £200,000 advance and a royalty rate said at the time to be the highest ever paid.

The Zeppelin Flies Over America

It must have come as something of a relief to Led Zeppelin when they flew out of grey, drab Britain two days before Christmas 1968, bound for the sunshine of California in preparation for their first American tour. They knew they were on to something, but their poorly-paid, sparsely-attended low-grade smattering of British concerts had been met with only polite applause and little media interest. Mick Jagger had snubbed them, the Press didn't get it, and nobody seemed interested. If the music press paid them any attention at all, it tended to be of the sneering "they're just a hype" kind.

What a contrast to America, where their record company had already put out a press release about their new signing, predicting Led Zeppelin would be "the next group to reach the heights achieved by Cream and Jimi Hendrix". A grand claim, for sure, but the size of the band's advance said that it wasn't just hype: Atlantic believed it, even if Britain remained sceptical.

Crucially, the band were coming to believe it, too. Jones, Plant and Bonham were all married, yet they batted not an eyelid when Peter Grant told them they would be spending Christmas away from home. "It's a sacrifice. But there's going to be a pay-off", Page reportedly told them.

Despite his disappointment at not spending Christmas with his month-old baby daughter Carmen Jane, for Plant, with his passion for Californian music and his romantic, wide-eyed attachment to the West Coast hippie ideal, it seemed as if he was being offered a free ticket to the **Promised Land**. "It was the first time I'd even had a passport, let alone the first time I'd been to America", he recalled in 2005. "To get off the plane in Los Angeles and to go with Bonzo to stay at the Chateau Marmont on Sunset Strip was amazing".

He relished the opportunity to taste at first hand a wild and bohemian lifestyle he had only read about. "We hooked up with Terry Reid and we ended up in the suite Burl Ives

Chateau Marmont, high above Sunset Boulevard, West Hollywood, beloved resort of fading Hollywood stars, and by the 1970s of aspiring rockers

had just vacated. Down the corridor were the GTOs, Wild Man Fischer and all those **Sunset Strip** characters of the time. Rodney Bingenheimer was making coffee. There was all this stuff going on all day and night and me and Bonzo walked in with a TV dinner in a tin-foil tray to put in the oven while we watched *Hawaii Five-O*. It was a complete gas and all that dour Englishness had just disappeared into this powder-blue, post-Summer of Love Californian sunshine. There were even showers in the hotel rooms! Within 48 hours of arriving, I was just teleported".

But there was work to do. According to Plant, Jones and Page bankrolled that first US tour out of their own pockets (despite the "Led Wallet" nickname Page came to acquire) and its pared-down nature was in stark contrast to later tours when they flew around America in their own privately-hired jet. "We went around just the four of us with one roadie, who was Kenny Pickett from The Creation and the tour manager Richard Cole. It was really very basic," Plant recalled.

The band's first gig took place on Boxing Day in Denver, Colorado supporting **Vanilla Fudge**

Vanilla Fudge, looking good, and not looking notorious, but now largely forgotten

and **Spirit** (whose song 'Fresh Garbage' was a prominent feature of Zeppelin's set). The band's name did not appear on the concert posters but they were warmly enough received. A colder reception awaited five days later in Portland, Oregon as the band spent New Year's Eve driving through blizzards of snow as they attempted to reach Seattle airport to catch a flight to LA. The weather was so bad that the roads were officially closed and at one point tour manager Richard Cole, who was at the wheel, was forced to pull over by state police and told to discontinue their journey. Once the police had gone, Cole drove on regardless over treacherous mountain passes and wildly swaying suspension bridges and Plant and Bonham were convinced on at least two occasions during the journey that they were going to die. When they eventually arrived in Seattle the weather had shut down the airport and, to add insult to injury, Bonham and Plant, still 20 years old, were refused drinks at the bar because they were under age.

When they got to LA for a four-night stint at the **Whiskey a Go Go** on Sunset with **Alice Cooper**, the rigours of the journey had laid Page low with a fever. Scheduled to play two sets a night, the guitarist gamely struggled through the first set each evening with a temperature of 104 but the second proved too much and the band's pay was docked accordingly.

The turning point in their fortunes came when the band moved up the coast to San Francisco for four shows at **Bill Graham**'s legendary Fillmore West with **Country Joe and the Fish** and **Taj Mahal**. Page was feeling better; Plant was in seventh heaven playing in a city which he had spent 1967's Summer of Love dreaming about from the distant greyness of the West Midlands and, for the first time, they were allowed longer sets, which provided ample room for the experimentation and improvisation that became the band's forte.

On bootlegs of the San Francisco gigs you can almost hear their confidence growing with each song. "We were playing all right before, but from that point it was really gelling", Page later recalled. "The rest of the boys had gotten more accustomed to the American audiences; they had never been to America before and they were able to gauge things a little better. They felt they could relax more on stage, so right there is when it started happening. From then on we could see that there was some sort of reaction to us. We got standing ovations for each set for the four nights at Fillmore West". Indeed, so well did they go down that, by the third night, an ecstatic Plant was telling the audience: "We've decided we're going to come and live here, because you're so nice!"

The Fillmore shows also saw some radical innovations to the set, including the introduction of 'Killin' Floor', which swiftly developed into 'The Lemon Song', and it was now evident that some serious momentum was now gathering behind Led Zeppelin. "It felt like a vacuum and we'd come to fill it. You could feel something was happening", Page noted. "First this row, then that row, it was like a tornado and it went rolling across the country".

Iron Butterfly, hairy, out there, and heavy, nevertheless failed to rise to the challenge of the Zeppelin

By the time they hit the **East Coast** in the last week of January for gigs in Boston, Philadelphia and New York, the balloon had gone up. Zeppelin were playing like champions and, over two nights at New York's Fillmore East where they were supporting **Iron Butterfly**, they just blew the headline act away. At The Boston Tea Party on 26 January, the band played their usual hour-long set, including everything from their debut album – and the crowd just kept on demanding more. They ended up playing for another three hours, reprising their own material alongside just about every other song they knew, from Beatles' covers and Elvis favourites to Chuck Berry and Little Richard songs. According to Jones, when they finally came off, Peter Grant was crying and hugging

them. "It was then that we realized just what Led Zeppelin was going to become", the bassist told *NME*'s Nick Kent in 1973.

By the time the tour ended in Miami in mid-February, the band's debut album was out. It entered the *Billboard* chart at 99, jumped to 40 and then to 28, before finally entering the Top Ten in May. In total, it stayed on the charts for 73 consecutive weeks. No single was released from the album, mainstream radio play was minimal, and many of the album reviews struck a distinctly sour note, led by *Rolling Stone* whose **John Mendelsohn** sneered that if Led Zeppelin wanted to succeed "they will have to find a producer, editor and some material worthy of their collective talents".

The live reviews from those who had actually seen them play were far better. On the evidence of their shows in Boston, the city's leading critic declared that Zeppelin were to rock "what Formula One cars are to road racing", while *Billboard* reckoned the way they had destroyed Iron Butterfly at the Fillmore East earmarked them as "**the next big super group**". The record was selling purely on the word-of-mouth enthusiasm generated by that first tour. "I think what did it for us was the live thing", Page observed. "We were unknown, we did our number and the word got out that we were worth seeing". And they now had a reputation to take back home to a previously uninterested Britain.

Back To Blighty: From Heroes To Zeroes

Strange as it may seem, when the band returned to Britain there were mutterings (if not open doubts) over Robert Plant's position in the band. The singer, who during the first American tour had earned the nickname "Percy" after the British TV gardener Percy Thrower (Plant – geddit?), was being singled out for criticism in some of the more negative reviews of the band, led again by *Rolling Stone*, which insultingly dubbed him "a pretty soul-belter who can do a good spade imitation".

According to Richard Cole, such comments also began to **gnaw away** at Page, who came to question whether he had made the right decision over his choice of singer. "It was a very touch-and-go thing whether Robert would even be in the group after that first tour, because he didn't quite seem to make it up to Page's expectation", the tour manager commented. "At the time there was a possibility he wouldn't do another tour. That's the truth". Plant has also confessed to having his own self-doubts: "I was very intimidated. Maybe I had a complex, maybe I was just neurotic or paranoid but I thought, 'this is all too much. Am I really here? Do I belong in this sketch?'"

To his credit, Page has always loyally denied in public that he ever had any doubts and has never offered anything but the highest praise for his colleague's vocal abilities, even when Plant himself has been highly self-critical of his early efforts. "I was very uncomfortable on stage and didn't know what to do with myself", the singer admitted in 2005. "I was really taken by the music but I was pleased when I was able to start crafting it a bit more. At the time I didn't even know what craft was. I was overwhelmed by it. There were much better singers at the time who could have brought it on home in a different way. If there had been Steve Marriott or Steve Winwood or Terry Reid, all of whom I considered to be far better singers than me, it would have had a different personality and the band would have gone a different way".

But when the comments were reported to Jimmy Page, he offered this sterling defence of his old colleague: "I know he's not happy with the ad-libs on *Led Zep I*, but I think he should be really pleased with his vocal approach.

British Top Twenty LPs

1	(2)	**GOODBYE**............Cream, Polydor	
2	(1)	**BEST OF THE SEEKERS**	
			Seekers, Columbia
3	(3)	**HAIR**............London Cast, Polydor	
4	(7)	**OLIVER**........Soundtrack, RCA Victor	
5	(5)	**SOUND OF MUSIC**	
			Soundtrack, RCA Victor
6	(4)	**SCOTT 3**..........Scott Walker, Philips	
7	(18)	**ON THE THRESHOLD OF A**	
		DREAM Moody Blues, Deram	
8	(6)	**20/20**..................Beach Boys, Capitol	
9	(9)	**GENTLE ON MY MIND**	
			Dean Martin, Reprise
10	(11)	**POST CARD**......Mary Hopkin, Apple	
11	(15)	**LED ZEPPELIN**	
			Led Zeppelin, Atlantic
12	(10)	**ROCK MACHINE I LOVE YOU**	
			Various Artists, CBS
13	(16)	**THE WORLD OF VAL DOONICAN**	
			Val Doonican, Decca
14	(12)	**ENGELBERT**	
			Engelbert Humperdinck, Decca
15	(8)	**DIANA ROSS AND THE SUP-**	
		REMES JOIN THE TEMPTATIONS	
			Tamla Motown
	(20)	**WORLD OF BLUES POWER**	
			Various Artists, Decca
17	(—)	**SONGS FROM A ROOM**	
			Leonard Cohen, CBS
18	(14)	**YOU CAN ALL JOIN IN**	
			Various Artists, Island
19	(—)	**ELVIS (NBC-TV SPECIAL)**	
			Elvis Presley, RCA Victor
20	(—)	**GRADUATE**...........Soundtrack, CBS	

two LP's 'tied' for 15th position

The *Disc* and *Music Echo* chart for April 1969 makes interesting reading, with the band whom Zeppelin would effectively succeed, Cream, posthumously heading a field heavy with musical scores and samplers

He was performing in a very inspired way, like everyone else in the band. What he did was really fitting, in terms of where we were going. It was an essential element. And millions would agree with me rather than with him on how great his singing was on those first couple of records".

If Plant's position was ever in any serious doubt, the **moment of crisis** passed swiftly as the band settled down to promoting their debut album, which received a belated British release on 28 March 1969. It entered the charts two weeks later and stayed there for the next 79 weeks, peaking at Number Six.

If some of the reviews were negative, and dwelt on the alleged hype surrounding the band, a few perceptive critics recognized that *Led Zeppelin I* represented a significant milestone in the development of British rock music. The ever-loyal **Chris Welch** chipped in with a brace of encouraging reviews, one in the satirical weekly *Punch*, which hailed it as the rock album of the year and another in *Melody Maker* under the headline: "JIMMY PAGE TRIUMPHS: LED ZEPPELIN IS A GAS."

In the underground magazine *OZ*, **Felix Dennis** wrote: "Very occasionally an LP record is released that defies immediate categorization, because it's so obviously a turning point in rock music that only time proves capable of shifting it into perspective. This Led Zeppelin album is like that". Even more presciently, he added: "Of course, as a result of this album we'll lose the group to the States and almost certainly within months the

Melody Maker letters page will headline 'Is Page better than God?'".

The band promoted the album with BBC radio sessions for **John Peel**'s *Top Gear* show and an R&B programme on the BBC World Service presented by Plant's old partner, Alexis Korner as well as virtually the only serious TV appearances of Zeppelin's career, for Swedish and German networks and on a new BBC2 show called *How Late It Is*, on which they deputized at the last minute for the Flying Burrito Brothers and played 'Communication Breakdown' and 'Dazed And Confused'.

Another short Scandinavian tour in March ended in near disaster with an emergency landing at Stansted on their return flight to Britain, the band dramatically exiting the plane via safety chutes. In an horrific imitation of the burning Zeppelin on the front cover of their debut album that might have spooked more superstitious souls, an engine had caught fire. Yet that same night Led Zeppelin were back on stage at The Marquee to commence a series of British dates which found them playing such venues as the Toby Jug, Tolworth, and Bromley Technical College. Fees were risible, one gig guaranteeing them just £60. The halls were mostly small but full, and the crowd reaction was increasingly enthusiastic, with the exception of a disastrous appearance at the Top Rank Ballroom, Cardiff, where an outdated dress code demanded everyone wore ties and jackets. Stewards even attempted to apply the rule to the group itself and they were initially refused entry for being **inappropriately attired**. When they were eventually allowed to play, their set was brought to an abrupt end when the revolving stage whisked them out of sight, halfway through 'How Many More Times'. The set was to last exactly 45 minutes and they were not even extended the courtesy of being allowed to finish the number, as they were replaced by an inane disc jockey playing that week's Top Twenty.

During the first two weeks of April, when not travelling between gigs, they began recording their second album at Olympic Studios, Barnes. Among the new compositions swiftly completed were 'What Is And What Should Never Be' and 'Whole Lotta Love'. Yet once again, it must have come as something of a relief when in mid-April they left behind uptight, stuffy, class-ridden, jacket-and-tie Britain for their second tour of America, where their debut album had now well and truly taken off.

From Success to Excess...
1969–1970

"Led Zeppelin is probably the most aggressive, masculine rock group anywhere. They batter at the mind and ear, insisting they will penetrate".

Live review in *The Edmonton Journal*, May 1969

From Success To Excess...
1969–1970

In what had seemed, to both the band and their critics, an amazingly short time, Zeppelin had moved from the shadows of presumptuous obscurity to the limelight. Their almost immediate success in the States while being coolly received in the UK oddly proving a mirror image to the Beat Boom bands of the previous generation. Suddenly, they were the hot ticket, with a follow-up album to beat all follow-up albums to boot.

The First Flush

Although it was less than four months since an untried and rather green Led Zeppelin had flown to America for its first tour, it was a very different band that returned to the US in April 1969. The first album was climbing the *Billboard* charts and there was a buzz about them, at least in all of the cities where they had already played. They were no longer the support but were now either headliners in their own right, or sharing top billing with such established acts as **Delaney & Bonnie** and **Three Dog Night**, as 27 shows across North America were crammed into a six-week tour.

They were further buoyed by the new material they had started recording for *Led Zeppelin*

II. Although their hectic schedule meant they would not finish recording the album until August, it was already obvious to all concerned that their sophomore effort was shaping up to be a classic. There was now a strutting, cocksure swagger about the group, both on and off stage and Plant in particular seemed to have shed his earlier insecurities. If they had been tentative on the first tour, they now believed not only that they were the loudest, horniest, most explosive rock band on the planet, but that it was only a matter of time before the rest of the world knew it too. With such an attitude, it was on this tour that some of the most outrageous incidents in the infamous catalogue of their **on-the-road excesses** took place and their reputation as "the hammer of the gods" was first forged.

From Success To Excess...

"We were hot and on our way up and nobody was watching too closely", tour manager Richard Cole later recalled. "All the Led Zeppelin depravity took place in the first two years in an alcoholic fog. Seemingly overnight, we found ourselves in a position to do almost anything we wanted and there seemed to be a tidal wave of free-spirited girls who were always cooperative and compliant".

Much of the debauchery was chronicled years later in his book by a boastful Cole, but more damagingly it was also observed at the time by **Ellen Sander**, a journalist with *Life* magazine who went on the road with the band. She was so disgusted with their behaviour that she refused to give the band the publicity of the planned cover story. Her edi-

Pamela des Barres, or "Miss Pamela" of the GTOs, one of a number of groupies who ligged with the Zep in LA, with Page outside Bingenheimer's English Disco

tors backed her and pulled the piece, and her observations eventually appeared in a book in 1973, in which she accused the band of "failing to keep their behaviour up to a basic human level". She also recorded Page's callous attitude to groupies ("girls come around and pose like starlets, teasing and acting haughty. If you humiliate them a bit they tend to come on all right after that. Everybody knows what they come for") and detailed such stories as a plot to gang-bang a pair of groupies and then stuff their orifices with cream doughnuts. She also claimed that two members of the Zeppelin circus ripped her dress and tried to rape her before Peter Grant arrived in the nick of time and pulled them off. "If you walk inside the cages of the zoo, you get to see the animals close up, stroke the captive pelts and mingle with the energy behind the mystique", she wrote of her encounter with Zeppelin. "You also get to smell the shit first hand".

Another who saw the hooliganism and excess at first hand was **Pamela des Barres**, a leading groupie known at the time as Miss Pamela. "As much as I loved Zeppelin, they kind of fucked things up in LA", she later observed. "Something about their energy really altered the *joie de vivre* of the scene. They thought they could get away with anything and they could, because everybody wanted to get near them. They were very debauched and the girls got younger and more willing to do anything. It got to be incredibly sick".

On their return to Britain they opened a short tour supported by **Blodwyn Pig** and the

The Bath festivals

The Bath Festival of Blues in 1969 was the first outdoor music event to be organized by promoter Freddie Bannister. It had a solid British line-up including Ten Years After, John Mayall, The Nice, Fleetwood Mac, Colossuem, Roy Harper and Taste, and with John Peel as MC. Played out on two tiny stages (above left) in Bath recreation ground, surrounded by Georgian buildings, and despite attracting a mere 12,000 people, the single-day event proved a significant outing for Led Zeppelin. Although appearing mid-afternoon, in covering most of Led Zeppelin I and

previewing much of Led Zeppelin II, they effectively stole the show. The event occurred in June, a week before the Stones played Hyde Park and two months before Woodstock and the Isle of Wight festival.

It was followed in June 1970 by The Bath Festival of Blues and Progressive Music (see page 76), again organized by Bannister, but on a much more ambitious basis, with US musicians such as Jefferson Airplane, The Byrds, Hot Tuna, Frank Zappa and The Mothers of Invention, Johnny Winter, Canned Heat, Dr. John, Santana and Steppenwolf. Apart from Led Zeppelin, among the British bands were Pink Floyd, Fairport Convention, Colosseum, John Mayall and The Moody Blues. Held over Saturday, Sunday and Monday on a greenfield site, an estimated 180–200,000 people attended, more than anticipated, which resulted in a general collapse in organization. Led Zeppelin appeared in the early evening of the Sunday, and once again their performance tend to dominate the memories of those who were there, although Zappa's set earlier that afternoon was remembered as the most professional.

Liverpool Scene in Birmingham on 13 June 1969, and reached a wider audience with no fewer than three sessions for BBC's Radio One that same month. Much bootlegged over the years, the best of the radio broadcasts were eventually officially released on the double-CD *Led Zeppelin BBC Sessions* in 1997 (see pages 191–193).

Their two-week sojourn in Britain, during which time they conducted further work on *Led Zeppelin II*, ended over the last weekend of June with performances at the **Bath Blues Festival** and the Pop Proms at the Albert Hall, the band's biggest two UK appearances to date. They also garnered some of their best British reviews. "When Zeppelin came on and played at a good ten times the volume of everyone else, the audience very nearly freaked completely", *Disc* reported of the **Albert Hall** show. "They stormed the stage, danced in the aisles and the boxes and were screaming so hard that the band did three encores. Jimmy Page, ex-Yardbird, who's got together one of the most exciting live bands playing anywhere right now, blew some really mean and fine guitar solos". Nick Logan in the *NME* concluded: "It is boggling that in a matter of months they have achieved such a high degree of musicianship and become one of the biggest crowd-pullers around".

Britain Catches On

The tour and the radio appearances helped propel the band's debut album into the Top Five of the British charts. But the weekend after the Albert Hall gig, they were back in America again for another barnstorming two-month coast-to-coast stint and more off-stage excess – and in one instance of on-stage excess an inebriated Bonham ran on stage and stripped naked during a performance by **The Jeff Beck Group** at the Flushing Meadows Festival, New York. He only escaped arrest when Peter Grant rugby-tackled him and then hid him from the police in a locked dressing room. Along with the booze, the endless supply of groupies also helped them unwind between shows and during the band introductions one night on stage in Toronto, Plant let the cat out of the bag when he candidly announced: "On lead guitar and as many chicks as he can find... Jimmy Page!" At the end of the tour, the guitarist went into a New York studio to finishing mixing *Led Zeppelin II*, before taking a holiday in Spain and Morocco while the other three band members enjoyed the group's first proper break of the year with their families. Back home, the wild, out-of-control, groupie-abus-

ing rock'n'roll studs found little difficulty, it seems, in transforming themsleves back into quiet and respectable husbands and fathers.

Virtually none of the material from the forthcoming new album had been played live during summer 1969 but, after their hard-earned break, Grant lined up another assault on American concert halls to coincide with the release of *Led Zeppelin II* in October 1969. Unlike the debut album, which had been recorded in such a tight time frame, work on the second album had sprawled over a period of almost six months, with songs written in hotel rooms while on the road and recorded in snatched studio sessions between live dates. Plant called it a "crazy" way to make an album – and yet it somehow worked to produce an era-defining record which created the template for a thousand derivative heavy rock bands to imitate. *Led Zeppelin II* marked the beginning of Plant's writing partnership with Jimmy Page, but it was still the guitarist's monumental riffs that dominated. Many of them were blues-based but Zeppelin's second album marked them out from the other British blues bands of the era such as **John Mayall, Fleetwood Mac** and **Chicken Shack**. Zeppelin were louder and heavier, for sure, but they were also somehow far sexier and more theatrical. As Plant put it in 2005, "It was still blues-based but it was a much more carnal approach to the music and quite flamboyant".

Aside from the mighty riffs of 'Whole Lotta Love' and Bonham's drum showpiece 'Ramble On', there were gentler moments, such as the acoustic part of 'Ramble On' and the lovely 'Thank You', with Plant making a major contribution as a lyricist. "I'd never really written a song until Zep got together, so the crafting of lyric and melody was developing all the time", Plant told this writer many years later. "The writing process is quite personal and intimate but working with Jimmy was very stimulating. He was my senior in every respect but the melding was good and by about the eighth song we wrote together I began to realize that I had something with this guy that was very special. I was no longer just chancing it so I was feeling better and better all the time. *Led Zeppelin II* was very virile. That was the album that was going to dictate whether or not we had the staying power and the capacity to stimulate. It had changed colour completely from the first album. It had become much more creative and imaginative".

"In the early days I was writing the lyrics as well as the music because Robert hadn't written before", Page recalls. "It took a lot of ribbing and teasing to actually get him into writing. And then on the second LP he wrote the words of 'Thank You'. He said 'I'd like to have a crack at this and write it for my wife'". Elsewhere, however, Plant's lyrics had an unfortunate tendency to "borrow" without attribution from his beloved blues heroes (see pages 222–223).

This became a particularly sore point on *Led Zeppelin II* when Willie Dixon, who wrote many of Muddy Waters' and Howlin' Wolf's greatest songs, subsequently sued and received

The double-page spread in *Melody Maker* for the band's early 1970 UK tour to promote *Led Zeppelin II* was unusual for the time, and again shows how Grant forcefully and rapidly built their reputation within the first 18 months of their existence

out-of-court settlements for segments from both 'Whole Lotta Love' and 'Bring It On Home' which were lifted without credit from his songbook. Certainly, Led Zeppelin weren't the only white rock band of the 1960s to steal from black blues artists. But on *Led Zeppelin*

Zeppelin: a singles band or not?

From the outset, Led Zeppelin adopted a "no singles" policy in accord with their self-image as a serious rock band rather than a pop group. In this respect, the band saw themselves as a very different creature from The Rolling Stones: "I always thought of the Stones as a pop group who made singles", Robert Plant noted in 2005. "The whole idea of what we did competing with Bobby Goldsboro for airplay as they were wasn't where we were at. What we said was there's no point putting out a single when the album is the statement of the band".

The deal Peter Grant had struck with Atlantic meant the band had the power to determine what was released under its name, and therefore had an effective veto on all singles. Yet, although they never released a single commercially in Britain, in America they did make several concessions to their rule. 'Good Times Bad Times' backed with 'Communication Breakdown' had appeared as a single in America in March 1969 and, although it didn't chart, it did get AM radio play which helped to promote the first album. Helpfully, both tracks were also short enough that they didn't require editing for the seven-inch single format.

Following the release of *Led Zeppelin II* in October 1969, Atlantic in America started pressuring the band to release another single, and suggested the five-and-a-half minute long 'A Whole Lotta Love'. According to an interview Bonham and Plant gave in *Melody Maker* at the time, the band agreed on the condition that the track was released in its entirety,

Despite the "no-singles" policy in the UK, viewers of BBC's weekly chart round-up *Top Of The Pops* got exposure to the band week in and week out, as Alexis Korner and CCS's cover of 'Whole Lotta Love' was adopted as the show's theme tune

complete with the sonic storm of its experimental middle section. However, the band hadn't asnticipated the enterprizing nature of American disc jockeys. Long before the remix became a standard practice, several AM station began playing their own edited version of 'Whole Lotta Love', omitting its unconventional middle. Retailers then started asking Atlantic to release it commercially in edited form, and the label petitioned Peter Grant to sanction it.

Grant stalled by telling them the band would record a custom-made single, although this may have been simply been a ruse that there was never any serious intention of fulfilling. Reluctantly, the band eventually gave in reasoning that, as the edited version was already all over the airwaves, they were merely accepting what was a *fait-accompli*. The edited single eventually sold almost a million copies, doing particularly brisk trade with juke-box companies. However, the band vetoed all plans to issue the edited single in Britain, where Atlantic had expectantly given it a catalogue number.

In later years the band resisted, with particular vehemence, sustained record company pressure to issue 'Stairway To Heaven' as a single. In America, however, Led Zeppelin actually released ten singles between 1969 and 1979. In addition to 'Whole Lotta Love', three more of them made the *Billboard* Top Twenty: 'Immigrant Song', backed with 'Hey Hey What Can I Do', the only non-album track ever to appear on a Zeppelin single (1970), 'Black Dog' (1971) and 'D'yer Mak' er' (1973).

II the band was more brazen than most and, as the writer **Barney Hoskyns** has noted, they appeared "callously indifferent to the implications of this purloining".

In later years, both Page and Plant have squirmed when questioned about it and, somewhat unedifyingly, attempted to blame each other. "I think when Willie Dixon turned on the radio in Chicago 20 years after he wrote his blues, he thought 'that's my song'" Plant said in 1985. "When we ripped it off I said to Jimmy, 'Hey, that's not our song'. And he said 'Shut up and keep walking'". Page claimed the problems were all down to Plant. "Robert was supposed to change the lyrics and he didn't always do that", he told *Guitar World*. "That's what brought us most of the grief. They couldn't get us on the guitar parts of the music, but they nailed us on the lyrics. So if there is any plagiarism, just blame Robert".

Yet such arguments were still in the future when *Led Zeppelin II* was released. Not all of the reviews were ecstatic and there were carping voices from the augustly hip (then) *Rolling Stone*, which for some reason had something against the band from the outset. But the critics could not prevent the album topping the charts and when *Led Zeppelin II* toppled The Beatles' *Abbey Road* from the Number One spot in America in December 1969, it somehow seemed to define the end of the 1960s and symbolize the rise of the new order. Inside a year, they had gone from earning $500 a night for their first US shows to a basic minimum guarantee of $100,000. A further indication of just how fast and how far they had risen was Grant's decision to turn down an invitation to appear at the **Woodstock** festival in August 1969, on a bill that included Jimi Hendrix, The Who and Santana. "Atlantic were very keen and so was our US promoter. I said 'no' because we'd have been just another band on the bill", he explained. Zeppelin now topped the bill or they didn't appear at all, it seemed.

A report in *The Financial Times* at the end of 1969 calculated that the group had generated $5 million in US sales. It didn't earn them MBEs like The Beatles, but their contribution to Britain's balance of payments was recognized when **Gwyneth Dunwoody**, a minister at the Board of Trade in Harold Wilson's Labour government, presented them with gold discs at a ceremony at London's Savoy Hotel the week before Christmas 1969. "You seem to be gas rockets rather than Led Zeppelins", she told them. Plant kissed the minister on the cheek and following the ceremony Page celebrated by popping around to an upmarket car dealership in Berkeley Square to buy himself a Rolls-Royce.

In America, the album's success had been helped by the release of an edited version of 'Whole Lotta Love' as a single. In Britain the band refused to sanction its release, insisting they were strictly an albums act. That may have slowed their progress but by early 1970, *Led Zeppelin II* had inexorably risen to the top of the British charts too.

Pomp And Circumstance

1970–1971

"I suppose it's a combination of a good band and the time it broke. Cream had gone and other groups had an even chance of getting in. But somehow we made it".

John Paul Jones, 1970

Pomp And Circumstance
1970–1971

With The Beatles no more, the Stones recovering from the horror of Altamont, in tax exile, and out of contract at Decca, and The Who wondering how to follow *Tommy*, 1970 was the year in which Led Zeppelin officially became the biggest British group in the world. What's more, rock's old guard didn't like being superseded one little bit. And they did their best to wrong-foot the young pretenders.

The Big Time

The year 1970 started with a brief British Zeppelin tour, which went some way towards mending bridges with the more hostile elements of the British rock press and those sections of its readership that felt aggrieved that the band had turned its back on its homeland. "I think our success in America had an effect on the critique over here", Plant noted. "It was like 'They've gone and who the fuck are they anyway?' Oh well, it's overblown". Highlight of the tour was a two-and-a-half hour show at London's **Albert Hall** on 9 January 1970 which Jones described as a "here-we-are type of show" to prove they hadn't deserted Britain. In fact, it was only seven months since their last British show – coincidentally also at the Albert Hall – but the statistics for once were revealing. Between December 1968 and April 1970, Led Zeppelin played 153 shows in America. During the same period, they played just 28 shows in Britain.

Just what Britain had been missing, and how spectacular a live act Zeppelin had become, can be seen in the film of the Albert Hall show, shot for a planned **documentary** (see page 264) which never happened but which eventually appeared on the *Led Zeppelin* DVD set in 2003. In the years since, we've got used to theatrical stadium shows with dry ice and inflatables. Yet, what is striking about Zeppelin circa 1970 is how simple, direct and yet intense was their stagecraft. As critic Barney Hoskyns put it, the DVD reveals a show stripped-down to "just four men, barely more than boys, bound together in intense rhythmic symbiosis, rooted in the most brutal, pulverizing grooves ever devised".

Sour grapes?

In early 1970, the writer Ritchie Yorke canvassed other prominent UK musicians for their views on Led Zeppelin, and the replies tasted more than a little of sour grapes. His experiment revealed a begrudging rock aristocracy deeply pissed off at the success of a bunch of upstarts.

– Keith Richards: "I played their first album quite a lot when I first got it but then the guy's voice started to get on my nerves".

– Eric Clapton: "I don't know about them. I've heard their records and I saw them play. They were very loud – I thought it was unnecessarily loud. I liked some of it but a lot of it was just too much. They over-emphasized whatever point they were making".

– Pete Townshend: "I'm not one of their biggest fans which doesn't mean that I don't like them, but means that I don't really get into their music a lot".

– John Lennon: "From what little I've heard, they sound all right".

It's also clear that there's a fair degree of spontaneity and improvisation going on. "You had to be on the ball, especially in the improvised parts", Jones says. "You' d have to watch each other for cues. Lots of things happened on stage to alter the songs. In the fast part to 'Dazed and Confused' John and I would turn the riff round backwards and Pagey would come across and shout, 'What the fucking hell do you think you are doing!' That was good fun".

Plant's presence is also impressively charismatic, even when playing air guitar during Page's solos. "At that Albert Hall show I was 21 and just a black country hippie", he now says modestly. "I was hanging on for dear life, weaving my way through the three greatest players of their time. It was an absolute shock when I first saw that footage. It's so disarming – not unnerving but kind of cute and coy, and you see all that sort of naïvety and the absolute wonder of what we were doing. And the freshness of it, because the whole sort of stereotypical rock-singer thing hadn't kicked in for me".

As usual, the reviews were mixed with *Disc* raving about the show and *Melody Maker* bizarrely claiming "it took them nearly the whole of their set to get the fires blazing", which suggests that their reviewer was at a different show to the one captured on film. But it mattered not. The UK music press is not always as powerful as it likes to pretend, and where Zeppelin were concerned, British rock fans had made their own minds up and no amount of sneering from critics who received their records and concert tickets for free was going to change their minds.

A mishap caused the **postponement** of the final date of the tour in early February, when Plant crashed his Jaguar on his way home after going to see the West Coast band Spirit playing at Mother's in Birmingham and was briefly hospitalized. But, by the end of the month he was fit enough for a short tour of Europe, which produced one of the group's oddest gigs when they were forced to appear in Copenhagen under the name 'The Nobs'. Before the show they were confronted by

The acoustic section, which was to become a staple of the live shows after *Led Zeppelin III*, gets an early outing in during "An Evening With Led Zeppelin" in the USA, 1970. Jones (left) is playing mandolin

Eva von Zeppelin, who claimed to be a relative of Graf von Zeppelin, who had designed the German airship that bore his name. Announcing that "They may be world-famous but a group of shrieking monkeys are not going to use a privileged family name without permission", she must have been a formidable lady, for the group were intimidated enough to change their name for the night – or perhaps they just enjoyed the joke. Nothing further was heard from Eva or her lawyers, and a week later they were back to being Led Zeppelin for

an appearance at the **Montreux Jazz Festival**, promoted by Claude Knobs, whose name they had borrowed in the panic in Copenhagen.

After another box office-breaking American tour in spring 1970, billed as "An Evening With Led Zeppelin" in recognition of the fact that their elongated sets now meant they had no need of a support act, they also started work on their third album. That it would present a different sound from the first two LPs had already been telegraphed by Robert Plant when he told *Melody Maker*: "We haven't prepared much material yet, but we've got a few things down and it's all acoustic, folks! You can just see it, can't you: 'Led Zeppelin go soft on their fans' or some crap like that". He also revealed that he and Page planned to rent a cottage in Wales "where we can lock ourselves away for a few weeks just to see what we can come up with when there's no one else around".

Back To Nature

He already had a location in mind. When he was a child, Plant had regularly spent summer holidays with his parents in a cottage called **"Bron-yr-aur"** (pronounced Bron-raar) just north of Machynlleth in Powys, central Wales near the river Dyfi, rented from friends of the family. It was rural and isolated, with no running water, heating or electricity – it could not have been further removed from the hedonistic pleasures of the Hyatt Hotel on Sunset Strip or the trials and tribulations of the just-completed American tour during which a promoter had pulled a gun on Peter Grant, a show had been stopped in Pittsburgh, and Bonham had vented his homesickness by systematically destroying hotel rooms. The tour had ended on another bum note with the cancellation of the final date, after Plant collapsed from exhaustion in Phoenix. In late April, a week after the band's return from America, the singer decamped to the Welsh cottage with his wife Maureen, daughter Carmen, and the family dog, **Strider**. Page arrived with his girlfriend Charlotte Martin and two Led Zeppelin roadies, Clive Coulson

and Sandy MacGregor, were also invited along to take care of the domestic chores and ensure that the drudgery of cooking, cleaning, lighting fires and fetching water from the stream didn't interfere with the serious business of strumming guitars and writing songs.

Coulson later insisted that the roadies weren't taken for granted. "Everyone mucked in really. I wouldn't take any of that superior shit. They were wonderful people to work for, normal blokes. They weren't treated as gods", he said. Nevertheless, there was never any doubt as to who were the paymasters and which members of the party were there as hired hands. "Pagey was two people – one of the lads and the boss", Coulson admitted. "Plant's speciality was posing and telling people how to do things".

As a working holiday it was highly productive in more ways than one: Page and **Charlotte Martin**'s daughter Scarlett (who later became a respected rock photographer) was conceived while there. But the songs also flowed prolifically. Page brought a portable tape recorder along so that no song or song fragment was lost. Among the songs that began to take shape at Bron-yr-aur were 'Friends', 'Celebration Day', 'Gallows Pole', 'That's The Way', 'Hats Off To (Roy) Harper', 'Bron-y-aur Stomp' ((sic) based on a song called 'Jennings Farm Blues' named after Plant's new home, which they had started the previous December). All were further developed to appear on *Led Zeppelin III*. Also products of the stay in the Welsh mountains were 'Hey Hey What Can I Do' (a rare non-album track that was the B-side to

Rural idylls

"Getting it together in the country" had already become something of a tradition in rock circles. Traffic had put together its debut album while staying in a country cottage in Berkshire and Plant was also much impressed by time spent hanging out with The Incredible String Band, who lived collectively in a row of cottages in the Scottish borders. There was also the role model of the San Francisco bands, who had retreated up the coast from the city and across the Golden Gate Bridge to the more bucolic surroundings of

Marin County, while The Band had recorded both their debut album *Music From Big Pink* and *The Basement Tapes* with Bob Dylan in a communal house in Woodstock in upstate New York. By 1971, even the urbane Paul McCartney was shearing sheep at his Scottish croft on the cover of *Ram*.

Although the Ordnance Survey shows Plant's retreat as "Bron-y-aur", as spelt on *Led Zeppelin III* (the "y" being typical in certain Welsh toponyms), the current owners (and *Physical Graffiti*) prefer "Bron-yr-aur".

'Immigrant Song' when released as a single in America) and pieces that later became 'Over The Hills' and 'Far Away' (on *Houses Of The Holy*), 'Down By The Seaside', 'The Rover' and 'Bron-yr-aur' (on *Physical Grafitti*) and 'Poor Tom' (on *Coda*).

Plant, in particular, was ecstatic about the whole experience, which represented the culmination of the **hippie dream** he had nurtured since 1967's "Summer of Love", and which had sustained him even when he was reduced to joining a road-gang laying tarmac in West Bromwich high street. "We wrote these songs and walked and talked and thought and went off to the abbey where they hid the grail", he later recalled of their Welsh idyll. "No matter how cute and comical it might be now to

look back at that, it gave us so much energy because we were really close to something. We believed. It was absolutely wonderful and my heart was so light and happy. At that time, at that age, 1970 was like the biggest blue sky I ever saw".

The sun was still shining when Page and Plant took the songs to Jones and Bonham and the four convened to begin rehearsing the material at Plant's farm in Worcestershire. In an attempt to replicate at least some of the spirit of Bron-yr-aur, they then decamped in June 1970 with some mobile recording equipment to **Headley Grange**, an allegedly haunted former workhouse. The sessions went well, Jones entering the acoustic spirit by introducing mandolin and with further work taking places in Island's London studios, the album was virtually finished by July, although other delays in the mixing and the gimmicky sleeve design with its revolving card disc delayed release until October. This meant its release missed their sixth American tour, which culminated with a brace of shows at **Madison Square Garden** on 19 September for which the band grossed more than $100,000. It was the day after Jimi Hendrix's death, and Plant paid tribute to him from the stage, calling his demise a "great loss for the music world".

Bigger Than The Beatles

Led Zeppelin's only British appearance during the second half of 1970 came at the Bath Festival of Blues and Progressive Music in June. With Page dressed in a "Farmer John" hat and tweed overcoat and Plant sporting a pointy, goatee beard, it was the biggest UK appearance of their career to date in front of an ecstatic 150,000 audience. Peter Grant had negotiated that the band would take the stage at sunset, which meant that the band's set was sandwiched by **Flock** and **Hot Tuna** leaving **Jefferson Airplane** as the nominal bill-toppers. But Grant had astutely calculated that with festival bills at the time habitually over-running by several hours, hitting the crowd when it was wide awake and ready to rock in the early evening was preferable to topping the bill in the early hours of the morning when every-

Page in farmer's tweeds, Plant in a Charles I "full set" at Freddie Bannister's seminal Bath Festival of Blues and Progressive Music in 1970 (see also page 63)

one was tired and exhausted.

The plan almost went wrong when Flock received an ecstatic ovation and were called back for two encores, but Grant ordered his roadies to start dismantling the American group's gear against the wishes of the festival organizers and the group itself who were planning a third encore. His hardball tactics won the day. The bewildered Flock were hustled off, Zeppelin went on as dusk was falling and proceeded to play like demons. The reception was phenomenal, and a set of glowing reviews hailed their set as the highlight of the weekend. For the first time, the band's detractors in the

UK music press were forced to admit that perhaps they had got Led Zeppelin wrong. Or perhaps they were simply bowing to the clamour of their own readership: in September, Zeppelin were voted best band in the annual *Melody Maker* readers' poll, displacing **The Beatles** from the top slot they had held continuously since 1963.

The fans who had catapulted Zeppelin to the top tended to be slightly younger than the average rock constituency, often still at school rather than college or university, and in some quarters were disparagingly referred to as "**headbangers**". In fact, it was an accurate description of the characteristic pose adopted by many fans, and the sight of the entire front row at a Zeppelin concert, with their heads weaving up and down with hair flying over their faces in time to the thundering riffs, made for an extraordinary sight. Were such fans ready for the subtler and surprisingly mellow sounds emanating from the Welsh cottage that were about to appear on *Led Zeppelin III*? Although they all faithfully bought the new record when it appeared in October 1970, many were undoubtedly disappointed that it was not a standard heavy-rock album. The riffs that the album did boast, such as the crunching opener 'Immigrant Song', were certainly spectacular. But such moments were tempered by the acoustic material born of the Bron-yr-aur sojourn, such as 'Friends', 'Tangerine' and the Crosby, Stills and Nash-influenced 'That's The Way'. "What came out on our third album was a reflection of the fact that the pendulum had swung in the total

opposite direction from all that *Led Zeppelin II* live thing, and the energy of being on the road", Page explains. "It was like, 'Oh we're here, we're in nature, we can hear the birds sing, there's not a car sound, there's no aeroplanes, there's no concert to do'. It was just fantastic".

According to Plant, they were "obsessed" with change and doing something different. "*Led Zeppelin II* was something we felt good about because it would have been more obvious to use 'Whole Lotta Love' as a kind of calling card and carry on in that direction", he observed. The "simple thunder" of the heavy riffs was easier to assimilate, he conceded. "But you can't just do that, otherwise you become stagnant and you're not really doing anything, you're just pleasing everybody else". Certainly, some fans were less than delighted with the change of direction and, although the *Led Zeppelin III* initially sold spectacularly and went to Number One on both sides of the Atlantic, in the long term it has remained the weakest seller among the band's first four albums.

The Genesis Of LZ IV

Yet, even as the album was hitting record stores, in the autumn of 1970 Page and Plant were on their way back to Bron-yr-aur to repeat the cottage experiment and begin work on material for the next album. "It was just the four of us this time", **Henry Smith**, one of the two roadies who accompanied them, recalls. "It just felt like a good thing. Like if you want to write you need to get away and this was a great place to get away because there was nobody around. It was so off the beaten path. We were in the middle of a sheep field, I remember, and the sheep would almost come into the house while Jimmy and Robert were working on songs".

It was a shorter stay than six months earlier, but among the material they worked on was the introduction of what was to become 'Stairway To Heaven'. Then as before, the pair took their ideas to Jones and Bonham at Headley Grange, where basic backing tracks were recorded before being further refined at **Island Studios** in London in December 1970. Those sessions were then followed in the New Year by a return to Headley Grange, where the band stayed for much of January and February 1971. Jones hated the place. "It was cold and damp", he complains, "virtually no furniture, no pool table, no pub nearby". He would no doubt have preferred to record at **Stargroves**, Mick Jagger's well-appointed country pile, but Page – living up to his "Led Wallet" nickname – had apparently baulked at the idea when the Stones' singer had quoted a rental of £1,000 a week.

But Jones' antipathy towards Headley Grange found him in a minority. "It was really great", Plant reported. "The mics coming in through the windows and a fire going in the hearth and people coming in with cups of tea and cakes and people tripping over leads and the whole thing in utter chaos. It was a good feeling and we did it as easy as pie". Road manager Richard Cole paints an equally bucolic picture: "There weren't any

serious drugs around the band at that point. Just dope and a bit of coke", he recalls. "We had an account at a shop in the village and we'd go down there regularly and collect huge quantities of cider. They were playing at being country squires. They found an old shotgun and used to shoot at squirrels in the woods, not that they ever hit any. And there was this lovely old black Labrador wandering around which we used to feed". The beast, of course, was commemorated in 'Black Dog', the opening track on *Led Zeppelin IV*. Plant also wrote the lyrics to 'Stairway To Heaven' at the house, and if the spirit of Bron-yr-aur ran through *Led Zeppelin III*, it was the ambience of Headley Grange that dominated the follow-up album.

With the record virtually finished, Peter Grant announced a "back to the roots" British tour for March 1971, culminating with a return to the legendary **Marquee** club on Wardour Street in London's Soho, where the band had last played in December 1968. It was a deliberate attempt to step away from huge venues such as Madison Square Garden and Grant further let it be known that the group had turned down $1 million for a show in Germany on New Year's Eve 1970, to be relayed by satellite coast-to-coast across America. He may well have exaggerated the figure, but the story helped to dissipate British resentment at the band's concentration on the US market, and allowed the band to claim that remaining in contact with their fans was more important than the money.

Page's guitars

The most enduring image of Jimmy Page on stage is of him playing the solo on 'Stairway To Heaven' on his custom-made double-neck Gibson. But needless to say, he owned an army of guitars which were deployed for different purposes in the studio and in concert.

On the first Led Zeppelin album and the band's early live dates he favoured a 1958 Fender Telecaster, given to him by Jeff Beck. In 1967, he had it painted in psychedelic colours and it was this guitar rather than the Gibson double-neck that was actually used for the studio version of 'Stairway To Heaven'. The guitar was subsequently 'retired' due to problems with the pick-ups.

By the time of *Led Zeppelin II* he had switched to a sunburst-finished 1959 Gibson Les Paul. During the early days he also used a Gibson "Black Beauty" Les Paul, but this was stolen on tour in 1970. He had bought the guitar in 1962 on hire purchase for £185 and used it extensively in his session work. He was devastated to lose it and, in 1973, placed an advert in

Rolling Stone offering a reward for its return with "no questions asked". There was no response.

The Gibson Les Paul remained his favoured instrument for the rest of the Zeppelin era, and the 1959 model was joined by a similar-looking 1958 model which he bought or was given by Joe Walsh of The James Gang and later The Eagles. It was this guitar which was copied at Gibson's custom shop to create the now discontinued Jimmy Page Signature Les Paul series.

The Gibson SG twelve/six-string double-neck guitar was introduced specifically to play 'Stairway To Heaven' on stage. It was also used live on 'Tangerine', 'The Rain Song', and 'The Song Remains The Same'. He seldom played it in the studio, the one exception being its use on 'Carouselambra'.

Towards the end with Led Zeppelin, he rediscovered his early passion for Fender guitars, playing a 1959 Telecaster in Botswana brown and a 1960 blue Stratocaster with tremolo arm. Both were used live with Led Zeppelin and remained favourites in the 1980s when Page used them with The Firm and on his solo tours.

For acoustic work, on the first Led Zeppelin album he used a Gibson J-200 that had belonged to Big Jim Sullivan. After 1970, he mostly played a Martin D28 both in the studio and during the acoustic set which became a key part of Led Zeppelin's live shows, although a Harmony Sovereign is used quite heavily on *Led Zeppelin III*. When a twelve-string was required, he mostly used a Rickenbacker. The pedal steel heard to prominent effect on *Led Zeppelin III* is a Fender ten-string model.

When it came to effects units, Page used a Roger Mayer fuzz box; a Sola Sound Tonebender; a Vox Cry Baby Wah Wah; the Maestro Echoplex; an MXR phaser; an Eventide clockwork harmonizer and, of course, a theremin.

"The boys came to me just after Christmas and talked about their next tour", Grant told *Melody Maker*. "We decided to do the clubs and forget about the bread and the big concert halls. We're going to play the universities and clubs and restrict prices to about twelve-bob a ticket. When I rang The Marquee, the manager refused to believe it was me offering him Led Zeppelin, so he had to call me back to be convinced".

"The audiences are becoming bigger and bigger, moving further and further away. We are losing contact, so by going back to places like The Marquee we aim to re-establish our contact with the people who got us off the ground in the first place", Page explained. "It will give the fans a chance to see a group which in the accepted tradition would be appearing only at large auditoriums for high prices". The tour also gave fans an early chance to hear some of the material from *Led Zeppelin IV*, which would in the event not be released until November. Foremost among the new numbers was 'Stairway To Heaven', which received its debut minus the recorders, but with the introduction of Page's soon-to-be-familiar custom-made **Gibson SG double-neck** at Belfast's Ulster Hall on 5 March. The song was described by *Melody Maker*'s Chris Welch as "an excellent ballad" which displayed Plant's "growing lyricism", a favourable enough response, but one which gave no indication that it was to become one of rock music's most epic and enduring landmarks. 'Black Dog' and 'Going To California'

were the other news songs unveiled on the tour, but although the band played well, the smaller venues cramped the theatrical swagger Zeppelin had developed on their American tours and the entire exercise left many feeling oddly underwhelmed. Richard Cole also suggests that after being treated like gods in America, they were unimpressed by the meagre backstage hospitality at such venues as the **Nottingham Boat Club** and the **Belfry** in Sutton Coldfield.

By the end of the tour, which took in a dozen dates in 17 days, Plant was also having voice problems, which resulted in the postponement of the recording of a BBC Radio One *In Concert* session. When it was rescheduled for 1 April, the band put in a bravura performance that compensated for any disappointments on the tour, and gave the broader listening public its first taste of 'Stairway To Heaven' when the show was broadcast in an hour-long edited version three days later.

The fourth album had originally been planned for a late spring or early summer release, to coincide with European dates and set up the band's seventh assault on North America, beginning in August. Unfortunately, a cock-up with the mixing nixed this plan and, when Page returned from **Sunset Sound** in Los Angeles with what was meant to be the finished album and played it to the rest of the band at Olympic in London, the entire group was in for a shock. They knew they had made a great album but nobody could understand why it sounded so terrible. The answer was a purely technical one: a mismatch between the tape machines on which the music had been recorded and mixed. Only the Sunset Sound mix of 'When The Levee Breaks' could be rescued, and the laborious process of mixing the album's other seven tracks had to begin all over again.

Italy Erupts

It was a morale-sapping blow, and another followed when they arrived in Italy for a show on 5 July in Milan's **Vigorelli Velodrome**. As Keith Shadwick perceptively analyzed: "At that stage in rock's history, concerts were perceived as a convenient theatre in which to act out some of the basic dramas affecting Western society. Throughout America and Europe in 1970 and 1971 the potential for violent confrontation was always lurking, with so much mistrust between youth and authorities". Certainly, it all boiled over in Italy. With more than 2,000 Milanese police on duty in anticipation of trouble, confrontation became almost inevitable and trouble started well before the concert when left-wing demonstrators chanting slogans outside the stadium were charged by riot police firing tear gas and water cannon. The skirmishes moved inside the auditorium but the band decided to go ahead with the gig in the mistaken belief that their music would have a calming effect. It might have worked on the 15,000-strong crowd, but the band's appearance seemed to have the opposite effect on the police. As soon

as sections of the crowd jumped to their feet to applaud Zeppelin's arrival on stage, the forces of law and disorder charged, wielding batons and releasing more tear gas. Plant appealed for calm but it was hopeless. Within a few numbers a full-scale riot had broken out, and when a tear gas canister exploded close enough to the stage to make the band's eyes water during Bonham's drum solo on 'Moby Dick', Grant ordered them off stage. In anticipation of trouble, he had perceptively demanded the money and the return first-class air tickets upfront. According to Bonham's drum technician Mick Hinton, "The roadies stayed on to protect the stage. I got hit on the head with a bottle and the next thing I knew I was on a stretcher. I remember we lost the hi-hat, but aside from that the kit was OK, incredibly".

Plant still sounded disturbed by the event when he described it to this writer almost a quarter of a century later. "We escaped down an access route and the troops pumped gas canisters at us", he recalled. "We managed to get in a dressing room and I barricaded the door with a medicine cabinet and got everybody in there with wet towels around our heads. Then they broke the windows and popped a couple of canisters in from the street".

The band never played in Italy again, and when their seventh American tour opened in August, their personal backstage security had been **discreetly doubled**. In the wake of what had happened in Milan, the habit of American audiences to let off volleys

Magick moments: Page and Aleister Crowley

Of all the lurid tales surrounding Led Zeppelin, none has provoked more controversy over the years than the sinister rumours that the group were "Satan's own band". The rumours began in the early 1970s as a direct result of Jimmy Page's growing interest in the magician and sexual libertarian Aleister Crowley (1875–1947, right). Dubbed by the press of the day "the most evil man in Britain", in the 1930s Crowley conducted black magic rituals and sex orgies at his "satanic temple" on London's Fulham Road and styled himself "The Great Beast".

The 'Great Beast': mad as a hatter

In the most extreme rumours, it was held that three members of Zeppelin (with John Paul Jones as the dissenter) had signed a pact with the devil. It was claimed that the words "Here's to my sweet Satan" could be heard if you played the "If there's a bustle in your hedgerow" verse in 'Stairway To Heaven' backwards. The disasters and mishaps that dogged the latter part of the band's career were all attributed to their liaison with Lucifer.

Total nonsense, of course. But Page's interest in the realm of magic was a matter of record. He had the phrases "Do What Thou Wilt" and "So Mote Be It",

scratched into the run-off matrix at the centre of the original vinyl release of *Led Zeppelin III*. Both were derived from the sayings of Crowley. He was also a collector of rare books and manuscripts connected with the magician and even bought the robes in which he had conducted his magic rituals. In 1975, he purchased the Equinox occult bookshop and publishing house, located in Kensington High Street, London and used it to publish a facsimile of a 16th-century magical text edited and annotated by Crowley in 1904. He also collected Crowley's paintings of magical subjects and pictures from his collection were displayed at London's October Gallery in 1998.

In 1971, Page also purchased Crowley's former home, Boleskin House, on the shores of Loch Ness in Scotland. The house had an evil reputation but Page was intrigued by its history. It was said to have been built on the site of a church which had been burnt to the ground with all its parishioners inside. A man had been beheaded there, according to local legend and, of course, his head was said still to roll around the halls at night. A lodge keeper had also gone berserk there and tried to murder his family.

of firecrackers in the auditorium caused some understandably jumpy moments and there were stage invasions in New York and Honolulu and serious crowd trouble in Boston. According to Richard Cole, there were also **death threats** and the band's collective sense of isolation and paranoia had never been higher. Despite such problems

the tour was deemed a success. Peter Grant had been desperate for Led Zep to return to the US. Ludicrous though it may sound now, he feared that in the eleven months since the band had last toured there, the pedestrian but briefly huge **Grand Funk Railroad** were on the point of stealing the band's thunder. Grant was satisfied that the band had reas-

Page had the house redecorated by a Satanist called Charles Pierce and the ill repute of the place continued to grow as one caretaker committed suicide and another was claimed to have lost his sanity. Page had his rather sinister fantasy sequence in the film *The Song Remains The Same* filmed near Boleskine House in 1973. He eventually sold the property in the late 1980s but, as far as is known, he still has his Crowley memorabilia, said to constitute the most extensive collection of the stuff in the world.

On stage with Zeppelin, Page often appeared with astrological symbols embroidered into his clothes (above), representing Capricorn, Scorpio and Cancer which are Page's sun, ascendant and moon signs. His 'Zoso' symbol for *Led Zeppelin IV* was also derived from occult sources (see page 85) while the painting of the hermit he commissioned for the album's inside cover (see page 17) was based on the Tarot.

When asked about his interest in the occult by interviewers in later years, Page has invariably been cautious and taciturn. Yet in the first flushes of his enthusiasm, he was quite open, telling one journalist:

The zodiac trousers

"You can't ignore evil if you study the supernatural as I do. I have many books on the subject and I've also attended a number of séances".

He also called Crowley "a misunderstood genius of the 20th century" and in a 1972 interview with *Disc & Music Echo*, he made clear his interest in Crowley's "sex magick" – and appeared to confirm the criticisms that Zeppelin's attitude towards women was deeply misogynist. "Magic is very important if people can go through it", he said. "I think Crowley is completely relevant to today. We're seeking for truth: the search goes on. Crowley didn't have a very high opinion of women – and I don't think he was wrong. Playing music is a very sexual act, an emotional release and the sexual drive comes in along with all the other impulses".

None of the rest of the band shared his fascination with the occult and he appears to have made no attempt to share his interest with them. "No one really delved into what Jimmy did", Richard Cole says. "He didn't really speak about it much. It was as much of a mystery to us as it was to everyone else".

serted its supremacy and GFR were sent down the track into oblivion.

The fourth album was still not out, but the band unveiled much of the new material, with the triumphant 'Stairway To Heaven' as the jewel in the crown. Plant repeatedly told audiences that the new album would be out in three weeks – which proved to be a hopelessly optimistic forecast while they battled with Atlantic over their desire not to put the band's name on the cover or to give the LP a title.

Frustratingly, there was still no sign of the new record when the band undertook its first-ever tour of **Japan** at the end of September. Although the band played just five shows in three cities, it was a memorable trip in several ways. On the first night in Tokyo, Plant complained about their recent American tour, which he compared unfavourably with the way they had been "having a ball" since their arrival in Japan. On stage, the band seemed relaxed and the sets were full of ad-libs and improbable **improvisations**. For some reason, Plant dedicated all the new songs to Cliff Richard, and sang a snatch of Simon & Garfunkel's '59th Street Bridge Song (Feelin' Groovy)'. Page responded by throwing in a few licks from the Stones' 'Honky Tonk Woman'. On another night, the 'Whole Lotta Love' medley included Cliff's 'Bachelor Boy', while elsewhere Plant offered up snatches of 'The Lady Is A Tramp' and 'Smoke Gets In Your Eyes'.

It was clear they were relaxed and having fun – which made the **fight** that erupted between Plant and Bonham in Osaka all the more strange. During the row, Bonham gave Plant a split lip and then refused to return to the stage while the singer led the crowd in a chant to persuade him to return and apologized: "Japan is a wonderful place and you're too much. You're putting up with a lot. We don't usually do things like this".

When Bonham finally reappeared, he initially refused to play his 'Moby Dick' showcase. Bootleg tapes reveal him saying: "I don't want to play it. I'm fed up playing it!" Grant later attempted to explain the problem: "It was over some dispute concerning some money from some tour. He still owed Bonzo some petrol money, seventy quid or something, but

that's how it was". Bonham and road manager Richard Cole were also involved in one of the most infamous tales of Zep's on-the-road excess when they used two samurai swords to slash everything in their hotel rooms to shreds at the **Tokyo Hilton**. In another misjudged prank, in Osaka the band invited Atlantic Records' UK boss Phil Carson to play bass while Jones was on keyboards. The band then disappeared, leaving Carson alone on stage – which Page, Plant, Jones and Bonham thought was a simply hilarious in-joke, but which left the audience feeling short-changed. On a more sombre note, in Hiroshima, where the Americans had dropped the first atom bomb just 25 years earlier, the band visited the Peace Gardens and played a benefit concert, donating all proceeds to the bomb's victims and received peace medals from the mayor in return.

Billy Boys

At the end of the tour, Bonham and Jones returned via Moscow while Page and Plant stopped off in Thailand and India. "In Bangkok all the kids followed us calling 'Billy boy, Billy boy', which means queer, because of hair, but they're laughing and happy all the time", Plant recalled. The pair apparently spent much of their time in various houses of ill repute. But in Bombay they also checked out the local music scene and the possibility of recording with Indian musicians, laying the groundwork for their return to do just that a year later.

Reading the runes

| Page | Jones | Bonham | Plant |

Strictly speaking, the band's fourth album is not called *Led Zeppelin IV*. Like the Beatles' *White Album* and the Byrds' double LP widely known as *Untitled*, it was the band's intention that their fourth LP should have no title at all. The only marking it bore on the cover was the four runes or hieroglyphs which appeared both on the label and the spine of its cover. "I think *Four Symbols* was how it was referred to by us at the time", Plant says.

On Page's suggestion, the runes – or at least two of them – came from a book called *The Book Of Signs* by Rudolph Koch. "At first I wanted just one symbol but since it was our fourth album and there were four of us, we each chose our own", Page explained.

"Jimmy showed me this book he had and said we should all chose a symbol from the book to represent each one of us", John Paul Jones remembers. The symbol he chose depicted a circle inlaid with three interlocking semi-circular arcs which, according to Koch's book, was used to ward off evil. According to Page, the bassist chose it because of the "precision and dexterity" required to draw it.

Bonham chose a simpler emblem of three overlapping rings, like a simplified version of the Olympic symbol and which represented his family. "I suppose it's the trinity of man, woman and child. I suspect it had something to do with the mainstay of all people's belief", Plant observes. However, the down-to-earth Bonham was far from disappointed when they subsequently discovered in Pittsburgh that it also resembled the symbol for Ballantine's beer.

Plant and Page's symbols did not actually come from Koch's book, but were custom-designed. "The singer's feather in a circle was inspired by native American symbolism. "My choice involved the feather, a symbol on which all philosophies have been based", he explained. "For instance, it represents courage to many Indian tribes. I like people to lay down the truth. No bullshit. That's what it was all about".

Most mysterious of all was Page's symbol, which appeared to read 'ZoSo', although the guitarist insisted it was never intended to resemble a word. "It's just a doodle. Although it looks more like writing than the other three, that wasn't the intention", he explained. There has been speculation that it was a reference to the work of the occultist and self-proclaimed 'sorcerer' Austin Osman Spare, who started a mysterious cult called Zos and designed a series of magical symbols or "sigils", with which it is almost certain that Page was familiar. According to the writer Kenneth Grant: "When vividly visualized, the emblem or sigil mysteriously stirs the sub-conscious and a corresponding image, or set of images, arises in the mind. In proportion to the power of belief in the sigil, so is the clarity of the image which it evokes. If the sigil taps a layer of ancient or cosmic memory, some astonishing images surge into the mind and the skilful sorcerer is able to project them into the astral mind-stuff of other individuals, so that they imagine the image to be a palpable presence". Such theories may well have influenced Page's thinking when he came up with the idea of the four symbols for the fourth album.

The Ten Best-Selling Albums of all Time*

1. Eagles *Greatest Hits 71–75*

28 million

2. Michael Jackson *Thriller*

26 million

3. Pink Floyd *The Wall*

23 million

4. *Led Zeppelin IV*

22 million

5. Billy Joel *Greatest Hits*

21 million

6. Fleetwood Mac *Rumours*

19 million

7. AC/DC *Back In Black*

19 million

8. The Beatles *The Beatles (White Album)*

19 million

9. Shania Twain *Come On Over*

19 million

10. Boston *Boston*

17 million

* based on US sales figures

Back in Britain, *Led Zeppelin IV* was finally ready for release – almost. Further wrangling over the artwork meant that it was November before it finally appeared, eight months later than originally intended. "The record company hierarchy aren't into the fact that covers are important to a band's image", Plant grumbled. They knew it was a great album, heavier than *Led Zeppelin III*, and with more riffs on tracks like 'Black Dog', 'Rock and Roll' and their astonishing version of Memphis Minnie's 'When The Levee Breaks', but tempered with the ethereal 'Battle Of Evermore', featuring Fairport Convention singer **Sandy Denny** and the epic 'Stairway To Heaven'. Bonham told *Melody Maker* it was the best album they had ever made, and Plant concurred. "It's strong stuff and exciting and the flame is really burning higher and higher", he said just before its release. He hadn't changed his view 35 years later when he said "I think it was beautifully written in most areas. It wasn't overstated. It was crafted".

The sense of mystery created by the four, strange runic symbols which were the album's only identification only helped to sell the record, particularly when they were used full-page in a strong press advertising campaign. The four symbols were also displayed prominently on stage when the band celebrated the album's belated release with a 16-date British tour, of which the centrepiece was two dates at London's **Empire Pool, Wembley**. Billed as "Electric Magic", the five-hour extravaganza included circus acts and even some performing pigs, dressed in hats and ruffles. The swine

Plant in full flight at the Empire Pool, Wembley – the "Electric Magic" event

proved something of a disappointment, but the band were not, earning some spectacular reviews for a bravura performance. "This was no job, this was no gig. It was an event for all", **Roy Hollingsworth** wrote in *Melody Maker*. "So they get paid a lot of bread. Well, people paid that bread, and I reckon they got every penny's worth".

It was a fitting end to a fraught year and *Led Zeppelin IV* topped the British charts, although the success of *Santana III*, Sly and The Family Stone's *There's A Riot Goin' On* and Carole King's *Tapestry*, all of which topped the American charts over the winter of 1971–72, meant that it failed to rise above Number Two in America. Nevertheless, it stayed in the American charts for two years and, ultimately, went on to become the fourth best-selling album in musical history. As John Paul Jones succinctly put it, after *Led Zeppelin IV*, no one ever again compared them to Black Sabbath.

The Hammer Of The Gods

1972–1973

"Give an Englishman 50,000 watts, a chartered jet, a little cocaine and some groupies and he thinks he's a god".

Rolling Stone magazine on Led Zeppelin

The Hammer Of The Gods
1972–1973

The trappings of success were mixed: financial and domestic security, respect from many of their peers and indeed adulation from their ever-growing number of fans. But manager Peter Grant was aware that the momentum had to be kept up, which meant more touring and all that this entailed.

Up And Down Under

Away from the madness and mayhem of touring, Led Zeppelin enjoyed playing the part of devoted dads and respectably settled family men. With the band's fourth album riding high in the charts on both sides of the Atlantic, the beginning of 1972 found all four band members relaxing at home and enjoying the sweet contentment of domesticity. Plant was ensconced on his Worcestershire farm, where his wife Maureen was about to give birth to their son **Karac**, joining their daughter Carmen. Bonham had bought a farm nearby where he bred Hereford cattle and his wife Pat was expecting their second child. Jones, the most private and self-contained member of the band, was at home with his wife Mo and their three children in their comfortable house in Rickmansworth, Hertfordshire,

where he had built a home studio. Page, the only unmarried member, now had a daughter by girlfriend Charlotte Martin and had sold his Pangbourne boat house and bought a country estate in Sussex called **Plumpton Place**, complete with its own moat. He would shortly add to his property portfolio with **Tower House** in London's Kensington, which he bought from the actor Richard Harris.

The idyll did not, however, last long for Peter Grant had lined up their first visit to Australia and New Zealand, starting in February 1972. Things got off to an inauspicious start when a planned concert in **Singapore** was cancelled due to the reactionary nature of the government, which refused admission to males with long hair. Around the same time, the British bubble-gum group Middle Of The Road which had enjoyed a British Number One with 'Chirpy Chirpy Cheep Cheep' cheerfully agreed to an

The Story

The Zep tearing it up over Australia in 1972. Bonzo's distinctive rune now appears on his bass drum, but in comparison to the Stones' elaborate stage outfits of the period, the boys retained considerable street cred by still looking as if they could have wandered onto the stage from the crowd

enforced short-back-and-sides in order to play in Singapore, but Led Zeppelin felt the prospect of beginning their first Antipodean tour looking like a bunch of skinheads was too high a price to pay. When their flight stopped in Singapore for refuelling en route to Australia, they sensibly stayed on the plane.

Initially, it wasn't much better once they reached Australia. After a first gig in Perth, which was marred by running fights between fans and police, their hotel was raided by the local drugs squad. Astonishingly, nothing was found and the rest of the tour was wildly received by Australian audiences, unused to

visits from rock royalty. On the way back, Page and Plant again stopped off in Bombay to tend the seeds they had sown a year earlier. Hiring a local studio, the Bollywood composer **Vijay Ragav Rao** assembled a group of string players and they recorded experimental East-West versions of 'Four Sticks' and 'Friends'. It wasn't entirely successful, and the results were never officially released, but the experience was to have a long-lasting influence on the musical development of both Page and Plant.

Back in Britain, thoughts turned swiftly to writing and recording the fifth album with initial sessions taking place both at Olympic

The Battle of the Bands

The rivalry between The Rolling Stones and The Beatles in the 1960s is legendary – but by the early 1970s, it was Led Zeppelin they were vying with for the title "the greatest rock'n'roll band in the world".

Although the Stones released chart-topping albums in *Let It Bleed* (1969) and *Sticky Fingers* (1971), after their 1969 American tour had ended in the disaster of Altamont, they stayed off the road for the next three years, leaving Zeppelin to rise to the top on the back of their relentless touring of the US.

Following the release of the double LP, *Exile On Main Street* in May 1972, the Stones embarked on their first American tour since 1969. It was a spectacular trek. Between 3 June and 26 July, they played 51 shows in 32 venues, drawing an audience of 750,000 people and grossing $4million. They also took a leaf out Peter Grant's book in demanding a high percentage of the takings, although not quite as high as Zeppelin's 90 per cent. "There was a 100 per cent gross due to advance sell-outs for every concert", tour manager Peter Rudge told *Billboard*. "The Rolling Stones took between 60 and 70 per cent of that amount, but that was a gross figure. All expenses came out of the Stones' earnings. And they spent a lot of money to put on good shows everywhere".

Every gig seemed to be followed by a celebrity-packed party with a guest list that extended far beyond the usual rock'n'roll set to draw in the great and the good of the literary, art, film and social worlds, and a string of beautiful women from Jackie Kennedy's sister Lee Radziwill to Zsa Zsa Gabor.

"They could play three months in San Francisco and probably six in New York and sell out every seat", the promoter Bill Graham asserted. "They are the biggest draw in the history of mankind. Only one other guy ever came close: Gandhi".

Zeppelin's tour, which took in 19 dates between 6-28 June, was spectacular in its own right and musically it was arguably the best they had ever played. Yet there's no doubt they were totally eclipsed by the Stones. *Melody Maker*'s Roy Hollingsworth (who covered both tours) noted of their date at New York's Nassau Coliseum: "It was one of the most amazing concerts I'd seen from any band at any time". But he topped his own hyperbole when he caught up with the Stones a week later and wrote: "This tour is going to go down as the rock'n'roll tour of all time".

Once the tour was over, Zeppelin could not disguise their bitterness. "We've just toured the States and done as well if not better than the Stones but there was hardly anything about it in the British press", Bonham complained to *NME*. "All we read was 'the Stones this' and 'the Stones that' and it pissed us off, made us feel what the hell, here we are flogging our guts out and for all the notice being given to us we might as well be playing in bloody Ceylon. Because the kids in England didn't even know we were touring the States".

Perhaps what hurt most, however, was not the respective column inches or even box office receipts, but the simple fact that while the Stones were being lionized by the likes of Warhol, Capote and American chic liberal society, Led Zeppelin were still regarded as the hooligans at the gate.

And hooligans they might have been, but stories from the Stones' 1972 tour reveal a band just as debauched and feckless as the "young pretenders". But there was little doubt, in the public's mind, that by the time the Stones had released *Goat's Head Soup* in 1973, the band was past its peak musically, if not in terms of earning power, meanwhile, Zeppelin had yet to reach their zenith.

The Story

The LA Groupie Scene

Los Angeles being what it is, by the 1970s the tinseltown city of tawdry dreams had developed an unparalleled and notorious groupie culture. The infamous "plaster casters" were still in action, although their most prized trophies (Hendrix, Noel Redding et al) were already history, although Richard Cole was to number among their victims. The GTOs (Girls Together Outrageously) had gone professional in 1969 under Frank Zappa's guidance as a pop band, releasing an album *Permanent Damage*.

By the time Led Zeppelin hit the scene a new and much younger breed were haunting the backstage entrances, and the lobbies of the Chateau Marmont and the "Riot House". The most high profile exponents of the art of creative ligging were former GTO Pamela des Barres, Bebe Buell, Penny Trumble ("Penny Lane") and the precocious teenyboppers Sable Starr and Lori Maddox (b. 1958, aka Lori Lightning, above right). The latter had allegedly been involved with David and Angie Bowie. By the time she ousted des Barres as Jimmy Page's regular LA squeeze she was still far too young for their relationship to become public knowledge, and Peter Grant went out of his way to ensure this didn't happen.

Among of the favoured groupie foraging grounds were the Rainbow Bar & Grill, the Whisky a Go Go, and Rodney Bingenheimer's English Disco in West

Hollywood; Maddox was photographed there with Page and Bingenheimer (left in picture), but also variously with Bonham, Plant and Roy Harper as well. But she was most regularly seen on Page's arm until she was ousted by Bebe Buell. The latter's string of conquests included Todd Rundgren, Mick Jagger, David Bowie and Iggy Pop, not to mention Aerosmith's Steve Tyler, by whom she had a daughter, the actress Liv Tyler.

Both des Barres and Buell have written highly successful memoirs of their rocking and rolling years, whereas Maddox withdrew from the limelight to work in the LA fashion retail industry.

Studios in London and Mick Jagger's country pile, Stargroves, with Page this time agreeing to the high rent. A dozen new tracks were soon in various stages of completion and with out-takes from the previous two albums also available, thoughts turned to the possibility of a double album. However, work was interrupted by the start of their eighth American tour in June 1972.

It was this tour that more than 30 years later was commemorated on the live album, *How The West Was Won* (pages 190–191), and the recordings reveal that Zeppelin were on fire, as plenty of new material from the uncompleted fifth album, including 'Over The Hills And Far Away', 'The Crunge', 'Dancing Days' and 'The Ocean', was incorporated into the set alongside often stunning versions of the now established repertoire classics. It was also a huge success commercially. "We finally saved up the air fare to get back", Plant told the crowd. The irony was delicious for, in fact, for the first time Grant had hired them a **private jet** to fly them around America. It was also the first tour on which he insisted on 90 per cent of the takings going to the band, leaving just 10 per cent for the promoter. The traditional split had been 50:50 but Zeppelin were such a draw that despite loud grumbles, promoters had little choice but reluctantly to agree.

The one problem was that the press chose virtually to ignore the tour. This was largely due to the fact that at exactly the same time The Rolling Stones had returned to the road for their first American tour since 1969, which had ended with the horror of Altamont. Unveiling the famous tongue logo for the first time, and with a galaxy of celebrities in tow, including Jack Nicholson, Goldie Hawn, Hugh Heffner, Andy Warhol, Truman Capote, Princess Lee Radziwill and Norman Mailer, the Stones gobbled up all the column inches, both in America and back home in Britain, while Zeppelin's record-breaking tour went virtually unreported. Perhaps it was payback for the hostility that had existed between Zeppelin and the media from the outset, but the band felt slighted and were furious. As Keith Shadwick puts it: "Zeppelin wanted their media egos massaged and were intent on throwing their toys out of the pram if no-one listened". To try and make them listen, Grant hired as the band's official publicist B.P. Fallon, whose previous clients had included **T. Rex**, whose *Electric Warrior* had just a few months earlier dislodged *Led Zeppelin IV* from the top of the British charts. Plant, with typical wit and bravado, later explained the band's change of tactics in its media relations: "We thought it was time that people heard something about us other than that we were eating women and throwing the bones out the window".

The Long Wait For *Houses*

With the tour over, at the end of June 1972 the band briefly went into **Electric Lady Studios** in New York to do some work on the album that would become *Houses Of The Holy*, before returning to Britain and their families. While Plant, Bonham and Jones relaxed, Page continued to work on the new album, determined not to repeat the mixing errors that had delayed *Led Zeppelin IV*. However, there were other delays as he overdubbed parts while the sleeve design also caused the usual headache. He also became distracted by accepting a commission from the film director **Kenneth Anger** to write the soundtrack for his film *Lucifer Rising*. The project would prove to be a disaster, with Page completing less than half an hour's worth of music and being unceremoniously sacked (see page 116). But at the end of 1972, he was still working hard and was enthusiastic about the project. "I wanted it to sound timeless in a way, not to sound dated by anything. I used a synthesizer on it, but I tried to use it in such a way that it didn't sound like a synthesizer, just that all the instruments didn't sound like what they ought to sound. You don't quite know what it is at any point".

Jones was also starting to use a synthesizer – or rather a mellotron, an early and somewhat temperamental machine that The Beatles had deployed on 'Strawberry Fields Forever' and which bands such as **The Moody Blues** and **King Crimson** had also used to good effect. It can be heard on 'The Rain Song' on *Houses Of The Holy* and he also took it on tour when the band headed back to Japan for a second Far Eastern tour in October 1972. When he used the mellotron during *Stairway To Heaven* on stage, Plant habitually quipped: "John Paul Jones was the rather cheap orchestra".

True to form, the new album still wasn't ready by the time of the Japanese dates, which went well – although, if Richard Cole is to be believed, a stopover in **Hong Kong** on the way back was later to have serious ramifications for the band when they were introduced to heroin for the first time. According to Cole, he had tried to obtain them cocaine but was given heroin instead. He didn't bother telling them and they snorted rather than injected it and were violently ill.

There was still no sign of the new album when they returned home and commenced a 24-date British tour, the longest they were ever to play on home soil and for which ticket prices were pegged at £1. The tour opened at the end of November in Newcastle and, with a ten-day break over Christmas, carried on until the end of January. Needless to say, it was not without incident. In Glasgow, the band's new publicist B.P. Fallon was beaten up by fans who had been sold **counterfeit tickets** and were looking for a scapegoat. In protest, the group refused to play an encore, a strange decision to punish a crowd that presumably did not contain the miscreants, who would have been unable to obtain entry without proper tickets.

Fallon's attempts to make the band more media-friendly included lining up an interview during warm-up gigs for the British tour in Montreux between Plant and *Melody Maker*'s **Chris Charlesworth**, who in his report then dared to suggest that the band's popularity was waning. Plant then took great delight in sarcastically relaying the comment to the crowds which gave them standing, stomping, storming ovations every night. Fallon also invited *NME*'s Nick Kent to accompany the band around the UK. He filed favourable copy at the time, but years later claimed that in all his years as a rock journalist he had never seen anyone behave worse than Bonham and Richard Cole. "I once saw them beat a guy senseless and then drop money on his face", he wrote". "It makes me feel sick when I hear Plant talking about what a great geezer Bonzo was, because the guy was a schizophrenic animal".

While Zeppelin travelled around America by private jet, in Britain it was a different story with band members driving themselves to and from gigs. On the way to a date at Sheffield City Hall on 2 January, Bonham and Plant broke down in the drummer's Bentley and were forced to **hitch-hike** in the rain. The singer caught a cold and although the show went on that night, the following two dates had to be postponed.

Almost unbelievably, the much-delayed new album – which had now been given the title *Houses Of The Holy* – was still not ready when Zeppelin began a European tour in March 1973. On their French gigs, the band were accompanied by **Benoit Gautier**, an executive from Atlantic Records' Paris office, whose recollections offer a fascinating insight into the mentality of the Zeppelin touring party at the time. "It was obvious that some of them were using drugs but they were very discreet", he reported. "They never asked for grass or anything; they asked for legal things, mostly girls. Prostitution is legal in France. They wanted good booze, nice parties and amusing people. Peter Grant would say, 'I want everybody to have a good time tonight; can you find six beautiful girls?'" On one occasion, he claims he was asked to arrange a lesbian sex show for the band to watch at their hotel, the swanky Georges V in Paris.

Equally revealing are his observations on the band's individual members. Page he described as "the mastermind of it all and very much in control", but he was shocked by the amount of cocaine he was taking. Plant, he noted, "never harmed anybody, had good manners,

was always smiling". He found Jones "bright, intelligent and cultured" and reckoned the bassist was the smartest member of the group. "He never got caught in an embarrassing situation. He would always show at the very last minute for anything. You'd never even know where he was staying. He drove himself and was independent from the rest of the band. Peter and the band were always saying, 'Where the fuck is he?' It upset them that they couldn't manipulate him".

The picture he paints of **Bonham**, however, is deeply disturbing. At one point the drummer offered Gautier a line of cocaine. He was about to snort it when he realized it wasn't

The talented but unpredictable Bonzo in action

cocaine at all but heroin. "He thought that was the funniest thing, offering you coke and giving you smack. He would take a chance of killing you!" On the other hand, he says that when he admired a particular shirt Bonham was wearing, he took it off and gave it to him. "Bonzo would cry when talking about his family. Then the roadies would start to push him to do something and he'd go crazy. He would throw drinks or dump food on somebody if Jimmy told him to. He had no natural defence against being manipulated and nothing to protect him".

Houses Of The Holy finally hit record stores towards the end of the European tour, 17 months after *Led Zeppelin IV*. Predictably, it went to Number One the world over, but it was an oddly unsatisfying affair. In some ways it found the band commendably attempting to break **new ground**, often going for mood rather than raw excitement. But the atmospheric power of the best tracks such as 'Dancing Days' and 'The Song Remains The Same' was offset by the throwaway frivolity of 'D'yer Mak' 'er' and 'The Crunge', which Page freely admitted had been recorded as "just a giggle". If the purpose of such songs was for Led Zeppelin to show the critics that the band had a sense of humour, arguably they worked. But musically they were lightweight and dragged the album down.

Page seemed to recognize this, too, when he told *NME*: "I'm deaf to the album because we made it such a long time ago but I know there's some good stuff there". Which, of course, there

was – but which is quite different from saying it's a great album. As a follow-up to the power and glory of *Led Zeppelin IV*, it was a disappointing and **heavily-flawed** exercise that betrayed the fact that it had been so long in the making and that much of the joy and spontaneity had been squeezed out of the grooves. Reviews at the time were mixed, and history has not been particularly kind to *Houses Of The Holy*, either. Ultimately, it's hard to argue with Keith Shadwick's conclusion: "If it had been released closer to the unfolding success of *Led Zeppelin IV* the line-up of songs would have been different and more tightly co-ordinated. The feel may well have been different, too, for there is a palpable air in the songs towards the end of the album of a band who have arrived, big time, and are surveying their domain".

Barney Hoskyns perceptively compares *Houses Of The Holy* to the Stones' *Goat's Head Soup*. Both bands had made acclaimed masterpieces in *Led Zeppelin IV* and *Exile On Main Street*; both had taken the best part of a year and a half to follow it up – and after the long wait both bands managed to miss the mark. However, there was at least one fundamental difference. After *Exile On Main Street*, the Stones' best work was already behind them. Led Zeppelin still had the triumph of *Physical Graffiti* to come, which many regard as their crowning glory.

Whatever the failings of *Houses Of The Holy*, they were also still **dynamite** on stage. "We're playing better than we've ever played before", Plant insisted. "It's working that does it. It's easy to get stale and some bands reach a peak and think that's it – the old country house bit and a year off. It doesn't work that way. There's only one way to function and that's on stage. We've reached a high and we ain't going to lose it. And no bad album review is going to change that".

Zeppelin Ascendant: The '73 US Tour

As if to prove it, their ninth American tour which opened in May 1973 set about redefining the parameters of rock as extravaganza – or as the estimable Dave Lewis put it, "With this tour Led Zeppelin graduated from being a mere rock band to something of an institution in America". Perhaps spurred on by the previous year's disappointment at being outdone by the Stones, they added lasers, dry ice, backdrops, mirror balls, exploding cannons, smoke bombs and giant screens relaying pictures to the more distant parts of the huge stadiums in which they played. "We felt the denim jeans trip had been there for a long time. It was time to take the trip a little further and these ideas fit perfectly with the mood of the new songs and the excitement of the old", Plant explained.

Chartering their own private jet again, they set about breaking attendance records set by The Beatles seven and eight years earlier. The marathon coast-to-coast trek was split into two legs. Opening on 4 May and closing 87 days

later on 29 July, with most of June taken off in the middle for their batteries to be recharged, by the end they had also topped the $4 million grossed by the Stones on their 1972 tour, setting another record.

A new addition to the touring party was American PR **Danny Goldberg**, who immediately proved his prowess as a spin doctor by "leaking" to *Rolling Stone* that Grant anticipated the biggest-grossing US tour of all time, with box-office receipts in excess of $5million and then extracting a quote from the mayor of Atlanta, where the tour opened, that Zeppelin were "the biggest thing to hit America since the premiere of *Gone With The Wind*". In their early days, Zeppelin had been attacked in the British music press as all hype and no substance. The band were hurt by such criticisms which they felt were unfair and ignorant. Now here they were paying Goldberg to hype to the heavens in the most calculated and cynical way. Perhaps it was a case, perhaps, of "if you can't beat 'em, then join 'em".

But it wasn't merely hype, of course. In **Atlanta**, they played to a crowd of 50,000. The next day in **Tampa, Florida** they topped that with a paying crowd of 56,800 – the largest-ever concert attendance for a single act, breaking a record set by The Beatles in 1965, even without counting an estimated 6,000 gatecrashers. Peter Grant later joked: "I didn't tell them really how big it was going to be, but when we drew up, Robert was going 'Fucking hell, where did all these people come from?' And I just said: 'Don't worry son. I know you're still on probation with the band, but you'll be all right'".

Playing three-hour sets featuring material ranging across their entire career, the band also used their soundchecks to work up new material that would eventually appear on *Physical Graffiti*, including 'The Wanton Song', 'The Rover' and 'Night Flight'. Off stage, there were the usual debauched goings-on, and for once the usually reticent Jones was caught out, passing out drunk in his hotel room in New Orleans with a pretty young woman who, to the general hilarity of his fellow band members, turned out to be a transvestite. Bob Hart, a journalist from the British tabloid *The Sun* chronicled some of the excesses, but kept his own counsel about the band's huge drug intake. It was only several years later that he admitted: "I saw quantities of coke on that tour that were truly remarkable. There was an English girl I'll call Jane who travelled on the tour and she was the coke lady. This was so that nobody else ever carried or touched the coke. When she was summoned she would apply the coke with the little finger of her right hand, then follow that up with a sniff of cherry snuff and, as a final touch, she'd dab the nostrils with Dom Perignon 1966, which was the signature drink of the tour".

Hart also noted that in San Francisco, alongside the lavish backstage food, drink and other refreshments, promoter Bill Graham's Fillmore provided a table "bearing a large pile of a certain white substance" as an unofficial extra on the band's rider. Despite Goldberg's efforts, press reaction was once again mixed. *Rolling Stone* typically sneered, reporting from the San Francisco show that "Zeppelin are back doing what they do best: converting heavy metal into dollars". However, the British music press had long got over its reservations about the band. Charles Shaar Murray reviewing the same show for

The 1973 US tour was the pinnacle of the band's touring excess

NME wrote: "Led Zeppelin and 50,000 San Francisco people got together to provide one of the finest musical events I've ever had the privilege to attend. There may be bands who play better, and there may be bands who perform better and there may be bands who write better songs, but when it comes to welding themselves and an audience together into one unit of total joy, Zeppelin yield to nobody. Altogether a magical concert. I suppose legions of diehard Zep freaks have known this all along, but for me it was a revelation".

After enjoying most of June off, during which time some of the band vacationed in Hawaii, the tour resumed in Chicago on 6 July 1973 for an equally successful second leg. After experiencing problems with the small private jet they had chartered for the first leg, they now had their own Boeing 720, known as the **Starship** with LED ZEPPELIN emblazoned on the fuselage, and which Cole had managed to hire at a bargain $10,000 a week. At Chicago's O'Hare airport they proudly showed it off to the party of travelling journalists and were particularly pleased that it dwarfed **Hugh Hefner**'s private jet parked alongside.

During the second leg of the tour, film-maker **Joe Massot** filmed the band over three sold-out nights at Madison Square Garden in New York for what was to become *The Song Remains The Same* movie. He asked the band to wear the same stage clothes each night so the footage could be edited together and all complied with the request except Jones, who perversely wore something completely different each night. Yet it would be another three troubled years before the unsatisfactory film was finally finished and released.

Bum Notes

The New York gigs made a fitting finale to a landmark tour, although the band's triumph was marred by a couple of off-stage incidents. First, just before the third gig, $180,000 dollars in brand new notes from the Madison Square Garden promoter went missing from the band's safe deposit box at the Drake Hotel. Tour manager Richard Cole discovered the theft and after getting the road crew to search all the suites in the hotel booked to the band, (and simultaneously cleansing them of drugs, with particular attention to the rooms occupied by Jane the "coke lady"), he called in the police. For his pains, he was then interviewed as a suspect, although he was not charged after taking a lie-detector test. The band later sued the hotel and received a settlement from the Drake's insurance company. It left a sour note but also put the band in a quandary. As Bonham put it, "If we make like we care too much, they'll say we're only in it for the money. If we say we don't care, they'll say it's because we're too rich". Asked by the Press why the band carried so much cash, Grant claimed it was to pay off the cost of hiring the Starship, although that still left $150,000 in spare change.

The police also got involved in a second incident at the Drake, when Grant was arrested for assaulting *New York Daily News* photog-

The Starship

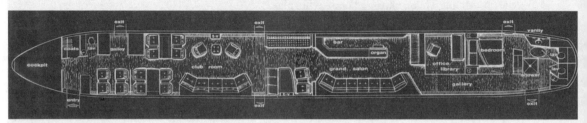

Hiring the Boeing 720 wasn't merely about celebrity one-upmanship. On a practical level, the Starship meant the band did not have to change hotels every night but could base themselves in large cities such as New York, Los Angeles, Dallas and Chicago and fly back in luxury on a plane fitted with revolving arm-chairs, a bar, club room, bedrooms and a shower. There was even an organ. After a gig, a fleet of limousines ensured that the band were frequently in the air before the audience had even exited

rapher Charles Ruppman and ripping the film out of his camera.

The day after the final New York concert, the band flew back to Britain. They were wrecked, probably in equal parts by the hard work and by the hedonistic excesses that followed when the night's graft had been done. Page was in a particularly bad way, described by **Stephen Davis** as "exhausted, malnourished, sleepless, raving". The guitarist's alarmed family suggested he went to a sanitarium and he admitted he felt he probably belonged in a mental hospital at the time. "I was thinking 'what the hell am I going to do?' because it seemed like the adrenaline tap wouldn't switch off", he told one journalist. "During those concerts to that many people, there was so much energy being stored up. I felt like a kettle with a cork in the top. I'd stay up for five nights on the trot. It didn't seem to affect my playing but I'd come off stage and I was not levelling off at all, not turning off the adrenaline. I couldn't. I felt I needed to go somewhere there was a padded cell so I could switch off and go loony if I wanted. I was quite serious about it".

On tour, of course, staying up for five nights was aided by the copious amounts of cocaine he was taking. On his return, it may well be that this was where Page's problems with heroin started. Rather than the padded cell, the drug became his way of turning off the adrenaline.

Jones responded in a different but equally extreme way. He went to Peter Grant and told him he was leaving the band. "He told me he'd had enough and said he was going to be the choir-

the venue. NBC News was invited to film on board the Starship and footage showed Page and Plant singing along to 'I Do Like To Be Beside The Seaside' accompanied by Jones on the plane's organ. In an accompanying interview, Plant complained: "I'm a bit upset there's not a pool table".

John Bonham, a notoriously uneasy and reluctant flier, found that if he sat up-front in the cockpit in the co-pilot's seat, some of his nerves evaporated. However, Grant's claim to journalist Chris Charlesworth that the drummer had once taken the controls to fly the band from New York to LA was probably a wind-up.

After Zeppelin had started using the Starship in 1973, it was subsequently used by The Rolling Stones and Elton John. By Zeppelin's 1977 tour, however, the

Starship was out of commission after an engine had fallen over. It was replaced by "Caesar's Chariot", a Boeing 707 chartered from the Caesar's Palace casino in Las Vegas.

master at Winchester Cathedral", he revealed. Jones says that the choirmaster line was a joke, but confirms the gist of the story. "I did consider leaving after our 1973 tour of America. I'd just had enough of touring and I did go to Peter and tell him I wanted out unless things were changed. There was a lot of pressure on my family, what with being away so long". Grant asked him not to do anything rash or hasty but to go away and reflect upon it and to think again. "It was kept low-key", Grant added. "I told Jimmy, of course, who couldn't believe it. But it was the pressure. He was a family man, was Jonesy. By that time the security thing in the US was getting ridiculous. We started getting death threats. It got very worrying after that and I think that's how we lost a little of the camaraderie". Jones sought further

assurances that things were going to change and, having received satisfactory answers from Grant, decided to stay.

Meanwhile, Plant was having **voice problems** and in 1988, he confessed: "Fifteen years ago I had an operation on my throat and couldn't speak for three weeks". At various times during the 1973 American tour he had sounded hoarse and strained and it seems almost certain that the operation he alluded to took place in the late summer or autumn of 1973. Clearly Led Zeppelin desperately needed a rest. Yet few could have guessed that it would be another 18 months before the band would be seen on a live stage again.

Wearing And Tearing

1974–1976

"I realized I really missed the unity of the four of us. I realized that above everything else, above record companies, above films, we were Led Zeppelin".

Robert Plant, 1975

Wearing And Tearing
1974–1976

Six years on the road, a load of cash in the band's account, and tax exile beckoning, things were getting tough. Everybody – the Inland Revenue, record labels, movie producers, roadies and groupies – wanted a piece of the action. But then a few nights at Earls Court did the trick. Can you fly any higher? For the faithful, probably not.

Coasting At Cruising Altitude

During the long sabbatical from live appearances that followed the 1973 American tour, Led Zeppelin were hardly inactive. There was a film to finish, a record label to launch and – without the interruption of endless live dates – a record to make that would see them realize the **double album** they had long talked about and which would match The Beatles' *White Album*, The Who's *Tommy* and the Rolling Stones' *Exile On Main Street* as a heavyweight statement of their abilities and intent.

It should have swiftly become apparent to a man as astute as Grant that the film was a folly. He had been a stuntman and bit-part actor before he went into rock management and perhaps this previous experience had coloured his vision, for he was besotted with the idea. After filming the Madison Square Garden shows in 1973, it was decided that each band

member should have his own fantasy vignette. Instead of telling them not to be ridiculous, Grant decided that he, too, should have his own fantasy scene, one of the few times he ever actively courted or encouraged the idea of himself as the "fifth member'" of the band. That the model for their cinematic venture was T. Rex's film *Born To Boogie* only seemed to emphasize that they were courting potential disaster: Led Zeppelin so despised the notion of being a pop band that they continued to refuse to release any singles in Britain. Yet here they were using the biggest teeny-bopper band in the land as a template. "They wanted to show themselves as individuals but not in the traditional way of interviews", director Joe Massot said. "They wanted more symbolic representations of themselves". From the moment this misconceived decision was taken, the film was doomed to resemble a self-indulgent **home movie** rather than a serious documentary about the greatest rock'n'roll band in the world.

The band and Grant each dreamed up their own sequences, and Massot spent the latter part of 1973 shooting their ideas, however weird and whimsical. Only the down-to-earth Bonham avoided pretension by choosing to be filmed with his family and on his farm with his tractor and his cows. In a way, this was his fantasy, but at least it was real and he was actually living it. By March 1974, the inexperienced Massot had been sacked – ironically not due to the ineptitude of the fantasy sequences but following a screening of the rough cut of the live footage from Madison Square Garden. The band didn't like what they saw, and Massot later famously quipped: "They thought it was my fault Robert Plant had such a big cock. It took them another year to recuperate". In his place came the more experienced **Peter Clifton**, who inherited not only a complete mess of a film but all the internal complications of the band politics which meant that, like Massot, he was never completely in charge of the footage.

At least in launching their own label, Led Zeppelin were on surer ground. If what they knew about film-making could be written on the back of a postage stamp, nobody could deny that they certainly knew how to sell records. With their contract with **Atlantic Records** expiring at the end of 1973, Grant wasted no time in negotiating a new deal under which Zeppelin would administer their own still untitled label and have complete control over artistic direction and signing policy, but which would be distributed worldwide

by Atlantic. Crucially, Zeppelin would be the label's main act, and this time the model was not T. Rex but The Rolling Stones, who had established a similar deal with Atlantic following the expiry of their original contract with Decca Records (London in America). The deal was announced jointly by Grant and Atlantic founder Ahmet Ertegun in January 1974, although formal launches did not occur until May (in the US) and October in the UK.

Yet both the American and British launches of **Swan Song** had unexpected bonuses. While in Los Angeles, Zeppelin received an invitation to meet Elvis Presley after the band had been to see him perform at the LA Forum. Meanwhile, The Pretty Things' performance at Chislehurst Caves, according to Plant, reminded the band that the main purpose for their existence was not to make films or run record labels but to create music in front of as big an audience as possible. As a result, Grant was asked to put together a major touring schedule for 1975.

Graffiti Artists

There was also the follow-up to 1973's *Houses Of The Holy* to concentrate minds. One might have thought that with their own label, the logistics of putting out an album would have been simpler, but it wasn't to be the case. Sessions for the new album had actually begun at Headley Grange in late 1973. The band reconvened there in February 1974 and, even though they were now thinking about a double album, they were optimistic about

Swan Song

Although the deal with Atlantic had been announced at the beginning of 1974, it was May before Swan Song was up and running, launched with a double celebration at the Four Seasons in New York and the Bel Air Hotel in Los Angeles, where Groucho Marx was among the unlikely guests.

The name had taken some to time to resolve. Only a month before Swan Song's launch, Plant was still saying the matter was unresolved. "We went through all the usual ones, all the ones that twist off your tongue right away, like "Slut and Slag": the sort of name one would associate with us touring America. But that's not how we want to be remembered. We want something really nice". The logo was based on the 1869 painting 'Evening, Fall of Day' by William Rimmer, depicting a winged Apollo, although it has often been misinterpreted as representing Icarus or Lucifer.

The British launch of Swan Song did not come until October, with a launch party for The Pretty Things' album *Silk Torpedo* on Hallowe'en night in Chislehurst Caves in Kent. It was one of the few occasions that Britain got a taste of the Zeppelin school of debauchery with which America had grown so familiar, with stripper nuns and all manner of other excess.

Unfortunately, the label's signing policy for the new label proved to be rather conservative. Instead of searching for fresh talent – and perhaps running the risk of discovering a new band that might eventually eclipse them – they created a rest home for their old friends and contemporaries, The Pretty Things, who had been around since the mid-1960s being a case in point. The most successful of their signings was Bad Company, fronted by former Free singer Paul Rodgers. But, whether as a deliberate act of policy or not, they never ran the risk of taking on anyone who might rival – let alone outstrip – them. Essentially, Swan Song was a plaything, but with Zeppelin themselves as the label's guaranteed multi-million selling lead attraction, it was an indulgence they could easily afford. However, to Plant's never-ending disappointment, when both the Chess and Sun back catalogues were up for sale, he and Page were overruled when they proposed buying them, with Jones, Bonham and a particularly hostile Grant outvoting them.

Swan Song ceased operations in October 1983. Robert Plant went on to start his own label Es Paranza, while Jimmy Page and John Paul Jones reverted to Atlantic Records.

getting it out that spring. By May, the sessions had been concluded and a track listing agreed that combined new material and some of the backlog of unreleased tracks from previous albums. "What we talk about is creating something as notable as Beethoven's Fifth. Not just something that would still be remembered in 50 years but something so mammoth that it would last forever", Plant even told one interviewer. Ominously, however, he also joked: "We haven't got around to our six-month decision on covers yet".

In the event, it took almost another year for the cover and other assorted problems to be ironed out and *Physical Graffiti*, their first double album and their debut release on Swan Song, did not eventually appear until February 1975.

The day Zeppelin met Elvis

By 1974, when Led Zeppelin got to meet Elvis, there was some confusion about who was now the king. Presley and Zeppelin shared the same American promoter, Jerry Weintraub, and so all concerned knew that outside of Las Vegas, in terms of pulling power the British group was the hotter ticket.

When Zeppelin turned up to see his show one night at the Forum in LA, Elvis was intrigued to meet this bunch of long-haired English barbarians who were selling out venues faster than he was. After singing 'Love Me Tender', he told the audience: "I want to let everyone know my favourite band Led Zeppelin is

here tonight. I'd like to have the spotlight put on them and I hope you'll join me in welcoming them". According to the not-always-reliable account of the band's road manager Richard Cole, when the lights came up, they revealed drummer John Bonham to be fast asleep.

Afterwards the band were shown up to Presley's penthouse suite at the Inglewood, over the street from the venue. Determined to show who was the real star, he kept them waiting until the room was full before making his entrance. While Bonham attempted to engage him in conversation about hot rods and Peter Sellers movies, Elvis asked if the wild stories about Zeppelin on the road were true. Robert Plant mumbled something about them all having families and how easily rumours were spread. Presley laughed – and the ice was broken.

"The four of us and him talked for a couple of hours", Plant recalls. "We all stood in a circle and discussed this whole phenomenon, this lunacy. You'd have to go a long way to find someone with a better idea of what it was all about. He was very focussed". Despite the mishap of Peter Grant sitting on Elvis's father, Vernon ("he was perched on the end of the settee and I just didn't see him"), they got on so famously that Plant and Presley were soon trading lines from 'Treat Me Like A Fool'. When they left Elvis asked Led Zeppelin for their autographs. Bonham was intensely embarrassed and only partly reassured when Presley explained that the signatures were apparently for his daughter, Lisa Marie.

For Plant the meeting was a particular thrill for his entire youthful desire to become a singer had been down to the first time he had heard Presley's voice. "It was the blue note, that mournful dip in the scale that you didn't hear in English music", he recalled in 2005. "It was the whole deal of that emotional delivery he borrowed from Arthur Crudup and Johnnie Ray. I was eight or nine and I didn't know anything about the technical ability of it. I just heard this sound that wasn't anything to do with childhood. I recognized the conviction, although I didn't even know it was called conviction. I didn't know anything about sexuality or the innuendo or that it was part of a movement called rock'n'roll. I just knew the call, the pleading in that voice".

The clever jacket art was intriguing enough, but the music inside – from the Arabesque thunder of 'Kashmir' to the cataclysmic bottle-neck blues of 'In My Time Of Dying' – was, and remains, simply awesome. There was no unifying theme to the album, but it really didn't need one. Drawing on material spanning four or five years, the album summed up everything that had taken Zeppelin to the top whilst at the same time mapped out new vistas and horizons for them. As with the Stones' double album *Exile On Main Street*, some critics took their time to take it all in, but the reviews were positive and the album topped the charts in both Britain and America, where it stayed in the Number One spot for six weeks.

By the time *Physical Graffiti* hit the shops, Zeppelin were already back on the road for their tenth American tour and they would not return to play live in Britain for the next twelve months. Three weeks before the tour was due to begin, the band's accountant **Joan Hudson** informed Grant that there would be "massive problems" with the Inland Revenue and a gargantuan tax bill to pay unless the band took a prolonged absence from UK shores. It was the price of rock'n'roll fame: like The Rolling Stones three years earlier, Led Zeppelin were now tax exiles.

Their tenth American tour was not a bad way to begin a year in a exile. Like its 1973 predecessor, it was split into two legs, running from mid-January to the end of March, with a twelve-day break in the middle. In its early stages there were health problems. Page had damaged a finger in a train door which restricted his dexterity on the fretboard. Plant caught 'flu (allegedly after arriving bare-chested at Chicago's O'Hare airport in January!) and Bonham complained of stomach pains. Page's injury in particular created a few changes in the set list, but any shortcomings were covered up by Zeppelin's most successful stage presentation to date, with a neon-lit backdrop, a massive light show and laser effects to heighten the drama of Plant's violin bow interlude.

By the second leg, which opened at the end of February, *Physical Graffiti* was finally out, the band were in much better shape, and the tour ended triumphantly in Los Angeles at the end of March wit, bizarrely, *Deep Throat* porn star **Linda Lovelace** introducing the band on stage. Off stage, allegedly heroin had now been firmly added to their usual list of debauched pastimes. "Although alcohol and cocaine were still much more prevalent, I frequently nourished my own smack habit, and at one time or another Jimmy, Robert and Bonzo tried some, too", Richard Cole recalled.

Unable to return to Britain for tax reasons, Grant decided to use the limited number of days they were allowed into the UK for a series of five dates at London's **Earls Court** in May 1975 – their first concerts on home soil since January 1973. With the full panoply of their American stage set on show, they played a series of barnstorming shows which included a fine acoustic set, as can be seen on footage included in the 2003 DVD. Plant couldn't help having a jibe one

The Swan Song family

THE PRETTY THINGS

Veterans of the British beat boom of the 1960s, The Pretty Things are one of the great hard-luck stories of British rock. Cast in the same mould as The Rolling Stones, they played an even dirtier, tougher form of rudimentary R&B but, despite a couple of classic hit singles with 'Don't Bring Me Down' and 'Rosalyn' (both later covered by David Bowie) they were swiftly eclipsed by Mick, Keith, Brian, Bill and Charlie. In 1967, they reinvented themselves as a 'Summer of Love' psychedelic band and the following year released the classic *Sorrow*, widely recognized as the first 'rock opera'. Yet it was virtually ignored at the time, and all of the plaudits went instead to Pete Townshend for The Who's *Tommy*. Even the endorsement of Led Zeppelin failed to bring them commercial success and, after two albums on Swan Song, founder member Phil May left in 1976, effectively bringing the band to an end. The remaining members changed their name to Metropolis and there was talk of Jimmy Page producing them, but nothing ever materialized.

On Swan Song:

SILK TORPEDO (1974)

SAVAGE EYE (1975)

DAVE EDMUNDS

Like his close friend and collaborator Nick Lowe, Edmunds had a brilliant ability to recreate classic rockablilly, rock'n'roll and country styles without ever descending into the realms of pastiche. He first came to prominence in the late-1960s with the blues-rock trio Love Sculpture, who scored a Top Ten hit with 'Sabre Dance' and then enjoyed a chart-topping solo single in 1970 with 'I Hear You Knocking'. His band Rockpile supported Led Zeppelin at Knebworth, and he recorded four albums for Swan Song that included such hit singles as 'I Knew The Bride' and 'Girl's Talk'. After building his own studio Rockfield in his native Wales, he became a top producer, helming albums by the likes of The Flamin' Groovies and Shakin' Stevens. Robert Plant has used his Rockfield studios regularly over the years.

On Swan Song:

GET IT (1977)

TRAX ON WAX (1978)

REPEAT WHEN NECESSARY (1979)

TWANGIN' (1981)

MAGGIE BELL

Coming on like a Scottish Janis Joplin, Maggie Bell's raw and earthy voice graced Stone The Crows until the band split in 1973. She then signed to Swan Song as a solo artist but, despite her debut album being produced by the legendary Jerry Wexler, and featuring the cream of America's session players, she enjoyed little commercial success. She subsequently fronted the band Midnight Flyer, who were also signed to Swan Song, releasing just one album.

On Swan Song:

SUICIDE SAL (1975)

MIDNIGHT FLYER (with Midnight Flyer, 1981)

BAD COMPANY

Formed in late 1973 by ex-members of Free, Mott the Hoople and King Crimson as an instant supergroup, Bad Company were by far the biggest success on Swan Song other than Zeppelin themselves. With the voice of Paul Rodgers as the main attraction, but ably backed by Mick Ralphs on guitar, Boz Burrell on drums and Simon Kirke on bass, they were one of the progenitors of stadium rock, with bands such as Foreigner and Bon Jovi taking their cue from Bad Company's power chords and testosterone-charged lyrics. Managed by Peter Grant, unlike his other charges they were very much a singles band, hitting the higher echelons of the chart with 'Can't Get Enough', 'Good Lovin', 'Gone Bad' and 'Feel Like Makin' Love'. They split in 1982 and Rodgers went on to form The Firm with Jimmy Page.

On Swan Song:

BAD COMPANY (1974)

STRAIGHT SHOOTER (1975)

RUN WITH THE PACK (1976)

BURNING SKY (1977)

DESOLATION ANGELS (1978)

ROUGH DIAMONDS (1982)

DETECTIVE

Discovered by Jimmy Page in a club in Los Angeles in 1976, Detective were fronted by ex-Silverhead singer Michael des Barres and also featured former Yes keyboard player Tony Kaye, Michael Monarch on guitar, Bobby Pickett on drums and Jon Hyde on drums. Clearly modelling their sound on Led Zeppelin, Page himself produced their debut album under the pseudonym Jimmy Robinson. Fame eluded them despite their illus-trious champion, although it did land them roles in an episode of the American TV comedy, *WKRP In Cincinnatti*.

On Swan Song:

DETECTIVE (1977)

IT TAKES ONE TO KNOW ONE (1978)

WILDLIFE

Discovered by Simon Kirke around the time of Bad Company's demise, Wildlife was a band based around the two young Overland brothers, who played music broadly in a style similar to Journey or Styx. "I was looking for a band to either join as a drummer or produce. I heard the tapes and thought, 'There's some really good stuff here'", Kirke recalls. In the end he became the drummer and their sole album was produced by Mick Ralphs. With Swan Song barely functional and on the point of winding up, the album and the band sank without trace.

On Swan Song:

WILDLIFE (1983)

Artists signed to the label but whose work was never released included New York singer-songwriter Mirabai, The Message (featuring future Bon Jovi members Alec John Such and Richie Sambora), and Itchy Brother. The label also had lengthy discussions about signing Roy Harper but, despite the close friendship between the singer-songwriter and members of the band, negotiations broke down. When the offices were cleared out in 1983, demos from Iron Maiden and Paul Young's Q-Tips were found unplayed in a filing cabinet.

For British fans, the extended run at London's Earls Court in 1975 (above and right) probably remains the high point of Zeppelin's achievement

night at Chancellor of the Exchequer Dennis Healey, whose tax policies had forced them into exile. "We're about a foot away from the chain gang with our dear Dennis", the singer noted on the first night before ironically dedicating 'In My Time Of Dying' to the Labour politician. At the very end of the last show, as the band took their bow, Plant quipped : "If you see Dennis Healey, tell him we're gone!"

With hindsight, the Earl's Court dates were "the last of Led Zeppelin's glory days before they were beset by tragedy", as **Dave Lewis** wrote in *Led Zeppelin: The Concert File*. After taking off with Page on a holiday to Morocco – "hunting in the jungle for new words and new songs for a new album", as Plant put it from the Earl's Court stage – the singer and his wife Maureen and three children continued their vacation on the island of Rhodes

The Story

in Greece. It was there on 4 August, with the band's next American tour due to start three weeks later, that the car in which Plant and his family were travelling collided with a tree.

Plant's wife, who was driving, broke her pelvis and leg and fractured her skull and required an immediate blood transfusion. She had a rare blood type which might have caused a life-threatening delay in locating supplies, but fortunately her sister, Shirley, who had the same blood group, was travelling behind in a second car with Page's girlfriend and their daughter Scarlett. The children, who had been sitting in the back, suffered only minor cuts, bruises and shock, but Plant in the front passenger's seat broke an arm and both his legs.

Charlotte Martin contacted Richard Cole back in London who immediately flew private doctors out to Greece. After emergency treatment there, Cole managed to get the entire party on a plane back to London for further surgery. The day after the crash, Grant cancelled all plans for the American tour and the band would not tour again until 1977.

In addition to his broken bones, Plant, however, had a further pressing problem. As a tax exile he could only spend the bare minimum of time in Britain and within days he had to be moved again. While his seriously-ill wife remained in hospital in London, he was flown in a wheelchair to Jersey, in the Channel Islands, which enjoyed offshore tax status. There he spent a month in recuperation isolated from all those he loved when they needed him most – and vice versa. What was to become known as "the curse of Led Zeppelin" had officially begun, a curse the band would fail to shake off for the rest of their career.

In The Presence

By September 1975, Plant had been moved again, this time to Malibu, California where he met up with Page. The singer was still in a wheelchair but keen to resume some kind of work, if only to take his mind off what had happened. They were soon joined by Jones and Bonham to rehearse the new material that was taking shape for the album that was to become *Presence*. "The whole band really wanted to play and had wanted to do that tour", Plant explained. "The same effort was put into the album".

Certainly, the new record was coming together surprisingly quickly by Led Zeppelin's standards, but there were still problems. Page complained that Jones was never around in LA and after nearly quitting in 1973, it seemed that the bass player was still feeling somewhat semi-detached. Bonham was missing home and taking exile hard. His reaction was all too predictable: he went on the rampage, drinking and fighting his way up and down Sunset Strip. American tax laws, however, meant that they couldn't stay too long in the US either, so the band decamped to Munich, Germany and the **Musicland** studio, located in the basement of the Arabella Hotel. Working faster than at any time since the first album, *Presence* was done and dusted in two weeks. Plant's problems seemed to have focussed the band. "It was really like a cry of survival", the singer said. "There won't be another album like it. It was a cry from the depths, the only thing we could do". Years later he was to tell this writer: "*Presence* has got some of the hottest moments Led Zeppelin ever had – agitated, uncomfortable, druggy, pained".

The album's speedy completion came despite a growing dependency on heroin, according to Richard Cole. "Bonzo, Jimmy and I used smack during the daytime hours in Munich and none of us seemed the worst for it", the tour manager later wrote. "No one ever talked about the possible risks and we probably didn't think about them, either. We felt trapped indoors by Munich's frigid air. Heroin, it seemed, made the time pass more quickly".

The year ended optimistically with the album finished and a one-off gig in Jersey on 10 December before a lucky audience of just 350 souls at **Beehan's Park West**, a night spot in the island's capital, St Helier. Plant was still in a wheelchair and although he took his first steps unaided shortly afterwards, he soon scotched any hope of a swift return to touring when he told a journalist: "I could do with just sitting down with all my family and thanking the gods", he said. "That doesn't mean to say I've lost the grease at the bottom of my shoes. It means I've got to go back to my corner for a while".

The end of the band's year-long tax exile helped. Plant talked enthusiastically of getting back to what he called the "Isle of the Blessed" and joked that once reunited with his wife he didn't plan on getting out of bed for the first three months. With a return to the road ruled out, *Presence* appeared in March 1976 to some of the most positive reviews of the band's career as critics recognized the edge and urgency of tracks such as 'Achilles Last Stand'.

Horror Movies

Needless to say, it went to Number One on both sides of Atlantic, although it lacked the sustained selling-power of some of its predecessors. The long-running saga of the film *The Song Remains The Same* was also reaching its end, although by now both the band and even Grant were heartily sick of the entire project. Plant was the most outspoken, declaring: "The attitude and the antics of the people involved with film, the way they follow their own odd trips are really beyond my comprehension". As *The Song Remains The Same* was the only film of which he had any knowledge, it was clear he was talking about director Peter Clifton. "The idea of the solitary man standing in front of the camera repeating himself time and time again to some irate lunatic sitting in a chair with 'director' written on the back – yuk". Page was equally disillusioned. "It's so time-consuming. It's a horrible medium to work in. It's so boring", he complained.

Even Grant had grown sick of the film, and made his feelings plain by failing to turn up when Clifton met **Warner Brothers** in America to thrash out a distribution deal for the film. In his place he sent Richard Cole and another roadie, who arrived totally off their faces on booze and cocaine and looking and smelling like they hadn't been to bed in days. Nevertheless, a deal was struck, and the film and accompanying soundtrack album were scheduled for an autumn 1976 release.

In the meantime, Grant sacked Clifton, as he had sacked Joe Massot before him. Only this time it turned nasty, with Zeppelin heavies being ordered to search Clifton's premises for "stolen" negatives or out-takes. To the director's fury, Grant then left his name off the film's posters and publicity. When the film eventually opened, the reviews were poor and after the briefest of runs, the film disappeared from sight. The fantasy sequences in particular were widely dismissed as risible – or worse. The highly-respected **Dave Marsh** wrote in *Rolling Stone*: "While Led Zeppelin's music remains worthy of respect – even if their best songs are behind them – their sense of themselves merits only contempt".

The soundtrack fared better. Although they certainly weren't Zeppelin's best performances, fans had long been demanding a **live album** and – bootlegs aside – *The Song Remains The Same* was the best they were going to get. "As regards the actual gig that was used in the film, it wasn't a terribly good night and it wasn't terribly bad. Certainly it wasn't a

Lucifer Rising

Jimmy Page began working on the soundtrack for Kenneth Anger's film *Lucifer Rising* in 1973, after the pair found themselves bidding against each other for a rare Aleister Crowley manuscript at a Sotheby's auction. Their shared interest in magic and the occult promised a fruitful collaboration.

Page was initially enthusiastic about the project, declaring that he felt it was "quite an honour that he asked me". He also enthused about early rushes of part of the film which Anger gave him: "It's just so arresting. I had a copy and while I was in the US I hooked it up to a big stereo and frightened the daylights out of everyone. I was on the sixth floor and there were complaints from the twelfth. There's a real atmosphere and intensity".

Yet, by 1976 their relationship had gone horribly wrong. Anger complained that Page had produced just 28 minutes of completed music in three years. Page countered that Anger hadn't given him enough material to work with. "I just wanted to see the bloke finish the bloody film", he said. "All I can say is that Anger's time was all that was needed to finish that film. Nothing else. I told him that he must put the music on after he put the footage together, so I was just waiting for him to contact me. I never heard anything".

In a full-frontal media assault on the guitarist in September 1976, Anger announced: "I haven't laid eyes on Jimmy Page since early June... All I've had is promises that the soundtrack is on it's way, but nothings materialized. I've got a fucking film to finish".

He went on: "The way he's been behaving is totally contradictory to the teachings of Aleister Crowley and totally contradictory to the ethos of the film. Lucifer is the angel of light and beauty. But the vibes that come off Jimmy are totally alien to that – and to human contact. It's like a bleak lunar landscape. By comparison, Lucifer is like a field full of beautiful flowers – although there may be a few bumble bees waiting to sting you if you are not careful". Asked whether he felt vindictive towards Page he said: "You bet I do. I'm not a Christian, turn the other cheek kind. In fact, I'm all ready to throw a Kenneth Anger curse". He further suggested that the "problem" that was dragging Page down was an addiction to heroin.

Page hit back: "What a snide bastard. I've got to get my side across because now it's just gone too far. His stuff was just all over the place. I had a lot of respect for him. As an occultist he was defiantly in the vanguard. I just don't know what he's playing at".

Anger eventually turned to Bobby Beausoleil to finish the soundtrack (left). A member of mass-murderer Charles Manson's notorious "family", Beausoleil wrote the music while in prison.

Page's partial score, haunting and disturbing and mostly played on an electric guitar run through an early ARP synthesizer, later appeared on a bootleg and the beginning of 'In the Evening' from the album *In Through The Out Door* is taken from the same source.

magic one, but it wasn't tragic", Page noted. He also admitted that "there are loads of howling guitar mistakes on there". Whatever its strengths and weaknesses, it was snaffled up gratefully and in sufficient quantities for the double album to go to Number One in Britain and Number Two in America, where Stevie Wonder's *Songs In The Key Of Life* kept it from poll position.

If the reception that greeted *The Song Remains The Same* was a disappointment, Page had another film-related shock in store when, in September 1976, director Kenneth Anger launched a very public attack on the guitarist who was supposed to supply the soundtrack to his film, *Lucifer Rising* (see opposite).

While Zeppelin was off the road for the duration of 1976, the musical landscape was changing dramatically, particularly in Britain where the **punk revolution** launched itself with a mission to sweep all the "dinosaur" bands and "old farts" into the dustbin of history. In September, the annual *Melody Maker* poll

found Zeppelin relegated to second place as best band, Page in second place in the guitarist poll, and Plant losing out as top British singer. Not that this was anything to do with the advent of punk and the rejection of the "dinosaurs": the band that beat them were ultimate triple concept album prog-rockers **Yes**, whose singer Jon Anderson and guitarist Steve Howe also topped their respective sections. Zeppelin's problem was that, due to circumstances beyond their control, they had simply been off the road and out of the swim for too long.

While many of the prog-rockers viewed punk with as much distaste as its safety-pinned disciples had for rock's old guard, Zeppelin's relationship to it was more ambivalent. Page and Plant expressed their admiration for its spirit and energy, although with Zeppelin's reputation for rock'n'roll decadence, there was little chance of much reciprocation. What was clear was that in order to reconnect with the changing musical climate, Led Zeppelin desperately needed to return to the road.

Crash Landing
1977–1980

"Fate is already written. I tried to pick myself up and as I did so slowly, I realized my family was way more important than the luxurious life I'd been living in Led Zeppelin".

Robert Plant

Crash Landing
1977–1980

For the last three years of their life as a band, it seemed all four members were dogged by misfortunes, some self-inflicted, some way beyond their control. Conspiracy theorists pointed to Page's interest in the occult, Plant blamed Fate, and times and audience tastes were changing, while more pragmatic critics saw the inevitable tensions between the high life and substance abuse, and the attractions of a more sober domestic existence as the factors lying at the heart of the problem. By no means a spent force, the arc of the Zeppelin's astonishing flight had passed its zenith, and little could be done to stop the inevitable descent.

Bad Luck And Trouble

By the time Led Zeppelin's return to active service was announced in early 1977, they had already spent much of the previous November and December rehearsing for a new tour in Emerson, Lake and Palmer's **Manticore** studio in Fulham, West London. Their eleventh American tour was scheduled to take in 49 dates in 30 cities in three legs across seven months with extended breaks. The anticipated gross was a mind-boggling $10 million – in financial terms double the business they had done in 1975.

Yet misfortune dogged the tour from the outset and those of suspicious disposition might regard some of the events that occurred before they had even played a note as doom-laden portents. With the tour due to open in late February, Plant contracted laryngitis, resulting in the start being delayed until April. Then they were unable to hire the Starship, their usual means of transport around America, because one of its engines had fallen off. Instead, they chartered a Boeing 707 owned by the **Caesar's Palace** casino in Las Vegas which, of course, was dubbed Caesar's Chariot.

Fitting them all on the flight became a problem, too, for by now Zeppelin's entourage of personal assistants, bodyguards, physicians and other flunkeys had grown to bloated proportions. "The entourage had grown to ridiculous numbers, which was one of the problems during that spring and summer tour", according to Richard Cole. "Cliques were formed and a very tight organization became fragmented".

Inexplicably, Cole himself hired **John Bindon,** a minor London mobster who lurked on the periphery of showbiz, and who had already served a jail sentence for murder, as head of security. He argued that the death threats that had accompanied Zeppelin on recent American tours meant that they required some serious muscle, but it was indicative of a culture of casual violence that now seemed to hover over the band, although apart form Bonham's occasional participation, none of the group's members sanctioned or liked it. However, it could be argued that even by turning a blind eye to what was being done in their name made them culpable. The promoter **Bill Graham** would certainly maintain so as a result of a vicious incident during the third leg of the tour and Grant, suffering under a dark cloud of depression brought on by his marital break-up and further destabilized by heroin addiction, was not really in any fit state to keep his unruly crew in any semblance of good order.

When the tour finally opened in Dallas on 1 April 1977, the band were understandably nervous. "We had to postpone a lot of dates and reshuffle them and I didn't touch a guitar for five weeks", a bone-thin Page noted. "I got a bit panicky about that – after two years off the road that's a lot to think about". Although Plant was fully recovered from the injuries he sustained in the car crash, during the first few gigs he experienced considerable pain in his right foot, which was permanently enlarged as a result of his accident.

The fifth show in Chicago had to be cancelled after 65 minutes because Page was visibly ill. The official reason was given as food poisoning but his drug habit had obviously weakened his never robust constitution. After this slow start, the band eventually moved into top gear with a set which reinstated a full acoustic segment for the first time in several tours. Partly it was to allow Plant a chance to sit down, but it was an artistic success, particularly with the introduction of 'Battle Of Evermore' into the set for the first time, with John Paul Jones singing Sandy Denny's part. Surprisingly, only 'Achilles Last Stand' and 'Nobody's Fault But Mine' from the current album *Presence* were included – but on the other hand, as the record had been out for more than a year it wasn't actually that "current". Elsewhere, material from every album but their debut was featured, plus a Page tribute to **Jimi Hendrix** with a version of 'Star Spangled Banner', along the lines of the one the guitarist had played at Woodstock. Even into the second leg a self-critical Page continued to complain that he was "still only warming up" and not operating at full capacity, but by the time the first leg ended at the end of April in front of 76,229 people at the Pontiac Silverdome in Michigan, it was clear that Zeppelin were almost back to their best.

During the two-week break before the next leg, Page took a short vacation in Egypt but he was back in London by 12 May to collect (with the rest of the band) an Ivor Novello award for their "outstanding con-

The 1977 US tour, climaxing with a string of dates at Madison Square Garden and the LA Forum, revealed a band whose glory days were fading

tribution to British music". The second leg of the American tour opened in Birmingham, Alabama six days later and continued through to the end of June, taking in six nights at New York's Madison Square Garden and another half-dozen at the **LA Forum**. Their triumph was only marred by a disastrous open-air appearance in front of 70,000 fans in Tampa, Florida, which had to be abandoned after three songs due to torrential rain, a decision which resulted in a riot which put 60 fans and several policemen in hospital.

By the time the third leg opened in mid-July, the band seemed tired and oddly dispirited. Despite the lengthy breaks in between the various legs, perhaps having been on the road since the beginning of April was simply too much. Whatever the reasons, the first two gigs in Seattle and Tempe were lacklustre. They then moved on to **Oakland** for two fateful concerts that would prove to be their last ever on American soil. On the first night, a local security guard had his head banged against a wall by Zeppelin's crew over some slight, real or imagined. Then Peter Grant's son Warren was apprehended by a security guard who tried to prevent him from removing a wooden "LED ZEPPELIN" sign from the band's back-stage dressing room. Cole, John Bindon, Grant himself and John Bonham then waded into the fracas which left security guard Jim Matzorkis in need of hospitalization.

Promoter Bill Graham – who had been putting on Zeppelin shows in the Bay Area from the beginning, and The Yardbirds before that – was furious, but refrained from immediate counter-action in order not to jeopardize the second night's show. The following morning, however, he filed charges and police arrived at the band's hotel to arrest Bonham, Cole, Bindon and Grant. "I watched those guys walk through with their hands cuffed behind their backs. That was worth everything", Graham later said. "I saw them with their heads bowed down and their tails between their legs. As far as I was concerned every one of those guys in the band was accountable for that shit, because they allowed it to go on. We weren't the only ones it happened to. We were just the last ones".

Bill Graham, promoter extraordinaire, whose patience with the band and their entourage was finally exhausted at the end of the 1977 tour

All four were subsequently found guilty , fined and given suspended sentences. They didn't contest the case against them but the closest Grant came to admitting culpability was that the incident had been "regrettable". Graham declared that he would never book Led Zeppelin again – not knowing that even if he had wanted to, the chance would never arise.

While some members of the entourage, including Zeppelin's attorney **Steve Weiss**, stayed in California to sort out the mess, on the day after the arrests, Robert Plant and others flew on to New Orleans, where the band were due to play in front of a crowd of 80,000 at the Superdome on 30 July. As soon as they checked in to the Royal Orleans hotel, the singer received a phone call from his wife Maureen back in England. She told him the devastating news that their five-year-old son **Karac** was near death after failing to respond to treatment for a respiratory infection. What followed must have been the worst two hours of his life, until a second call came through from Maureen informing him that Karac had died.

Cole, Plant and Bonham took the next available flight back to Britain while Grant stayed behind to cancel the remainder of the tour. Plant's father was interviewed in the British press and declared: "All this success and fame, what is it worth? It doesn't mean very much when you compare it to the love of a family. Karac was the apple of my son's eye. He was a strong child, mischievous, bright and full of life. He had never been ill before. His death seems so unreal and so unnecessary".

Down To Earth

In a way, Plant never got over his loss: what parent could? The realization that his fame and money and being the golden god of rock did not make him immune from the most appalling personal tragedy shook him to the core and changed his outlook forever. "The perspective of that, losing one's child, is the bitterest pill to take", he told this author almost 30 years later. "I've got two more boys now who are gems – different kinds of guys but really good friends of mine. But at that time nothing was in my favour at all". He was further hurt by "the sensationalism and the cheap shots that followed it" as the more irresponsible sections of the media suggested Page's interest in magic and the **occult** had brought down some sort of demonic curse on Led Zeppelin. "The comments about it at the time all connected it to Jimmy's dalliances and preoccupations with the dark side and whatever. I've never shared those with him and I don't really know anything about it. Fate is already written. I tried to pick myself up and as I did so slowly, I realized my family was more important than the luxurious life I'd been living in Zeppelin".

It was a terrible, shocking price to pay for such a realization, and his disillusionment with his old rock'n'roll life was no doubt deepened further when Page, Jones and Grant failed to make it back to Britain for the funeral. Nothing would ever be the same again – in more ways than one. "I haven't taken a drug since that day", Plant told *Uncut* in 2005. "I thought 'How am I ever going to deal with the next moment and put my shoulders back and be a man?' I thought I'd better refocus the whole deal".

Inevitably, the rumour mill that Led Zeppelin were breaking up went in to overdrive, while adherents of the curse theory claimed further dubious "evidence" when a month after the death of Karac Plant, Bonham crashed his Jensen car and broke two ribs. Page kept his spirits up by talking to *Melody Maker* about plans for the next album. In truth, there was virtually no communication between Plant and the rest of the Zeppelin camp throughout the winter of 1977–78. Sensibly, his colleagues realized that he needed **time and space** and that any pressure on him to resume his career would probably be counter-productive.

The go-between was John Bonham, and the rest of the band relied on him to judge when the time was right to try to lure the singer back into the fold. "He encouraged rather than coaxed me back", Plant says of the drummer's role. "He was very gentle because Bonzo was my pal and we had a lot of love for each other. We'd known each other since we were 16 and he spent a lot of time coming over to see Maureen and me with his missus, Pat. I really didn't want to go back. But eventually he said 'give it a whirl again. You've got to sing. You're a big head'".

The reunion came after Grant eventually convened a band meeting at the end of April 1978 at London's Royal Garden Hotel.

"That was after a long uphill battle to get him to work again", Grant later recalled. "Robert kept saying he'd do it and then back down, but Bonzo was a tower of strength. We had a meeting and they started talking about **Bad Company** and **Maggie Bell** and all that with their Swan Song hats on and I said: 'What the fuck are you talking about? You should be worrying about your own careers'. So I suggested Clearwell, because Bad Company had been there. So Robert says he'd just like to do some jamming, so that's what they did".

Clearwell Castle was situated in the Forest of Dean on the English/Welsh borders, conveniently near Plant's own home, but it swiftly became clear that the singer was still not ready to concentrate on music again. "I felt quite remote from the whole thing", he recalls. "Everybody was very gentle and respectful, but it still felt very tenuous. They knew that after you've had an event like that in your life you start measuring your time and what you do with it and your focus is changed forever. But I wasn't comfortable in the group at all, then. We'd gone right through the hoop and because my hoop was on fire, I didn't know if there was enough in it any more".

In the end, it was October 1978, some 15 months after the death of his son, before Plant finally felt able to face the prospect of working again. After rehearsals in London the band had ten new songs ready to record and moved to Stockholm where they took over **Abba**'s studio in Stockholm and wrapped up the sessions in just three weeks, with group members commuting back to Britain each weekend. Although they worked fast, the recording was not without its problems. Page was clearly hampered by his heroin addiction and the band divided into two factions, with drugs the dividing line between them. In the "clean" corner were Plant and Jones; in the narcotics corner were Page and Bonham.

Many of the tracks began with Jones and Plant recording keyboards and guide vocals as the bass player increasingly stepped into Page's shoes in the songwriting stakes. An unhappy Page complained that Jones was also "trying to take over as producer", but the simple truth was that he was stepping into a vacuum of the guitarist's own making. According to Dave Lewis, throughout the sessions the guitarist was "distant, less enthusiastic and not entirely comfortable" and showed a particular antipathy to Plant's more mellow songs such as 'All My Love'.

Despite such problems, the album was finished ten days before Christmas. In fact, the band had more than enough material and three of the strongest tracks, 'Wearing And Tearing', 'Ozone Baby' and 'Darlene' were omitted from the album's running order with the idea that they would appear instead on a **souvenir EP** intended to coincide with the band's return to the live stage. However, in early 1979, Maureen Plant gave birth to another son and her husband's determination to give his family priority complicated Zeppelin's live plans. The singer simply didn't want to tour, particularly in America, which he would have taken him away from home for too long. On the other hand, a tour of Britain and/or Europe hardly offered the venues to stage the barnstorming return Grant desired. "It seemed logical to me that if we were going to regain our position as the world's top group, we'd better play the biggest place possible", he said.

In the end he came up with the idea of the band headlining a major summer festival, extracting an asking price of £1 million for two appearances over consecutive weekends in early August 1979 at **Knebworth House**, near Stevenage in Hertfordshire. Zeppelin's long-awaited return to the live stage was announced exclusively by Annie Nightingale on BBC Television's *Old Grey Whistle Test* on 22 May, and by the end of June the band were already rehearsing at Bray Studios, near Maidenhead, Berkshire.

Although long-finished, various delays meant the new album was still not yet in the shops, and it was decided its release should coincide with the Knebworth appearances. After album titles such as *Look* and *Tight But Loose* had been considered and rejected, the band eventually settled on *In Through The Out Door* because, as Page put it, "that's the hardest way to get back in". In the event, they just missed the deadline to get the album out for Knebworth but it hardly mattered. A festival triumph was almost guaranteed to catapult the album to Number One anyway – and so it proved.

Knebworth

As they hadn't played live in two years, before appearing in front of more than 200,000 fans a brace of low-key warm-up gigs were arranged for late July in a **Copenhagen** theatre seating just 2,000. Despite obvious and understandable nerves and some equipment problems, the shows went well enough, although *NME*'s reviewer was vitriolic. "They appeared sloppy and unrehearsed, sometimes seeming awkwardly lost, bewildered, stiff and reluctant to play", **Eric Kornfeldt** wrote. "They were no more than a quartet of uninspired old men, a relic from the past. There was so little feeling inherent in the set that it was like watching a fully-automated factory producing an endless string of chords that neither musicians nor audience cared about". It was the sort of review that frankly told you more about the politics of *NME* at the time than how Led Zeppelin actually played, and many of the ripest phrases smacked of having been written even before the gig started.

Despite such predictable sneering, all was set fair for an emotional return to the UK stage after a **four-year absence**. Before the gig, Plant observed: "We're not heroes anymore. Heroes are in books – old books". That wasn't how the fans saw it and on 3 August, the night before they played, Plant toured the festival site in a jeep and was overwhelmed by the enthusiasm he found. "People had pushed down the stone pillars to get in early. It was a phenomenally powerful thing", he reported.

The tension rose throughout the day on 4 August as a support bill that included Chas

On stage and on screen and in new outfits at Knebworth, August 1979. Page felt the sheer scale of the event meant that the Zeppelin had met its match

& Dave, **Fairport Convention,** Commander Cody, Southside Johnny and the Asbury Dukes and **Todd Rundgren's Utopia** did their best to entertain the impatient crowd. When Led Zeppelin eventually took the stage, they looked quite different from the four hippies who had last played on a British stage at Earl's Court in 1975. Page wore white chino-style pants and a smartly tailored shirt, Jones wore a white suit and Plant looked sharp in cords and an expensive designer shirt.

The set had its high points and its failings. Page was not always on top of his game and Plant was clearly on edge. "That was a very twitchy time for me. I was wracked with nerves", he confessed many years later. "We could have gone back to the Queen's Head pub. Instead we went back to hundreds of thousands of people. Nobody's big enough to meet those expectations. It didn't work for us. We played too fast and too slow and it was like trying to land a plane with one engine. But because there was some chemi-

Bucolic frolics at Knebworth

The country pile of the Cobbold family, lying some 45 miles north of London just off the Great North Road (A1), became one of the UK's major rock venues during the 1970s, when even stadiums like Wembley were proving too small to meet the demand for lavish live rock events. Kicking off with "The Bucolic Frolic" in 1974, headlining The Allman Brothers, Van Morrison and The Doobie Brothers (attracting a modest 60,000), the venue went on to host a dozen or so major events over the next 30 years. Pink Floyd headlined the next event, in 1975, pulling over 100,000, while 1976 the Stones, 10cc, Hot Tuna and Lynyrd Sknyrd managed a hotly-debated 120,000. 1978 saw Genesis and Jefferson Starship, and later that summer the venue hosted Frank Zappa and The Tubes, underperforming with barely 100,000 between them. The Led Zeppelin concerts were held over two consecutive weekends in 1979, adding up to around 200,000 capacity

Never a festival in the Glastonbury sense, but a one-day venue, by the 1980s public performance licences became more difficult to negotiate; nevertheless the decade saw a Beach Boys/Santana double bill, a couple of Capital Radio Jazz Festivals, a Christian "Green Belt" event headed by Cliff Richard, a 1985 heavy metal jamboree with Deep Purple and Meatloaf, culminating with Queen's final concert in 1986 with 120,000 jammed into the natural greenfield bowl. Knebworth's website claims that after the 1980s, few bands were capable of filling the venue, although Pink Floyd returned in 1990, on a British bill which included Paul McCartney, Eric Clapton, Elton John, Genesis and Plant and Page...not to mention Cliff Richard, which again pulled 120,000 souls up the A1.

The heyday seemed over for country house rock until, in 1996, Oasis headed a Brit Rock line-up including The Manic Street Preachers, Ocean Colour Scene, The Charlatans and The Chemical Brothers, playing two consecutive days, and drawing an estimated quarter of a million people, with only about one in ten of the 2.6 million ticket applicants being successful. By then though, the festival ethos of the 1960s had been thoroughly reinvented, with multi-stage events, innumerable acts, usually themed according to taste and preference, and presented among a host of other distractions, becoming the order of the day.

cal charge in the air, it was fantastic for those who were there. It was definitely intense".

The following weekend was inevitably something of an anti-climax, even if Zeppelin arguably played better and were more relaxed. Plant sniped from the stage about some of the less than adulatory press reviews that had greeted the previous weekend's gig, but the crowd was far smaller, which had unfortunate consequences. Led Zeppelin's guaranteed fee was renegotiated and reduced but it still wasn't enough to prevent the promoter Freddie Bannister's company from going into liquidation.

In Through The Out Door was eventually released the week after the second Knebworth date, packaged in a **brown paper bag** with a series of six different sleeves inside. The trick was that the purchaser didn't know which sleeve they were getting, and the somewhat cynical hope behind this marketing ploy was presumably that diehard Zeppelin fans would try to collect all six covers. Ultimately, the packaging suggested confusion, and the music inside similarly lacked cohesion or unity, although album sales were more than respectable, and spectacular in America.

Yet instead of building on Knebworth and the release of *In Through The Out Door*, Zeppelin retreated once more. Page hinted at all kinds of touring plans and Plant had promised from the stage at Knebworth that fans would get an opportunity to see them again before Christmas. Yet in reality there was little will within the band to take to the road again. The mood in the camp wasn't helped by the continuing escalation of Page's drug problems and, in October 1979, a 19-year-old boy died of an overdose at his house in Sussex. All of the band minus Page appeared with Dave Edmunds as guests at a London benefit concert for UN relief in **Kampuchea** at the end of December, but 1980 arrived with still nothing scheduled in Led Zeppelin's empty diary.

Last Flight: Over Europe

Grant's determination to get them back to America met with implacable resistance from Plant. Eventually he got the singer to agree to a short European tour and the band reconvened to rehearse at **The Rainbow** in North London in April 1980.

Symbolically, Page suggested that they tried to capture their early fire and enthusiasm by rehearsing the old Yardbirds' number 'Train Kept A-Rollin", the first number they had ever played together back in 1968. It opened every show on what was to be their final tour.

When the tour commenced in Germany in mid-June, it was for the first time without **Richard Cole**. Grant had finally had enough of his increasingly unreliable tour manager and decided that his spiralling heroin habit had made him a liability. "I'd paid for the doctor's bills and all that and it just wasn't getting better", he said. "He had a massive problem so I thought the only way to shake him up was to blow him out. So I told him I wouldn't want him in Europe and he says: 'You can't do it without me'. I said 'Well, we've got to'". He was replaced by **Phil Carlo** from Bad Company's road crew, much to the relief of the now firmly anti-drug Plant, who had lobbied Grant to have Cole removed. "There were personalities I didn't take kindly to in the end", the singer said. "I found it very difficult to be a doting father on the one hand and to deal with people like Richard Cole on the other".

With 14 dates inside three weeks across Germany, Belgium, Holland and Switzerland under the slogan "Over Europe 1980" in venues with an average capacity of around 4,000 and using a much reduced PA system, the tour was intended to have a "back to roots" feel

that would recreate the excitement of the early 1970s. Grant also hoped that it would rekindle Plant's taste for performing and lead to an American tour that autumn. "I hoped being up there would give him the necessary lift to do it", Grant confessed.

The gigs, with the acoustic set reduced only to Page's guitar showcase 'White Summer/ Black Mountain Side' and some of the longer pieces dropped in favour of a tighter, leaner approach, were mostly excellent. Plant was fighting fit and in great voice after his long lay-off and Jones, too, was in good shape. Page, dressed in baggy suits that looked even baggier as the tour went on as his frame became even more emaciated, was erratic, either inspired or sloppy, depending on his drug intake and Bonham was his usual self, equally capable of playing up a storm or falling off his drum stool dead drunk, as he did in Nuremberg. The tour wound up on 7 July in **West Berlin**, as it was then still known. Is it just misty-eyed nostalgia and hindsight to suggest that there was a renewal of the old camaraderie at what proved to be Led Zeppelin's final ever gig? It's impossible to say unless you were there, but many like to think so. Certainly, it was the longest set of the tour, as if they genuinely didn't want it to end, Page playing a lengthy and lyrical solo in 'Stairway To Heaven' that extend-

The last tour in 1980 saw a slicker, tighter Zeppelin playing to smaller venues, as here at Rotterdam

ed the song to 14 minutes, while 'Whole Lotta Love' clocked in at more than 17 minutes. Plant's final words from the stage as the front man of the mightiest rock'n'roll band in the world were: "Thank you very much everybody who's worked with us and put up with us and all those sort of things and goodnight!"

Not, of course, that anyone knew it was the end. In fact, quite the opposite for just as Grant had hoped, as they landed back in England, Plant told him walking across the tarmac that he would tour America again, but only for a maximum of four weeks. Grant immediately set about arranging a tour which he optimistically dubbed "Led Zeppelin The 1980s – Part One". He swiftly had a 19-date itinerary in place that would begin in Montreal on 17 October and wind up with four nights in Chicago, ending on 15 November.

The band dispersed for summer holidays and Page spent August moving out of Plumpton Place in Sussex and in to the **Old Mill House**, a mansion on the River Thames at Windsor, which he had just purchased from Michael Caine. They agreed to convene there on 24 September in preparation for rehearsals at the nearby **Bray Studios**, which they had used before the Knebworth gigs.

The week before they did so, Page visited Swan Song's London offices to look at a model of the stage set and lighting rig it was proposed they would use. He also began to draw up a potential set list, which showed a greater sense of adventure than that summer's European dates, and included a number of songs previously never played live, headed by the epic 'Carouselambra' from *In Through The Out Door*.

On the morning of 24 September, Plant and Bonham arrived in Windsor together and, according to the singer, the drummer was in a dark mood. "Bonzo was in one of those periods where he thought he was no good", he recalled. "We drove down to rehearsals together the morning before he passed away. He was saying 'I don't want to do this. You play the drums and I'll sing'. We got to the studio and that's what happened. I played the drums and he sang a bit".

Bonham had been drinking since early in the day and it was an unsatisfactory rehearsal. Nevertheless, it seemed to have blown a few cobwebs away and the entire band returned for a celebration at Page's house, where Bonham continued drinking heavily. By midnight he was in a drunken stupor and roadie **Rex King** carried him upstairs and laid him on a bed. They had seen him in a similar state many times before and nobody was particularly worried. Two roadies apparently checked on him on different occasions the next morning. When he hadn't appeared by the afternoon, John Paul Jones went to "kick him out of bed" – and swiftly realized that he was dead, having choked on his own vomit. He went downstairs to break the news to Page and Plant. "I think he had been drinking due to some problems in his personal life but he died because of an accident", the bassist said later. "He was lying down the wrong way, which could have happened to anybody who drank a lot. At first the main emotion for me was anger. It seemed such a waste".

The shadow of Bonzo

There was never any question that Bonham's death meant an end to Led Zeppelin. Two years earlier, The Who had lost Keith Moon in not dissimilar circumstances. The rest of the band pronounced him "irreplaceable" – but two months later replaced him with Kenney Jones of The Faces. This time, there would be no repeat of such behaviour. "I always say to Roger Daltrey, 'how could you do that?'", Plant said in 2005. "We desperately needed to come together again and create a new direction, which we might have been able to do. We may well have made it better and more constructive and focussed again. But as it happens we couldn't. For me there was no debate".

Nor indeed, was there any desire elsewhere in the Zeppelin camp to carry on. "We had to stop as a mark of respect to John's contribution", Page said. "We could not have gone on without him. It would have been dishonest. Nobody else could have fitted into his role". According to Jones: "He was so integral, to have gotten someone else would have made it more of a tribute band if you were playing Led Zeppelin songs, because anyone else would have to be in his shadow all the time".

The coroner subsequently concluded that Bonham had drunk the equivalent of 40 measures of vodka in the 24 hours before his death. He was just 32. "It could have happened to any one of us", Jones concluded. Ironically, on the day he died the first adverts were appearing in the American press with mail-order ticket application forms for the shows that were being cancelled even as the papers were rolling off the presses.

After the funeral, held at Bonham's local parish church on 7 October, the band took a swift break in Jersey while they tried to come to terms with what had happened. When they returned, Grant summoned a meeting at London's **Savoy Hotel**. "They all looked at me and asked me what I thought. I said it just couldn't go on because it was the four of them and they were all relieved because they had decided the same. For Led Zeppelin to make that music it needed the four of them to do it. And now that was gone".

Despite Press speculation that Bad Company's Simon Kirke, Cozy Powell, Aynsley Dunbar, Carmine Appice and Roxy Music's Paul Thompson were all in the frame as Bonham's replacement, on 4 December Grant issued a statement in the names of the three remaining members which read: "We wish it to be known that the loss of our dear friend and the deep respect we have for his family, together with the deep sense of harmony felt by ourselves and our manager, have led us to decide we could not carry on as we were".

Disembarkation: The Solo Years
After 1980

"Ahmet Ertegun always used to say to me 'Hey man, if you want to do well, you got to put the band back'. I had to tell him, 'This isn't a movie'".

Robert Plant

The Story

Disembarkation: The Solo Years
After 1980

Although their millions of fans fervently expected some form of reunion, the fact of John Bonham's untimely check-out meant that for Plant at least this was never really going to happen. The remaining band members' paths have crossed at various times, but with a powerful royalty-earning backlist none of them needed to work, and all could afford to pursue their own interests, some more fruitfully than others.

New Directions

Since the death of John Bonham, the remaining three members of Led Zeppelin have been unswervingly true to their word and resisted all attempts to put the band back together. In 27 years, there have been just three one-off reunions – at *Live Aid* in 1985, the **Atlantic Records 40th** birthday party in 1988 and their induction into the **Rock And Roll Hall Of Fame** in 1995. And all of these were the surviving band members' decisions. Of the three of them, only Robert Plant's solo career has really fired, but then with the royalties still flowing profusely from one of the mightiest and most enduring back catalogues in rock, none exactly needs either the money or further celebrity and fame.

As rock music – once imagined to be a totally disposable and transitory form – has grown

as a "heritage industry" so too has Zeppelin's stock. Arguably, their influence is as strong today as it was 30 years ago, and their formidable back catalogue continues to sell to new generations of fans. Every new format, from CD to DVD, has offered an opportunity to re-package and re-sell some of rock music's most memorable moments all over again.

When the band announced they were folding, **Atlantic Records** were swift to point out that they still owed the label one more record under the contract Swan Song had signed for five albums in 1974. Plant, Page and Jones spent some time in early 1981 debating what to do, with the guitarist keen on a chronological live double album, featuring performances from the Albert Hall in 1970 through to Knebworth and the final European tour. It was a project Page had been talking about ever

The Story

since the disappointments of the soundtrack album *to The Song Remains The Same* but for some reason Plant was against the idea and effectively vetoed it.

However, Swan Song's lawyers could find no way around the fact that they still owed an album and, determined to resist the personal pressure Atlantic founder Ahmet Ertegun was exerting for the group to re-form with a new drummer, Plant compromised on an album of unused studio out-takes. Page set to work and rescued the three tracks from the *In Through*

A 1980s Led Zeppelin?

The American tour for which the band was beginning rehearsals when John Bonham died, was optimistically to be called "Led Zeppelin The 1980s: Part One". What they might have sounded like during that generally dire decade for music, we shall never know – but the surviving members agree that they were in a good frame of mind and keen to find a new approach that reflected the changing spirit of the times. "We desperately needed to come together again and create a new direction, which we might have been able to do", Plant says. "We may well have made it better and more constructive and focussed".

Page claims that he had already discussed a new direction for the next album with Bonham. "We said we were going to resort to some really intense riffing. I don't want necessarily to call it heavy, but you know what I mean by that" he told this writer in 2005. "That's the way I figured the next album should be because the music had started to lighten up on *In Through The Out Door* and I wanted to get back to that sort of urgent intensity we managed to evoke. That was the discussion I had with Bonzo, anyway. Who knows? But the potential was definitely still there".

One strong possibility is that they would have stripped away some of the pomp and circumstance and returned to a more raw and simple approach under the belated influence of punk. "I don't know where it would have gone or for how long, but it certainly had gotten a new lease on life", reckons John Paul Jones. "Morale was very high. We were in really good spirits. Punk had severely embarrassed us. We'd stripped it down and just went, 'OK, right. This is over, off we go again'. It was a very hopeful time".

One possibility is that Zeppelin might have gone the other way and drowned themselves in synths and drum machines, as so many of their contemporaries did in the 1980s. By 1982, Page was experimenting with a Roland guitar synthesizer on the *Death Wish 2* soundtrack and Plant also admits that he was fascinated by "all that strange questionable technology that was coming on the scene", and which even led to him using a drum box on *Pictures At Eleven*. And, of course, a revival in "Pomp" was just around the corner anyway with Simple Minds and U2 in the wings.

Somehow it was never on the cards that Zeppelin would go down the disco/soul route of the Stones, nor, given Plant's antipathy for extended touring, would they emulate the Grateful Dead's phenomenal longevity as a seemingly constantly touring band playing ever-more extended and largely improvisational sets. Given that it was a decade in which even the likes of Bob Dylan and Neil Young lost their way, perhaps with hindsight Zeppelin broke up at exactly the right time....

The Out Door sessions that had been kept back for the aborted EP, plus further material from *Led Zeppelin III* and *Houses Of The Holy* sessions. As a tribute to the band's departed drummer he also added 'Bonzo's Montreux', a percussion track recorded in 1976. Ironically, however, the best two tracks were probably the two live takes from the Albert Hall concert in 1970 which were used to fill out the album and which left Zeppelin fans salivating for an official full-length live recording, a desire that would not be fulfilled until 2003. The album, *Coda*, eventually appeared in November 1982, making Number Four in Britain and Number Six in America. Finally, with contractual obligations fulfilled and tax bills paid, Led Zeppelin was able to rest in peace. While Page, Plant and Jones pursued separate lives and their own careers, Swan Song was wound up, and Peter Grant relinquished all management responsibilities and retreated into what he later described as "a period of blackness".

Crossing Paths

Of course, that didn't stop the rumours, or the wishful thinking, or former band members running into each other via guest appearances with mutual friends such as **Foreigner, Roy Harper** and **The Pretty Things**. They even helped out from time to time on each other's projects, Page playing on a couple of tracks with Plant's Honeydrippers project and on Jones's *Scream For Help* soundtrack. Then, in late 1984, the BBC broadcast a report by Michael Buerk on

the plight of starving children in Ethiopia. The film prompted **Bob Geldof** to put together the largest benefit concert ever organized, with simultaneous events in Britain and America to be televised around the world.

In early 1985, Robert Plant rang Bob Geldof and offered his services for the American leg of *Live Aid*. The timing fitted neatly with his *Shaken 'N' Stirred* tour and the initial plan was for Plant to perform with **Eric Clapton**. Yet when he realized how big the event was going to be, he began to wonder whether a grander gesture was required: "It seemed to be one of the two or three times in my life when I should consider it", he said. "The event was far more important than my determination to steer clear of something, so I called Jimmy up and said 'Let's do it'".

Jones also readily agreed and ex-Chic drummer **Tony Thompson**, who was on the road in America with **Power Station**, was asked to fill the sensitive John Bonham role. It was also decided to add bassist Paul Martinez so that Jones could play keyboards and a second drummer in **Phil Collins**, who flew the Atlantic by Concorde to become the only artist to perform at both the British and American concerts.

With Plant in the middle of a tour and booked to play in Detroit the night before, the line-up was unable to rehearse until the morning of the gig. When they came to perform it showed, but it hardly mattered. After Collins had finished his solo set, he announced that he would like to introduce "some friends of mine" – and there were Page, Plant and Jones together again on

The Story

The *Live Aid* appearance in Philadelphia, 1985, with Phil Collins in one drumseat, fresh from his transAtlantic Concorde flight

a stage for the first time in five years. Plant's voice was hoarse, Page's Gibson was out of tune and the sound wasn't working properly. Plant shouted: "Good evening!" only for Page to respond with "There'll be a short intermission while I get some monitors".

Plant later recalled: "It was so much like a lot of Led Zeppelin gigs. One and a half billion people and Page is swanning around with no guitar and I'm wondering how my voice is going to stand up and thinking 17 years and we still can't get it right!" With two drummers pounding away to replicate Bonham's thunder, they opened with 'Rock And Roll',

and it was an irresistible choice as Page sang the opening line "It's been a long time since I rock and rolled..."

When they'd finished, Plant teased the crowd by asking for requests, at which Page broke into the riff of 'Heartbreaker', before switching into 'Whole Lotta Love', played in shortened form along the lines of the edited US single. "OK, that was kind of up tempo. This is something that takes the mood down a little, and yet, then again, lifts everything up, maybe. Who knows?" Page strapped on the famous double-necked guitar and it could only be 'Stairway To Heaven'.

In all honesty, due to technical problems and an understandable rustiness, it was not a good performance – so poor, in fact, that when *Live Aid* eventually appeared on DVD 20 years later, Led Zeppelin were the only act to refuse to allow their contribution to be included. At the time, the **sheer emotion** carried them through, as Plant explained: "I'd be lying if I said I wasn't really drunk on the whole event. The rush I got from the audience, well, I'd forgotten how much I missed it. I'd also forgotten how Led Zeppelin and Bonzo could never be replaced. The fact that they were still chanting for us 15 minutes later and that people were crying all over the place was something more powerful than words can say". Their performance aided the cause, too, for the monies being pledged by telephone increased dramatically following their appearance.

Once the emotion had subsided, Plant was far more critical. "*Live Aid* was a fucking atrocity for us", he claimed in 1995. "It made us look like loonies. I was hoarse and Pagey was out of tune. We had no monitors and the idea of playing 'Stairway To Heaven' with two drummers while Duran Duran cried on the side of the stage, there was really something quite surreal about that". He went on to liken the performance to **Frank Sinatra** singing 'My Way'. They refused to allow the footage to be used in the 2005 DVD, released to raise money for refugees in Sudan. Inevitably, the decision brought a hail of criticism down on their heads, forcing them to issue a statement which read: "Jimmy Page, Robert Plant and John Paul Jones are in absolute full support of the fundraising project for the people of Sudan. However, Jimmy, Robert and John Paul found that both the sound and general reproduction of their performance at *Live Aid* Philadelphia was sub-standard". They went on to pledge **financial support** for the campaign in other ways.

The Page/Plant Nexus

Despite the shortcomings of the *Live Aid* set, the emotional power was undeniable and they began to think about playing together again. On finishing his American tour in September, Plant sacked the band he had been touring and recording with since 1981. By January, he was in rehearsals with Page, Jones and drummer Tony Thompson at a village hall near **Peter Gabriel**'s Real World Studios near Bath, reputedly trying out new music with Jones on keyboards and Plant taking over the bass. However, the singer almost immediately got cold feet and when, on the second day, Thompson was involved in a car crash, all the singer's worst suspicions seemed to be confirmed. Plant had never subscribed to the "curse of Led Zeppelin" theory, but Thompson's mishap brought unwelcome memories of former such catastrophes flooding back. "The second day we got to play, it really started to cook", Page recalls, "and that very night Tony Thompson was injured in a car accident. I just thought, 'Wait a minute, this just isn't meant to be'. We tried playing along with a drum machine after that and then a roadie took over the drums for a bit. I just felt completely, 'What's the point', y'know?".

In truth, the guitarist himself was not in great shape, as Plant obliquely acknowledged. "Two or three things were quite promising, a sort of cross between David Byrne and Husker Dü", he remembers. "But for it to have succeeded I would have to have been far more patient than I have for years".

Nevertheless, both Page and Plant made cameo appearances on each other's next albums and, in 1988, came the second Led Zeppelin gig of the decade, when they re-formed for an appearance at a twelve-hour concert to mark Atlantic's 40th anniversary at New York's Madison Square Garden. This time, the familiar name of Bonham was back on drums once again – **Jason Bonham,** the 20-year-old son of the late drummer. Like *Live Aid*, it was Plant who first put his name forward. The most reluctant to turn the clock back, his reticence basically meant that Zeppelin reunions only happened on his instigation. Page and Jones readily agreed and, with the *Live Aid* fiasco much in mind, determined this time to rehearse fully. With Plant on tour in America, Page, Jones and Bonham spent a week rehearsing in London's Nomis Studio, running through between 15 and 20 old Zeppelin numbers. Jones was particularly impressed with how much Bonham had absorbed of his father's playing. "I went in to a very old fill I used to do and he's right there with me", Jones

marvelled. "It's one of those things that a bass player and a drummer only do when they've been married for ten years but we just went straight into it".

The trio finally met up with Plant for a day's rehearsal in New York prior to the concert on 14 May 1988. Yet once again, the gig, which was **broadcast live** on HBO, was a bit of a mess. Subsequently, Page and Plant publicly blamed each other for the show's disappointments. The only thing they could agree on was that Jason Bonham had acquitted himself with great credit. "It was Jason's dream to play with Led Zeppelin. It was so important to him, something he'd always hoped for", Page said. "I was looking forward to it, too, because I knew how good a drummer he'd become. Jones and I had rehearsed with Jason and it had gone particularly well. We'd agreed on what we wanted to play and the soundcheck at the Garden sounded really good. Then at the eleventh hour, Robert decides he doesn't want to do 'Stairway', so there's this running confusion and harsh words between us right up to literally the last minute, and that shook me up quite a bit. The whole thing was one big disappointment, especially since I knew I wasn't playing well. It was so upsetting because we really put work into it and it should have been really good. All the last minute dramatics about not doing 'Stairway' suddenly threw the whole thing up in the air. I was trying to cool it out at the end but it was like, 'Thanks a lot, pal!'"

The Plant/Page Unledded world tour outing in 1998. Page elegantly coiffed, Plant less so

According to Plant: "Page and I had our usual touchy vibration-filled moment when I didn't want to sing 'Stairway To Heaven' and he said it was a necessity for the Western world and I said that I didn't think it was that important. So the rehearsal was good, the soundcheck was good – and the gig was foul. However, I must say that Jason Bonham was stunning. I've always tried to clip him around the back of the head and tell him to get his act together and stuff, but he really was the king-pin of the whole delivery".

In the end, Plant did sing a perfunctory 'Stairway To Heaven' at the end of a 28-minute set in which the singer had messed up the lyrics to 'Kashmir' and Page had played a limp solo in 'Heartbreaker'. 'Whole Lotta Love' and 'Misty Mountain Hop' were better, but it was far from the triumph that it should have been.

The Story

Oddly, the row and the erratic performance did not drive an insurmountable wedge between them. Behind closed doors and strictly for family and friends, they were more than happy to play together. Plant, Page and Jones all jammed together at the 21st birthday party of the singer's daughter **Carmen** in late 1989. After the harsh words of the previous year, this time Plant said: "Pagey was playing so good, I had a big lump in my throat. That little time of playing with him gave me something I hadn't had for a long time". Without the pressure, it seemed the **chemistry** was still there, and the following year they did it again at Jason Bonham's wedding reception.

A more public reunion between Page and Plant in June 1990 took place at **Knebworth**, the scene of Led Zeppelin's final British gig ten years earlier, with the guitarist joining Plant's band for 'Misty Mountain Hop', 'Wearing and Tearing' (never previously performed live) and 'Rock And Roll'. Once again, it led to feverish speculation that a full-scale reunion was on the cards and Page himself did everthing he could to make it happen. Plant was as usual reluctant but agreed to consider it when told an offer worth several million dollars was on the table for an American tour. The singer even suggested **Faith No More**'s Mike Borodin as a drummer – but then, according to Page, changed his mind again "the very next day" and threw himself back into his solo career.

Mining The Back Catalogue

Atlantic Records were particularly keen on a reunion because it would have helped to sell the digitally remastered, 54-track 4-CD boxed set Page spent the spring and summer of 1990 compiling for them. It included one previously unreleased item, Page's acoustic 'White Summer/Black Mountain Side' sequence from a 1969 BBC radio broadcast. Even without the support of live gigs, the set sold a million, the highest-selling such project until EMI began raiding its archives for The Beatles *Anthology* series five years later. A second boxed set followed in 1993, and included 'Baby Come On Home', a "lost" out-take from the first album, plus a gargantuan, 10-disc *Complete Studio Recordings* set the same year.

In late 1993, Plant was approached to contribute a Led Zeppelin-based set to MTV's highly successful *Unplugged* series. At first he was uncertain. "Then mysteriously Jimmy turned up at a gig I was playing in Boston and it was like those difficult last days of Led Zep had vanished and we had this understanding again without doing or saying anything. We talked about the MTV thing and decided to see if we could present Zeppelin's music in a broader light. It would have been incredibly facetious if I thought I could carry any thread of the Zeppelin history on my shoulders outside of a live gig. The only answer really was to see if I could team up with the one bloke who knew where I was coming from. I felt very good about it". Page, too, was delighted at the prospect, ditching the singer **David Coverdale**, with whom he was working at the time, and throwing himself wholeheartedly into the project. "The MTV thing was a catalyst", he said later. "It gave Robert time to think about things and get in contact. It was really the first time we had a chance to think about the future constructively – to kick it around, see how to do it and how not to do it".

In February 1994, they began working in a studio in London's King's Cross with looped backing tapes prepared by French World Music producer, Martin Meissonnier. Other musicians were added, including bassist **Charlie Jones** and drummer **Michael Lee** from Plant's backing band and an Egyptian ensemble led by **Hossam Ramzy**. Asian singer **Najma Akhtar**, hurdy gurdy player Nigel Eaton and ex-Cure guitarist **Porl Thompson** also joined the party, although there was no call to John Paul Jones. "Nobody rang me to tell me they were doing it, which I found a little odd", he later complained. "I saw it in the papers and called somebody up, and said, 'God, I see all of the rumours are all starting again. Here we go', because it happened regularly. I thought it was just more rumours. And this person said, 'Haven't they told you?' 'Told me what?' I asked. 'Oh, they're going out on the road again together'".

In early August 1994, Page and Plant flew to **Morocco** to record and film a sequence for the upcoming *Unplugged* show. The full recording of the show took place over two nights in a TV studio on London's South Bank at the end of the month. The new arrangements of songs such as 'Thank You', 'Battle Of Evermore', 'Gallows Pole', 'Friends' and 'Kashmir' were radically different from the originals, but in their way quite inspired. The show was broadcast on MTV two weeks later and the resulting album, *No Quarter: Unledded*, made the Top Ten in Britain and in America.

In February 1995, Page and Plant launched a year-long tour during which they played 115 shows in 19 countries and performed new versions of 34 Led Zeppelin songs. Some fans were disappointed at the non-inclusion of Jones in the "reunion" and the bass player himself made his disgruntlement known when a month before the tour started, Led Zeppelin were inducted into the Rock And Roll Hall Of Fame at the Waldorf-Astoria Hotel in New York. "Thanks to my friends for finally remembering my telephone number", he quipped from the stage, although his annoyance didn't prevent him from joining in a jam session with Page and Plant, which was also joined by **Neil Young**. It was only the third time all three surviving Zeppelin members had played together in public in 15 years.

Without Jones, the Page and Plant tour went well enough for them to consider further collaborations. For Page it was the most creatively satisfying project he had been involved in since the demise of Zeppelin. "It's fucking great and it comes from a good chemistry and a lot of straight-talking now", Page enthused. "There's a sensitivity that we've got between ourselves

At The Rock And Roll Hall Of Fame presentation, with Pat Bonham, and Aerosmith

which I think has taken a while to kindle in these new times. But it's good stuff and there's no better place to be". For Plant, it was the first time he had felt totally at ease with his past. "There's still an extraordinary energy, it's just that it's a bit more manageable and a bit more enjoyable. There aren't so many loose cannons or grey areas", he observed. "We know where we are and what we're doing".

The pair spent much of 1997 writing *Walking Into Clarksdale*, although the album was then recorded at **Abbey Road** in just 35 days. Sadly, their first full songwriting venture together since *In Through The Out Door* was a disappointing effort, with few outstanding

songs and was easily outsold by *Led Zeppelin: The BBC Sessions*, a 2-disc compilation of their early radio recordings which had been much bootlegged but was not given an official release until 1997.

When they took the new record on the road in 1998 on the '*Walking Into Everywhere*' tour, playing another 89 gigs in 18 countries, including Eastern Europe, audiences showed little or no interest in the new songs and they fell back increasingly on Zeppelin classics such as 'Rock And Roll', 'Babe I'm Gonna Leave You', 'Gallows Pole', 'Heartbreaker' and 'Whole Lotta Love', although they were now mostly being played as straight rock songs again rather than in the intriguing *Unledded* arrangements. By the end of the year, to the surprise of nobody, a disenchanted Plant pulled the plug and plans for a 1999 tour of Australia and the Far East were cancelled. "Jimmy and I were kind of marooned. We were still surrounded by the protective shield of who we were and it meant we were playing big arenas around the world and I realized again there had to be another way of singing than doing it in front of a great black abyss", Plant later explained. "It was when we did an Amnesty International benefit in Paris with Bruce Springsteen, Radiohead and the Dalai Lama that I knew it was getting absurd again. Only 'The Laughing Policeman' was missing. Then it was suggested we played New Year's Eve in Guam and then on to Hawaii and I knew I had to get back to playing clubs and remembering what the pulse was all about. To sell 200 million albums with Zeppelin was chance. But to say goodbye to the large arenas I played with Jimmy was a very purposeful move. I just didn't think there was anything left for me to project to the back of an ice hockey arena. So I had to go off play little places on the Welsh borders. And that gave me a new life".

In public, both sides claimed there was no animosity, but it was noticeable that when the two were booked to appear separately at a charity concert organized by **Roger Daltrey** at the Albert Hall in February 2002, Page jammed with **Paul Weller** and **Ocean Colour Scene** but not with Robert Plant. It was the first time the pair had not played together when sharing the same bill.

Page meanwhile turned his attention to putting together the *Led Zeppelin* DVD. He had begun assessing the archive of film material as early as 1997, but it took the rapid development of DVD as a format before the project took full shape and, in 2002, he hired director **Dick Carruthers** to help with the task of digitalizing the available material. He even swallowed his dislike of bootleggers and put out a call for audience-shot cine footage, an appeal that produced further interesting material. The 2-disc DVD set appeared May 2003 and became the biggest-selling music DVD at that time. During his trawl of the archives, Page also came across the multi-track tapes of Zeppelin's LA performances from the 1972 tour, which he cleaned up and issued as the live double CD, *How The West Was Won*.

Jones, Plant and Page all attended special premiere screenings in London and New York but, typically, guitarist and singer derived different messages from watching the old footage. "If we got back in a room and played a Zeppelin number and there were smiles behind our eyes, then maybe it could happen", Page said with a considerable degree of wishful thinking. "It could be possible. I wouldn't discount it. I just don't know". Plant, however, was far more decisive. "The DVD really opens and closes the issue because it's so explicit of what it's about", he said forcefully. "It's the epitaph of Led Zeppelin – stunning, a lot of energy, a roller-coaster ride, four guys melding in this great fusion of music. And it's gone".

Solo Flights

It would be fair to say that Jimmy Page found the demise of Led Zeppelin harder to take than either of his surviving colleagues. Plant was full of ideas and threw himself swiftly into a busy and productive solo career, determined to prove that the most significant part of his life was not over at 32 years of age. The self-contained John Paul Jones was more than content to disappear into obscurity, spend time with his family and tinker for his own amusement in his home studio. Page, it seemed, simply didn't know what to do, although he was able to delay thinking about his post-Zeppelin future for a while as he set about compiling the posthumous *Coda* album.

Jimmy Page

Living in the house where Bonham had died can hardly have helped Page's state of mind and rumours were rife that his health was in a perilous state as a result of his heroin addiction. "There was a period after John died that I didn't touch a guitar for ages. It just seemed to relate to everything that had happened", he admits. When he eventually asked his road manager **Tim Marten** to retrieve his favourite Les Paul from storage, the guitar case was found to be empty. "I thought, 'That's it, I'm finished'" was Page's immediate reaction. Fortunately, it transpired that the guitar had been borrowed not stolen, and it was swiftly returned. In March 1981, he made his first post-Zeppelin appearance on stage, jamming

with **Jeff Beck** during the encore at a gig by his old Yardbirds sparring partner at London's Hammersmith Odeon.

Meanwhile, at his Sol studio in Cookham, Berkshire he was working with Chris Squire and Alan White from Yes. Seven tracks were recorded but were never released amid rumours that he was trying to get Plant to sing with them and the band would be called **XYZ** (ex-Yes and Zeppelin). Such plans came to nothing but in the late summer of 1981, he was approached by the film director **Michael Winner**, who was a near neighbour in Kensington, to provide a score for the film *Death Wish 2*. Despite his disastrous experience over the *Lucifer Rising* project, he accepted and, working with alacrity, the soundtrack album, which found him experimenting with the Roland guitar synthesizer for the first time, was released in February 1982. "I was at a very low ebb but then a great challenge came up to do a film score", he recalls. "I had eight weeks on that project, that's all I had to deliver the whole thing. That's what got me back into it without a doubt".

If so, his return to the fray wasn't immediately evident. A drug bust in 1982 was depressing proof of his continuing problems and it was well into 1983 that there was any serious sign of further activity when he performed music from *Death Wish 2* and an instrumental version of 'Stairway To Heaven' at a brace of benefit concerts at London's Albert Hall that September for the multiple sclerosis charity ARMS. They were successful enough for Page to agree to nine similar shows in America. **Steve Winwood** had sung with him at the Albert Hall, but with the former Traffic man unavailable for the American dates he turned to **Paul Rodgers**, footloose and fancy-free after the break-up of Bad Company. It ushered in a far more productive period in Page's post-Zeppelin life and 1984 found him appearing at folk festivals with **Roy Harper**, playing on albums by Harper and Stephen Stills and aiding both John Paul Jones and Robert Plant on their respective solo projects.

The big news, however, was the band he was putting together with Paul Rodgers. Rehearsing under the name the McGregors (Page was also introduced by Roy Harper during their joint appearances as 'James McGregor') among those who came and went during early rehearsals were **Rat Scabies**, drummer with The Damned, and **Bill Bruford** from Yes. However, the line-up eventually settled on included **Chris Slade** on drums and **Tony Franklin** on bass and the quartet made their live debut in Stockholm in November 1984 under the name **The Firm**. British gigs and an American tour followed with a set that largely avoided old Zeppelin and Free material, but many of the dates were less than sell-outs, hardly helped by a lacklustre debut album with few stand-out songs. A second album was even less well-received, and after a further American tour the band split in May 1986. "The Firm was originally going to be a one-album project and then it went to two and then Paul and I agreed it had run its course, really", Page commented. Given the tal-

ent involved, it was all rather a waste, but even musicians of the ability of Page and Rodgers could not carry a band that displayed such a chronic inability to write memorable songs.

Uncertain what to do next, and with the attempted Zeppelin reunion with drummer Tony Thompson having collapsed in early 1986, Page decided to record his first proper solo album. Originally intended as a double LP with one side of rock'n'roll, one of blues, a third of acoustic material and a fourth experimental side, it was eventually cut back to a single album, in part because demos of some of the material were stolen from Page's home. *Outrider* eventually appeared in June 1988 and featured a guest appearance by Robert Plant. Page later admitted that the album sounded "a bit like a glorified demo" but it was better received than the misconceived efforts of The Firm, and Page toured the record successfully in Britain and America, also taking the opportunity to reprise favourites from the Led Zeppelin songbook. He also seemed at last to have laid some of his demons to rest, having married and become the proud father of a son, **James Patrick**.

After the *Outrider* tour had wound down, he talked about another album project and suggested he was putting together a new band with "a lot of young blood". Yet he put all such thoughts to one side when Atlantic asked him to oversee the remastering of the band's back catalogue. Frustrated by Plant's vetoing once again another attempt to reunite Led Zeppelin, in 1992 Page took the surprising step of teaming up with the former Deep Purple and Whitesnake singer, David Coverdale. It was also provocative, due to a long-running feud between the singer and Plant, who regarded him as a shameless copyist. "I'd been looking for a singer to work with and gone through scores of demo cassettes with no luck. Then someone from my record company, Geffen, suggested I team up with David", Page explained. "Initially we tried a few ideas and then the stuff began pouring out. We knew we had something good".

A routine heavy rock album followed but a planned tour of America in 1993 was cancelled, allegedly due to poor ticket sales. They did play seven dates in Japan at the end of the year but a proposed second album was scrapped when Page teamed up again with Plant for the MTV-*Unplugged* project. There were more than a few who believed that his dalliance with Coverdale had been deliberately conceived to rile Plant and force him, like a jealous lover, back into resuming their old partnership.

Page and Plant worked together again for the best part of the next five years, producing two albums, 1994's *No Quarter/Unledded* and *Walking Into Clarksdale* three years later, and touring extensively. However, when Plant tired of the reunion at the end of 1998 and pulled the plug, Page took it badly. His response was to go on the road in America with **The Black Crowes**, a liaison that lasted into 2000 and produced a live album full of old Led Zeppelin material.

Since then Page has once again gone quiet. Now in his sixties, at an age when most are settling into

becoming grandparents, he has three young children by his current partner, **Jimena**, and enjoys taking and collecting them from school and fulfilling his paternal duties in a way that he wasn't always able to with his two children by previous relationships. Impressively, his extended family, which includes three different mothers and five children, are all on good terms. "Every Christmas we are all together, all the mums and all the children", he told *The London Evening Standard* in 2004. "We are a close-knit family".

Musically, he remains happiest when working on Zeppelin-related projects such as the 2003 DVD, which he spent hundred of hours assembling. While Plant is terrified of being seen to rest on the laurels of Led Zeppelin, Page can't think of anything grander. He's delighted every time Zeppelin are given some new honour or award and invariably turns up to accept in person, beaming with pride and pleasure. When asked in 2005 if he was frustrated that the media were obsessed with his role in a band that had split up a quarter of a century earlier, he seemed baffled by the question. "Not at all, because if you look at it from my point of view, it was a great life in Zeppelin", he responded. When it was pointed out that his time in the band constituted less than one-fifth of his life and had come to an end when he was just 36 years old, he answered: "But it's what Led Zeppelin means across the board – the playing, the writing and the fact we made so many groundbreaking statements at the time". Implicit in the reply was a recognition that nothing he had done since had come close to matching it.

Yet in the same interview, he insisted that there would be a new Jimmy Page solo recording. "What I need to be doing is trying to make a new musical statement", he said. "My main intention this year is to get up to speed. The way to look at it is that I took a year out. I had some things to sort out and that's done and now it's time to get back on a serious roll this year. And hopefully there will be some music. Now's the time to do something that makes people say, 'I didn't think you'd do that, but I can really see why you've done it'. We'll see what we come up with. I'm not retired yet if that's what you're thinking". Two years later, the world was still waiting.

Robert Plant

Devastated as he was by John Bonham's death, Robert Plant could hardly wait to launch his solo career. A new band and a new method of working in which he called the shots were his way of wiping the slate clean and putting behind him both the pain of losing his friend and what he has called the "psychosis" that surrounded Led Zeppelin. The details of the launch of his solo career were imbued with considerable symbolism: on 9 March 1981 he turned up with a bunch of local blues players dubbed **The Honeydrippers** at a wine bar in Stourbridge and played a set of vintage R&B and blues standards with not a Zeppelin number in sight, other than a reinterpretation of Sonny Boy Williamson's 'Bring It On Home'. The contrast with his last performance on British soil at Knebworth could not have been greater.

During the short club tour that followed, Plant began writing new material with guitarist **Robbie Blunt**, an old friend from the Midlands and a veteran of several bands including the criminally underrated early-1970s roots-rockers **Bronco**. Before long they were at Dave Edmunds' Rockfield studio in Wales, recording with a new band that included **Paul Martinez** on bass and Black Sabbath drummer **Jezz Woodruffe**. Released in June 1982, Plant's solo debut *Pictures At Eleven* represented a deliberate break with the past as he experimented with a drum machine and other programmed elements and supported the album with singles and videos, activities that had been anathema to Led Zeppelin. There was a new look, too, although Plant had already hinted at a change of image at Knebworth. Gone were the hippie threads to be replaced by smart designer labels, while the once unruly hair was expensively coiffed 1980s-style.

Pictures At Eleven made the Top Five on both sides of the Atlantic and proved to Plant's delight that there was life after Led Zeppelin. A second album, *Principle Of Moments*, followed in 1983 and included the hit single 'Big Log', which he even performed on *Top of The Pops*, "with a lemon in the trouser pocket of my silk jumpsuit", he recalls. "In fact there were lemons in both pockets and they were swinging around. Big bollocks. And that's exactly what it was. Big bollocks. Going along with those funny hair-dos and mohair jumpers! But there were some fantastic moments". With a band that initially included **Phil Collins** on drums, he also toured the album in Britain and Australia and Japan, although he assiduously avoided Led Zeppelin material.

Before recording his third solo album proper, *Shaken 'N' Stirred*, Plant indulged himself on a handful of vintage R&B standards with a stellar pick-up band that included **Nile Rodgers**, Jeff Beck and Jimmy Page. Released at the end of 1984 as *The Honeydrippers Volume One*, the 5-track mini-album was a huge success in America, where 'Sea Of Love' was a surprise Top Five single, although it fared less well in Britain. *Shaken 'N' Stirred*, however, found Plant moving in the opposite direction on his most 1980s-sounding set. The album has not stood the test of time well, but the supporting tour, which included his first American dates since 1977, was a more engaging affair, incorporating a Honeydrippers sequence and an inflatable Cadillac car as a backdrop.

In the middle of the 1985 tour he reunited briefly with Led Zeppelin at *Live Aid* but after vetoing plans to re-form on a more permanent basis, the following year he ended his three-album partnership with Blunt, broke up his band and went back to the drawing board. He didn't re-emerge until early 1988 with the release of the album *Now And Zen*, which included a guest appearance by Jimmy Page and sampled Zeppelin on the track 'Tall Cool One'. It was an indication that he was beginning to come to terms with his past and on the accompanying *Non Stop Go* tour for the first time he incorporated Zeppelin material into his solo shows, including 'Rock And Roll' and

'Communication Breakdown'. "I guess I'm eating a sizeable portion of my own words", he confessed at the time. "But these are great songs and I think enough time has now elapsed. Some of them are sacred still, but if I want to romp through 'Misty Mountain Hop' again, well it's my prerogative". Predictably there was no 'Stairway To Heaven', which he now regarded as nothing but an **albatross** around his neck. Indeed, he showed what he thought of the song by having an easy-listening cocktail version played as the outro music as the lights went up at gigs where sections of the audience had irritated him by calling for him to sing it.

His fifth solo set, *Manic Nirvana*, appeared in 1990 and was a harder-edged affair that echoed the relief of many that the 1980s were over. The accompanying tour included half a dozen Zeppelin numbers as rumours of a reunion reached fever pitch. Instead, Plant assembled a new band for 1993's *Fate Of Nations* and the accompanying tour found him visiting **South America** and **Mexico**, as well as the more usual European and North American venues. It was the last time he would be seen as a solo artist for six years, when in 1994 Zeppelin fans finally got their wish and he teamed up with Jimmy Page again.

It was a very different Robert Plant who returned to the stage in 1999. Just as in 1981 he had picked up his solo career playing R&B with a bunch of local musicians he dubbed The Honeydrippers, this time he assembled **Priory of Brion**, featuring a bunch of part-time musicians which included his former Band Of Joy colleague,

Kevin Gammond. The repertoire consisted entirely of covers of late 1960s psychedelic classics by the likes of The Youngbloods, Buffalo Springfield, Tim Buckley, Love and Jefferson Airplane, mostly delivered from a seated position. Promoters were forbidden to advertise his name as the band made its way around tiny pubs and clubs, mostly near the Welsh border. The only publication he invited to cover the venture was the specialist magazine *Folk Roots*. When the magazine's interviewer turned up backstage at a gig at The Cheese and Grain in Frome, Somerset, Plant quipped: "It's a

long way from the golden god of cock-rock, eh?" *Folk Roots* duly featured him on its cover with a long interview in which he talked about his desire to get back to his roots and his love of **Arabic** music and singers such as the late Egyptian diva **Oum Kalthoum**.

In 2000 Priory of Brion played festival dates at **Glastonbury,** the **Cambridge Folk Festival** and Fairport Convention's annual **Cropredy** get-together, where Plant had guested several times over the years. In all, he played more than 70 gigs with the band in an 18-month period,

The Priory of Brion ensemble. Plant's shorts (but not his hair) show that this is a very different gig from the good old days

much to the exasperation of his manager **Bill Curbishley**, who wanted him back in a studio and doing something a little more high profile. "Bill said it was like Arkle pulling a milk float or Seb Coe running down the chip shop", Plant later observed. "But Priory of Brion was a bit like musical sorbet. It cleared my palette for the next thing that was going to happen".

In 2001, he dispensed with Priory of Brion's part-timers and assembled a more serious band of seasoned professionals which he dubbed Strange Sensation. Key to the line-up was Justin Adams, a guitarist who had worked with **Jah Wobble** but whose interests in North African music provided a strong foil for Plant's own World Music passions. Others on board included keyboardist John Baggott, who had worked with **Massive Attack**, drummer Clive Deamer, from **Portishead**, Charlie Jones on bass and second guitarist **Porl Thompson**. Citing Julian Cope as an influence, Plant's debut album with the band, 2002's *Dreamland*, was a modest return, consisting mostly of covers done with a decidedly psychedelic twist.

After travelling to Mali in 2003 with Adams to perform at the **Festival in the Desert**, where he also jammed with African musicians, Plant began recording a second album with **Strange Sensation**. *The Mighty Rearranger* appeared in 2005 and was his most significant statement in years. In an echo of *Led Zeppelin III*, most of the lyrics, which found him both commenting on the post-9/11 world and reflecting on his own past, were written in a remote cottage in Snowdonia. Musically the album was a thrilling fusion of styles. "I've spent time in northern Mali and in Morocco and I've got this wanderlust and muse that is part of my being now", he said, sounding more enthused than in years. "It could have been cabaret, singing ballads at The Albert Hall. Instead we have a collision of Western rock and roll with this Malian/Tuareg rhythmic stuff where neither element of the music is compromised. It's an absolute collision without trying to make it a cosmic progressive rock album. It's a new place to go".

On tour the band has worked up almost a dozen Led Zeppelin numbers, which took their place comfortably alongside the new material and covers. "I can now sing 'hey hey mama said the way you move' without feeling bad about it", he noted. "It's no longer sexist or tired. Strange Sensation have created an environment where the door is always open to adventure so there's a whole new shift to a song like that. We've found all the combinations".

With Strange Sensation Plant has also instituted a policy of attempting to play in places he had never performed before, taking the band to the **Arctic Circle** and playing gigs in **Estonia, Latvia, Ukraine** and **Tunisia**. One rock critic disparagingly described the latter-day Plant as resembling "a middle-aged backpacker". He himself would surely regard the comment as a compliment.

The end of 2006 found him in Nashville recording with **T-Bone Burnett** and bluegrass singer-fiddler **Alison Krauss** for a possible album. "We were pushing ideas around. The combination of my voice with Alison's voice and T-Bone's spookiness – well, I'll just say it's very encouraging", he told *Rolling Stone*. He

The Story

also confirmed that he was working on a new album with Strange Sensation. After Nashville, he took a pilgrimage to the Delta to visit the birthplace of the blues and played his harmonica at **Sonny Boy Williamson**'s grave. "Now I'm free", he announced. "I can drive through Mississippi, use my credit card and nobody even looks at it. And it doesn't matter to me if things are successful or not. Because I can walk away feeling I haven't wasted my time".

John Paul Jones

After Led Zeppelin, John Paul Jones slipped back into the anonymity he had enjoyed pre-1968. Based initially in **Devon** where he had built his own studio, he spent the post-Zep years in happy obscurity, only reappearing once for an encore jam with Robert Plant when his *Principal Of Moments* tour hit Bristol at the end of 1983. The following year he stirred himself to score **Michael Winner**'s film *Scream For Help*, a gig he got on the recommendation of Jimmy Page, who played guitar on two tracks. Elsewhere on the soundtrack, Jones played most of the instruments himself with Yes's Jon Anderson and Madeline Bell helping out with the vocals and his daughter Jacinda contributing lyrics.

A brief appearance followed in **Paul McCartney**'s film *Give My Regards To Broad Street* on the track 'Ballroom Dancing'. Donning his producer's hat, he then worked with **Ben E. King** on his comeback album *Save The Last Dance For Me* (1987), the **Mission**'s 1988 album *Children* and an album by his daughter Jacinda (1990).

Together again for the launch of the DVD. Your time is gonna come...

In 1991, he built a new studio near Bath, where he worked on various commissioned pieces, including the renaissance-influenced 'Amores Pasados '(1991) and a composition called 'Macanda' (1992), both of which were premiered at London's South Bank. Throwing himself a little more into the mainstream, he played on albums by **Peter Gabriel** and **Brian Eno** and contributed arrangements to **REM**'s blockbuster album, *Automatic For The People*. During the 1990s he also produced the Butthole Surfers, Heart and **Diamanda Galás**, with whom he subsequently toured. By 1996, he had built yet another studio, this time in London, where he recorded his first proper solo album, *Zooma*, released in 1999. "I spent all my time producing, arranging, starting classical composition. I was just working on everything else I suppose. I never really got around to it", Jones said when asked why it had taken him 19 years since the demise of Led Zeppelin to make a solo record. The all-instrumental set was followed two years later by a second album, *The Thunderthief*, which found him singing and writing his own lyrics for the first time. He also toured both albums – and performed a number of Zeppelin songs – before returning to production duties, working on albums by New Zealand rockers The Datsuns (2004) and American bluegrass act Uncle Earl (2007). In recent years he has been a regular attender and enthusiastic performer at the **Lunel Mandolin Festival** in France, and at the end of 2006 he reported via his website that work on the follow-up to 2001's *The Thunderthief* was almost completed.

Epitaph

If there were any lingering hopes that Led Zeppelin might get together again – even for one last farewell concert – they were probably finally dashed in 2005 when the band significantly failed to come together to receive a lifetime's achievement award at the Grammies in Los Angeles, with only Page and Jones attending while Plant stayed at home. The guitarist was clearly delighted with the award, which he felt represented long overdue recognition by an American music record industry that had always seemed to begrudge Led Zeppelin its success. "I'm sure people thought we'd been nominated in the past", he told *Uncut* magazine "But you know, we never even got a single Grammy nomination until now. I never thought it would happen, so of course I really enjoyed it". But he was spitting blood at Plant's failure to show. "I'm sure he had his reasons", he grumbled moodily, "but it wouldn't have taken much for him to pop over and meet everybody, would it?"

The very morning after the award, Led Zeppelin's former singer was sitting several thousand miles away drinking tea with this writer in the kitchen at Peter Gabriel's Real World studios in Box, Wiltshire, where he was rehearsing with his band Strange Sensation. "I saw Jimmy had a bit of a go at me for not being there", he said. "But what can you do? What I'm doing now is more important to me. This veneration of one period of one's life is pointless. It's great to look back and smile. But middle-aged self congratulation is very dangerous".

Part Two:
The Music

"*I'd love to meet a chick who could fuck like* Led Zeppelin I, *but she'd wear me out in a week*".

OZ review, quoted by the prosecution in the infamous obscenity trial, 1971

The Albums

The Music

This section catalogues all albums released by Led Zeppelin, including solo work and other major side projects since the band's break-up in 1980. All albums are available on CD unless indicated.

LED ZEPPELIN

UK, Atlantic, 28 March 1969; US, Atlantic 17 January 1969

GOOD TIMES BAD TIMES/BABE I'M GONNA LEAVE YOU/YOU SHOOK ME/DAZED AND CONFUSED/YOUR TIME IS GONNA COME/ BLACK MOUNTAIN SIDE/ COMMUNICATION BREAK- DOWN/ I CAN'T QUIT YOU BABY/ HOW MANY MORE TIMES

Recorded: Olympic Studios, Barnes, London, September–October 1968
Produced by Jimmy Page
Engineer: Glyn Johns
Cover design and photography: George Hardie, Chris Dreja
Highest chart position: UK 6; US 10

When Led Zeppelin went into Olympic Studios in September 1968, the album they recorded was essentially the live set they had worked up for and during their first tour of Scandinavia earlier that month. Some of the material had its roots in the repertoire The Yardbirds had played on their final tour of America earlier in the year. The rest may have been somewhat hastily cobbled together, but it had all been well-rehearsed and fully-arranged by a meticulous Page, who seems to have known exactly the sound he wanted. As a result, they were just 30 hours in the studio, only nine of which were actually spent laying down the tracks, all paid for out of Page's savings. The Plant/Page writing partnership that would serve them so well on later albums was not yet fully operational, but that there was an energy and dynamism about the new group. The sense of drama was something out of the ordinary. Interestingly, Bill Wyman had encountered Page at Olympic the previous month and Page played him some preparatory tapes. Wyman recalls: "they sounded so powerful, in a completely new style".

The album is often cited as "the birth of heavy rock", a somewhat misleading description when Cream, The Jimi Hendrix Experience and The Jeff Beck Group had already preceded it. Yet what was undoubtedly fresh and exciting was Page's vision to use dynamic contrasts of light and shade, quiet and loud, an approach perhaps most evident on the stunning acoustic-electric arrangement of 'Babe I'm Gonna Leave You', a version of which by Joan Baez Page had played to Plant during their bonding session at his Pangbourne home. The track was also the most notable example of what would become the trademark Plant vocal style, with

Crashing on Take Off?

The cover of the first album was designed by George Hardie, whose striking Rapidograph treatment of an historical image pre-empted Punk design by almost a decade, and remains iconically graphic. However, the dramatic choice of a photograph of the fated German passenger airship Hindenburg exploding following a transatlantic flight as it docked at Lakehurst Naval Air Station, New Jersey, on 6 May 1937, may be thought a strange choice for a launch album. Perhaps the key lay in the airship's serial number, LZ 129, the album indeed containing the band's first nine released tracks.

its repeated "baby, baby, baby" mannerisms, which he now wishes he could remove from the record completely.

Now widely recognized as one of the great debut albums, 'Good Times, Bad Times' kicks off proceedings and has a close affinity with the old Yardbirds, particularly in its catchy pop chorus. But it's given an astonishing kick by Bonham's drums, making his presence as the loudest, heaviest sticksman of them all felt from the outset. Plant gives us the first taste of his primeval scream, and Page cuts loose with a soaring Telecaster solo before the show fades out after a terse two minutes 46 seconds, like a jukebox hit that leaves you wanting to put

a coin in the slot and play it all over again. After the staggering, hair-raising intensity of 'Babe I'm Gonna Leave You', the band's blues roots come to the fore in a version of Willie Dixon's 'You Shook Me'. The slow groove is never plodding and, according to Jones, was a *tour de force* for Bonham. "He kept a really straight groove on slow numbers and there aren't many that can", the bass player said. "To play slow and groove is one of the hardest things in the world, so it was a joy to sit back on a beat like 'You Shook Me' and just ride it". Page switches to a Gibson Les Paul to effect the blues-drenched sustain on his solo, Plant wails away on harmonica and Jones' organ swirls around magnificently, before the track ends with guitar and vocal trading licks off each other in breathtaking fashion.

'Dazed And Confused' also had its roots in The Yardbirds' repertoire, when Page had taken a folk song by Jake Holmes and rearranged it as 'I'm Confused'. Here it's transformed into the first great Zeppelin epic with Plant moaning over some echoing Page guitar effects and a powerhouse rhythm provided by Jones and Bonham. Its power was sufficient to ensure its presence in every Led Zeppelin live show until 1975. Jones' childhood history as a church organist is evident on the intro of 'Your Time Is Gonna Come', and the track builds into a gospel-styled chorus with Page – who came up with a different guitar sound for almost every track on the album – this time adding pedal steel.

His acoustic guitar showcase 'Black Mountain Side' is, in effect, a homage to the folk fingerpickers he admired so much, such as Bert Jansch and Davy Graham, and recalls the similar 'White Summer' which had appeared on The Yardbirds' *Little Games* album. It cuts abruptly and dramatically straight into Jones' throbbing bass line to the album's other major epic, 'Communication Breakdown', a masterful fusion of heavy rock and a brutal Stooges-style stacatto riff that pre-dated punk by some eight years. Listen to it and you can hear how Plant could keep a straight face many years later when he claimed Led Zeppelin had welcomed the mid-1970s punk revolution because it reminded him of early Zeppelin.

'I Can't Quit You Baby' is another slow Chicago blues work-out written by Willie Dixon with arguably Plant's finest vocal on the record, although the album's closer 'How Many More Times' also retains a strong claim to this honour. The track was another that had its origins in the old Yardbirds repertoire, but Plant transforms it as he ad-libs wonderfully, borrowing freely from several other songs including 'Rosie' and 'The Hunter', while Page creates one of his most experimental Hendrix-style solos, before getting out his violin bow to add some even more extraordinary sounds.

One of the most overlooked aspects of the album is the sheer brilliance of Page's production. If the album isn't intrinsically any heavier than Cream's *Wheels Of Fire* or Jeff Beck's *Truth*, it sounds as if it is simply because of the stunning and dynamic contrasts between the quieter moments and and the manic, dense quality of the louder passages which his pro-

duction deliberately sets out to emphasize. In particular, nobody had ever recorded drums like that before and he made it sound as if Bonham is setting off volleys of cannon fire. "I had been on so many sessions where the drummer was stuck in a little booth and he would be hitting the drums for all he was worth and it would just sound as though he was hitting a cardboard box", Page later recalled. "I knew that drums would have to breath to have that proper sound, that ambience. So consequently we were working on the ambience of everything, of the instruments, all the way through". The use of stereo panning and other effects such as the backwards echo at the end of 'You Shook Me' is staggeringly sophisticated for its time too, given the relatively rudimentary equipment on which the album was recorded.

As a template, Led Zeppelin's debut album was raw and flawed and, in many ways, the next album would be a far superior effort. On the other hand, it is possible to make out a case for the first album as the purest expression of their art that the band ever made. "There was a naiveté", says Robert Plant who is highly critical of some of his own singing on the album and with the benefit of hindsight has described his vocal style as over-hysterical. "But that's what was splendid about it in a way. I was 19 or 20 when we started nuancing those songs, so I don't have a problem with any of it, really. I just prefer the way it grew later. But the spontaneity of the band was phenomenal. It's simply kicking through the grooves of *Led Zeppelin I...*"

LED ZEPPELIN II

UK, Atlantic, 22 October 1969; US, Atlantic, 31 October 1969

WHOLE LOTTA LOVE/WHAT IS AND WHAT SHOULD NEVER BE/ THE LEMON SONG/THANK YOU/HEARTBREAKER/LIVING LOVING MAID (SHE'S JUST A WOMAN)/RAMBLE ON/MOBY DICK/ BRING IT ON HOME

Recorded: Olympic Studios, Barnes, London; Mirror Sound, Los Angeles; Mystic Studios, Hollywood; Juggy Sound, New York; Morgan Studios, Willesden, London; Atlantic Studios, New York; A&R Studios, New York, April–August 1969
Produced by Jimmy Page

Engineers: George Chkiantz; Chris Huston; Andy Johns; Eddie Kramer
Cover design: David Juniper
Highest chart position: UK 1; US 1

It was not unusual for hard-working groups to record their albums in snatched windows of opportunity while on the road. The Rolling Stones, for example, had regularly recorded in studios such as Chess in Chicago and in Hollywood while touring America between 1964 and 1966. *Led Zeppelin II*, however, was an extreme case by anyone's standards. "It was crazy really", Robert Plant remembers. "We were writing the numbers in hotel rooms and then we'd do a rhythm track in London, add the vocal in New York, overdub harmonica in Vancouver and then come back to finish mixing in New York".

Road manager Richard Cole pointed out that this placed a particularly heavy load on Page, who again produced. "On several occasions Jimmy and I would catch a plane into New York from a gig in Minneapolis or Chicago,"

he has written, "I would carry the unfinished tapes on the plane with me, wrapped in foil. We'd grab a taxi to A&R Studios, spend half a day there and then fly out to the next concert". Page, as Cole noted, was also a hard taskmaster in the studio: "He would become much more nervous than he ever did on stage. No matter how well prepared he was, he rarely seemed completely satisfied. He always wanted something a little closer to perfection. It was long, exhausting work and as much as he enjoyed the creative process, it would sometimes overwhelm him". Yet his attention to detail paid off for, out of such far from ideal circumstances, he crafted a record that is regularly voted as one of the greatest rock albums of all time.

By the time of its release in October 1969, the band were already well on the way to becoming rock gods, although the artwork

Continuing the historic German theme with the second album sleeve, the band here were integrated into a group shot of WWI flying aces, whilst the combo's name erupted in psychedelic clouds above them

of the inside cover of the gatefold sleeve is somewhat over the top: a huge zeppelin picked out in spotlights above a Greek temple topped with the band's logo and four plinths in front of it bearing the names of Page, Plant, Bonham and Jones, as if they were Olympian deities. That the plinths were empty was pre-

The gatefold image for Led Zeppelin II announced the advent of pomp rock in no uncertain terms

sumably meant to indicate that there were at least hard-working gods, far too busy to hang around on Mount Olympus and rest on their laurels when there was a gig to play. Yet if it was intended as a prediction of Led Zeppelin's elevation to the very top of the rock pile, it was unerringly accurate. By the end of the year the album was sitting at Number One in America, having dislodged The Beatles' *Abbey Road*. By February 1970, it was also Number One in Britain, where *Led Zeppelin II* eventually spent 138 weeks on the album charts.

Inside, the riffs were as monumental as the cover's imagery. The album opens with 'Whole Lotta Love', which became not only the band's signature but came to define heavy metal, a phrase which, as Dave Lewis points out in his excellent survey *Led Zeppelin: A Celebration*, was not yet in usage. Page's three-note riff was a killer, and the descending chord structure irresistible, while the middle section was nothing short of apocalyptic, with Plant squealing orgasmically over a palette of extraordinary sound effects created by Page and engineer Eddie Kramer at the mixing desk. Inevitably,

this section was edited out of the shorter version which became a Top Five single in America. More problematic were the lyrics. After Plant had failed to come up with any new words, he simply started singing the words from 'You Need Love' as recorded by Muddy Waters and written by Willie Dixon. That they then forgot to credit the bluesmen caused the band no end of legal trouble in a dispute that was not settled until 1985, and earned Zeppelin an unwelcome reputation for plagiarism.

That there was much more to Led Zeppelin than heavy rock was evident from the next track, 'What Is And What Should Never Be'. This time Plant did manage to come up with some words on the first song he wrote for the band. The track begins in mellow mood over an almost jazzy chord progression and Jones' arresting bass part which is almost a counter-melody in its own right, before Bonham's drums explode and introduce another classic Page riff.

'The Lemon Song' is a part-rewrite of Howlin' Wolf's 'Killing Floor' with some dirty blues guitar from Page and with Plant sounding every inch like a gnarled old Delta bluesman rather than a 20-year-old newcomer, as he pays homage to one of Robert Johnson's classic metaphors in the line "squeeze my lemon 'til the juice runs down my leg". 'Thank You' is a heartfelt tribute from the singer to his wife, Maureen, with some gorgeous swirling, psychedelic organ from Jones and delicate acoustic lead picking from Page, proving that Led Zeppelin were not merely a heavy rock monster but could make great and highly accessible pop music. Indeed in many ways, the arrangement brings to mind Rod Stewart's version of 'Handbags and Gladrags'.

In its original vinyl format the LP was cleverly sequenced to allow for a pause after 'Thank You', before the listener turned the record over for a return to the relentless riffing. On CD, the listener is abruptly bounced back into the heavy blues-rock of 'Heartbreaker', a track which seems to have divided authors of books about Zeppelin. The extended guitar solo which commences unaccompanied by the rest of the band is, according to Dave Lewis, "a platform for Page to express his guitar virtuosity with a breathtaking exercise in string bending technique". Keith Shadwick, on the other hand, reckons it's one of Page's poorest on any Led Zeppelin record, "repeating time-worn fingerboard patterns rather than attempt anything fresh". Most fans will surely side with Lewis's favourable assessment.

'Heartbreaker' is followed by 'Living Loving Maid (She's Just A Woman)', allegedly written about a lady of the night with whom the band had got acquainted in Los Angeles. Plant has identified it as one of the weakest songs in Zeppelin's canon both lyrically and musically; today it sounds distinctly clichéd, although the riff is sharp enough. By contrast, 'Ramble On' is one of the album's highlights, the quiet passages contrasting dramatically with the uplifting chorus and Plant singing his Tolkien-inspired lyrics with great expressiveness. With Bonham's extended drum solo already a highlight of Zeppelin's live show, it was inevitable that he would be given a similar showcase on the record and it comes on 'Moby Dick'. On stage the number could go on for half-an-hour or more but here is mercifully truncated at less than four-and-a-half minutes, and is introduced and closed by a potent Page riff that frankly seems to have little to do with the assortment of rolls and paradiddles in the middle. The album closes with 'Bring It on Home', another homage to Plant's blues roots which begins with his rather good Sonny Boy Williamson harp imitation and a slurred pastiche of a Jimmy Reed vocal over a repetitive twelve-bar motif played on Jones' bass, but then drives into a storming heavy rocker with some great multi-layered guitar from Page.

More than three decades later, Barney Hoskyns described *Led Zeppelin II* as a "tour de force of pulverizing riffs and febrile bluesology that stands at the gateway to the 1970s as a monstrously powerful record". All true, of course. Yet listening to it more than three decades on, one is also struck by the fact that the record has little in common with the sins subsequently committed by so many heavy metal bands in Zeppelin's name. Compare Led Zeppelin II, for example, to the first Black Sabbath album released only a few months later. Not only did Page, Plant, Jones and Bonham have the better riffs, but they also boasted a subtlety, sophistication, eclecticism and musicality at which few of their imitators could ever even hint.

LED ZEPPELIN III

UK and US, Atlantic, 5 October 1970

IMMIGRANT SONG/ FRIENDS/ CELEBRATION DAY/ SINCE I'VE BEEN LOVING YOU/ OUT ON THE TILES/ GALLOWS POLE/ TANGERINE/ THAT'S THE WAY/BRON-Y-AUR STOMP/HATS OFF TO (ROY) HARPER

Recorded: Headley Grange, Hampshire; Olympic Studios, Barnes, London; Island Studios, London; Ardent Studios, Memphis, May–August 1970
Produced by Jimmy Page
Engineer: Andy Johns
Cover design: Richard Drew
Highest chart position: UK 1; US 1

Probably the must misunderstood album in the group's entire canon, *Led Zeppelin III* confused critics and fans alike on its release in October 1970 – although that did not stop the album topping the charts in both America and Britain, where two weeks before its release Led Zeppelin had been voted "best group" in the *Melody Maker* poll, displacing The Beatles from Number One for the first time since 1963.

Mostly conceived and written by Page and Plant at the cottage they rented in Snowdonia, Wales in the spring of 1970, the material subsequently changed shape and character in the studio and yet retained strong elements of its acoustic guitar origins amidst the riffs to create the strongest expression yet of Page's vision of a new kind of rock music, rich in dynamic contrasts. Or, as the notes on the cover put it: "Credit must be given to Bron-y-Aur, a small derelict cottage in South Snowdonia for painting a somewhat forgotten picture of true completeness which acted as an incentive to some of these musical statements".

Yet, although Page once again took the producer's chair and had the final say in most matters, his role was less dominant than it had been on the first two albums and there were considerably few set-piece Page guitar solos. Led Zeppelin had hit its stride as a collective

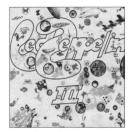

An intricate sleeve for a change of pace, the front sleeve had punched holes and an inner illustrated cardboard wheel, so the design could be varied

via its endless touring, particularly in America, and Plant had visibly grown in confidence. "It'll be acoustic as well as electric with the emphasis on everyone in the group", the singer told *NME* while they were still recording the album. To *Rolling Stone* he enthused about "the trip into the mountains" and the beginning of the new "ethereal Page and Plant".

Released in an elaborate gatefold sleeve designed by Richard Drew, a friend of Page's who was a lecturer in Fine Art at Leeds Polytechnic, the CD reissue is a pale imitation of the packaging of the original vinyl LP, which contained a rotating inner wheel. Echoing the rural origins of the songs on the album, the wheel was based on crop rotation charts, although in the end it didn't come out quite as the band had planned or hoped. A crestfallen Page lamented that it looked "teeny-bopperish" but by the time the band saw the finished artwork, they were on top of a deadline and it was too late to change it.

The Music

The inner gatefold maintained the theme with a surreal choice of images, of course including various flying machines

The album kicks off with the galloping fury of 'Immigrant Song', a classic Zeppelin pile-driver telling of a Viking force of invaders raping and pillaging across the land ("We come from the land of the ice and snow, from the midnight sun where the hot springs blow/ The hammer of the gods will drive our ships to new lands"). At two minutes 23 seconds its brevity is commendable, but it packs an astonishing punch as Plant howls like a testosterone-doped Valkyrie. He later suggested that the lyric – which gave Zeppelin one of its enduring nicknames as "the hammer of the gods" – was tongue-in-cheek, although this was probably lost on most of the band's fans who did not expect humour from a heavy rock band.

'Friends' is in dramatic contrast, introduced by ringing Crosby, Stills, Nash and Young-style acoustic guitars, which are soon joined by Indian-influenced strings and an ethereal Plant vocal that owes more to his West Coast influ-

ences than his blues roots. It segues straight into the slashing slide guitar of 'Celebration Day', with a funk-blues riff that is reminiscent of Jimi Hendrix's 'Freedom'.

At seven-and-a-half minutes, 'Since I've Been Loving You' is the album's longest track by almost two minutes and it's also one of the highlights. A slow blues, on which Page's guitar in places sounds rather like Duane Allman, it is complemented by Plant's most assured blues shouting to date; but it's also a superb ensemble piece, with Jones and Bonham making major contributions. 'Out On The Tiles' is the album's second signature Zeppelin riff after 'Immigrant Song'. Led by Bonham's drum pattern, it's not one of their most inventive riffs, but the production is inspired and there were few technicians at the time who could match Page's ability to capture such raw energy in the studio. He later explained that the sound was based on a combination of close and distant miking: "That's ambient sound. Getting the distance of the time lag from one end of the room to the other and putting that in as well. The whole idea, the way I see recording, is to try and capture the sound of the room live and the emotion of the whole moment and try to convey that".

'Gallow's Pole' is an extraordinary hybrid that confused fans as much as anything else on the album. Based on a traditional song popularized by Leadbelly in the 1930s, instead of the blues-rock riffing one might have expected from a Zeppelin transposition, it's delivered initially by just voice-and-acoustic-guitar before Jones adds some mandolin and Page joins in on banjo and pedal steel. By the end, the whole things sounds more like Traffic than Led Zeppelin. There's more pedal steel on 'Tangerine', an acoustic tune Page had first worked up with Keith Relf while he was still in The Yardbirds, when it went under the title 'Knowing That I'm Losing You'. Plant adds a new and simple romantic lyric which he sings with a double-tracked vocal and, in retrospect, the song's more baroque elements can be seen as something of a dry run for 'Stairway To Heaven' on the next album.

'That's The Way' is the third consecutive track to feature Page's new toy, the pedal steel guitar, although this time he plays it in a spacier, more echoing style that owes more to Jerry Garcia's use of the instrument rather than the standard country style he had employed on 'Tangerine'. Perhaps the finest composition to come out of the Bron-yr-aur experience, its wistful, bitter-sweet quality owes much to Plant's obsession with Neil Young's early solo albums. 'Bron-y-Aur Stomp', as its name suggests, is another track that has its roots in the Welsh mountains as a fireside jam, although it was initially titled 'Jennings Farm Blues' after the farm Plant had just bought in Worcestershire. Jones plays a fretless bass and Bonham adds spoons and castanets. The album

closes with 'Hats Off To (Roy) Harper', dedicated to the maverick singer-songwriter whom the band had befriended, but is actually based on an old blues tune called 'Shake 'Em On Down' first recorded by Bukka White in 1937. Plant's vocal is a highly convincing recreation of the style of a pre-war Mississippi country bluesman, and Page's acoustic bottleneck guitar makes all the right noises but it sounds like little more than a demo. Page admitted it was taken from "a whole tape of us bashing out different blues things" and it's a low-key and slightly puzzling way to end an album by the biggest, loudest, heaviest rock band in the world – which is, no doubt, exactly what Page and Plant intended.

Many of the reviews that greeted the album were dismissive. In some cases, it was the same critics who had attacked them for being too loud and bludgeoning who now pilloried them for "going acoustic". However, speaking in 2005, Page was magnanimous about the bad reviews. "With hindsight, I can see how if somebody got *Led Zeppelin III*, which was so different from what we'd done before, and they only had a short time to review it on the record player in the office, then they missed the content," he told *Uncut* magazine. "They were in a rush and they were looking for the new 'Whole Lotta Love' and not actually listening to what was there. It was too fresh for them and they didn't get the plot. So in retrospect it doesn't surprise me that the diversity and breadth of what we were doing was overlooked or under-appreciated at the time".

Yet at the time the criticism undoubtedly hurt, for the band regarded the "cottage album" as an absolutely critical step in their development. Plant later described the LP as the band's "single most important statement", and noted that "it wasn't until *Led Zeppelin III* that I was able to calm it down and have the confidence to sing in a different style".

Although it topped the charts, ultimately *LZ III* was the poorest-selling of Led Zeppelin's first four albums. As Keith Shadwick noted, "its radicalism proving a long-term problem for the band's less adventurous fans" while, on the other hand, fans of the folk-rock groups such as The Incredible String Band and Fairport Convention – which had inspired much of the record and might have provided the record with a new constituency – remained suspicious of Zeppelin's reputation as monsters of the all-conquering mighty riff.

LED ZEPPELIN FOURTH ALBUM (FOUR SYMBOLS, IV)

UK, Atlantic, 11 November 1971; US, Atlantic, 8 November 1971

BLACK DOG/ROCK AND ROLL/THE BATTLE OF EVERMORE/ STAIRWAY TO HEAVEN/MISTY MOUNTAIN HOP/FOUR STICKS/ GOING TO CALIFORNIA/WHEN THE LEVEE BREAKS

Recorded: Headley Grange, Hampshire; Island Studios, London; Sunset Sound, Los Angeles; December 1970– February 1971
Produced by Jimmy Page
Engineers: Andy Johns; George Chkiantz
Cover design/artwork: Graphreaks/Barrington Colby Mann
Highest chart position: UK 1; US 2

After the mixed reaction that had greeted their third album, Led Zeppelin took their time over the follow-up, although the delay was also exacerbated by horrendous technical problems with the mixing. At one time they considered releasing a double album and then toyed with the idea of issuing the material on four EPs. Once they had reverted to the concept of a standard LP, the band then sought other ways to make their fourth album distinctive and hit upon the idea of not giving it a title but presenting it under the banner of four symbols, each representing one of the group's members. This has led to considerable confusion over the years: the album has variously been referred to as *Led Zeppelin IV*, The Fourth Album, Untitled, Four Symbols, Zoso (an approximation of the non-existent word that Page's symbol resembled) and The Runes.

LED ZEPPELIN

The CD spine added the band's name to the notorious "runes"

The front cover, with its depiction of a character from Britain's rural past, came from a print found by Plant in an antique shop in Reading, and its use resembled the cover of Fairport Convention's 1969 album *Liege and Lief*. However, it was then contrasted with a scene of 20th-century urban decay shot in Dudley in the West Midlands on the back cover, while inside a drawing of a hermit was inspired by Page's interest in the mysteries of the Tarot pack. For the first time, the band also allowed

The sleeve design of this apparently anonymous album could be read as a "State of the Nation" address. The front featured peeling wallpaper and a hark back to the country's rural past...

a lyric to be printed on the inside sleeve, with the words of the key-note track 'Stairway To Heaven' singled out for the honour.

Faced with the problem of how to market a record that lacked a title, Atlantic placed a series of full-page ads in the music press featuring each of the four symbols, which generated a sense of mystery and intrigue around the album, which went straight to Number One in Britain, and where it remained in the charts for a total of 62 weeks. In America, its chart residency was even longer, although surprisingly it was kept from the top spot by Carole King's *Tapestry*.

Once again, Page and Plant had begun

...the back an equally depressing image of urban blight in the early 1970s

writing the album by retiring in the autumn of 1970 to the cottage at Bron-yr-aur. Before Christmas they had enough material to go into Island Studios. In January they transferred to Headley Grange, using The Rolling Stones' mobile recording truck, although when the rambling old house proved a tad too cold in winter, they then moved back again to Island.

A screw-up in mixing the tapes in Los Angeles resulted in a delayed release when the band rejected the muddy sound and the tapes were remixed again in London. Then there was a prolonged fight with Atlantic over the band's insistence that neither their name nor that of the label should appear on the album's cover. "I remember being in an Atlantic office for two hours with a lawyer who was saying 'you've got to have this'", Page recalled. "It was a hard job but fortunately we were in a position to say, 'This is what we want', because we had attained the status whereby that album was going to sell a lot anyway". At a concert at New York's Madison Square Garden in September 1971, Plant actually apologized to fans for the delay of the album, telling the audience, "We've got problems trying to get a record cover that looks how we want it". They won the battle by telling the label "they couldn't have the master tapes until they got the cover right", although the band climbed down in one small detail. They had originally not wanted the record to even have a catalogue number, but the point was conceded when Atlantic pointed out that it would mean record stores would not be able to order the record. "The whole story of the fourth album reads like a nightmare", Plant later observed.

Yet as they would do so often in their career, out of the jaws of disaster, Led Zeppelin fashioned a triumph. The album kicks off with the turbulent, supercharged groove of 'Black Dog', based on a bass riff that Jones developed from a track on Muddy Waters'

1968 experimental blues-rock album, *Electric Mud*. Plant contributes one of his most swaggering, carnal vocals ("Hey, hey mama said the way you move, gonna make you sweat, gonna make you groove") and Page overdubs multiple guitars.

With the bassist having come up with the riff on the opening track, it was the drummer's turn on 'Rock and Roll, which came out of a jam inspired by Bonham playing the intro to Little Richard's 'Good Golly Miss Molly/ Keep A Knockin". Page added a guitar riff, Plant improvised some suitable lyrics ("Been a long time since I rock and rolled") and within 15 minutes the band effectively had the song in place, a perfect example of Zeppelin at their most inspired and spontaneous. The song became the opening number, or was used as an encore, in their live set at every show for the next six years.

After two classic pile-driving Zeppelin anthems comes the ethereal, mandolin-driven 'Battle Of Evermore'. One of Page and Plant's most haunting and understated songs, it has inevitably been overshadowed down the years by the iconic status of the track that follows it on the album, but unfairly so. The tune was composed by Page playing around on Jones' mandolin while Plant added a lyric inspired by a combination of *The Lord Of The Rings* and a book of myths and legends about the Scottish border wars. It was also Plant's idea to invite Fairport Convention's Sandy Denny to duet with him: "Sandy and I were friends and it was the most obvious thing to ask her

to sing on it", he recalled in 2005. "It's pretty, and if it suffered from a naiveté and tweeness, it makes up for it in the cohesion of the voices and the playing".

And then comes 'Stairway To Heaven'. If anybody had said in 1971 that a song that opened with the pastoral sound of overdubbed school recorders would come to be regarded as one of the greatest rock tracks of all time – "a mystical epic beloved of suburban metal-heads from sea to shining sea" as Barney Hoskyns memorably put it – the laughter would surely have been loud enough to drown out not only its initial gentle chord progression but the soaring electric guitar solo which closed it as well. 'Stairway To Heaven' is dealt with at length in the 50 Greatest Tracks section (see below) and so suffice it to say here that however hackneyed it may now sound due to over-familiarity, it is a breathtaking piece of music, and Page's internal construction of the song is inspired. It's more than four minutes before Bonham makes his entrance on drums and almost six minutes before Page's dramatic electric guitar solo cuts loose. Regardless of its commercial success, Jones is surely right to claim it as one of the band's proudest musical moments in which pop music attained a previously unknown peak. "Everything built nicely", the bass player says. "Both Jimmy and I were quite aware of the way a track should unfold and the various levels that it would go through. I suppose we were both quite influenced by classical music and there's a lot of drama in the classical forms. It just seems natural for music to have that as opposed to everybody starting and just banging away and finishing. That's part of song structure. It's also part of pop music". At least, it was after 'Stairway To Heaven'.

Side Two of the original vinyl release opened with 'Misty Mountain Hop', driven by a crashing riff played on guitar, bass and keyboards over which Plant sings a salutary, of-its-time tale about a bunch of hippies smoking dope in a park and getting busted. It's followed by 'Four Sticks', another crunching riff but without much of a tune, other than in the rather pretty but slightly incongruous bridge. Featuring Jones on synthesizer, it's basically a studio exercise in playing in a 5/4 time signature with Bonham crashing around not to the best effect. It's the album's weakest moment and, perhaps unsurprisingly, was only ever attempted once in concert and then swiftly dropped.

Far more successful is the wistful 'Going To California', all mandolin and acoustic finger-picking born of "a late-night guitar twiddle" at Headley Grange. Plant's lyric pays tribute to Joni Mitchell ("there's a girl out there with love in her eyes and flowers in her hair") and is arguably the singer's most effective expression of his ongoing romantic attachment to the ideals of 1967's 'Summer of Love'. Indeed, he has cited it as his favourite among Zeppelin's softer numbers, claiming: "It's a really nice song, so simple, and the lyrics just fell out of my mouth". Several years later, the writer Cameron Crowe asked him how he felt about being criticized for writing such "dated flower-child gibberish". Plant was unrepentant: "The essence of the whole trip was the desire for peace and tranquillity and an idyllic situation", he reasoned. "That's all anybody could ever want, so how could it be dated flower-child gibberish? If it is, then I'll just carry on being a dated flower-child".

The album closes with the primeval blues of 'When The Levee Breaks', based on a song written by Memphis Minnie and her husband Kansas Joe McCoy about the flood that devastated Mississippi when the river burst its man-made banks (or levees) in 1927. Plant's vocal and the monolithic riff, with Page's slide guitar to the fore, seem to echo the dread of the elemental forces the song is describing.

Although Led Zeppelin's unnamed fourth went on to become the fourth best-selling album of all time (behind only The Eagles, Michael Jackson and Pink Floyd) with US sales alone of 22 million, once again many of the critics didn't initially appreciate either its power or its range. In Britain, the music weekly *Sounds* declared it a "much overrated album", reckoned 'Black Dog' had all "the grace and finesse of a farmyard chicken" and declared 'Stairway To Heaven' so dull that its reviewer suffered "first boredom and then catatonia". *Melody Maker* sat on the fence and judged it "not their best or their worst". Ironically, *Rolling Stone*, for so long Zeppelin's leading press tormentor, for once liked the album and praised its "low-keyed and tasteful subtlety"

HOUSES OF THE HOLY

UK, Atlantic, 26 March 1973; US, Atlantic, 18 March 1973

THE SONG REMAINS THE SAME /THE RAIN SONG /OVER THE HILLS AND FAR AWAY/THE CRUNGE/DANCING DAYS/D'YER MAK'ER/NO QUARTER/THE OCEAN

Recorded: Stargroves, Berkshire; Headley Grange, Hampshire; Island Studios, London; Olympic Studios, Barnes, London; Electric Lady, New York, April–August, 1972
Produced by Jimmy Page
Engineers: Eddie Kramer; Andy Johns; George Chkiantz
Cover design/artwork: Hipgnosis
Highest chart position: UK 1; US 1

How to follow *Led Zeppelin IV*? The answer is that they didn't – at least not for almost 18 months, by the standards of the time an astonishingly long gap. The long wait hadn't been planned and Page had originally hoped to release the album as early as June 1972 in time for the eighth American tour, on which they previewed much of the material. By then large chunks of the album had been recorded, after they had convened in the studio at Stargroves, Mick Jagger's country pile at Newbury, Berkshire. (They had initially planned to record *Led Zeppelin IV* there, but Page, living up to his "Led Wallet" nickname, had balked at the cost). Several other locations were also used and deadlines came and went as the band could now afford to work at its own pace and – in stark contrast to the rush of the first album – Page "demanded that the final product have decimal-point precision", in the words of Richard Cole.

In the event, by the time the tour started Page had concluded that there was still a lot

of further overdubbing and re-recording necessary before the album was ready and the band was still some way off making the final track selection. They concluded that there was no point in rushing the album out to meet a tour deadline (particularly when *Led Zeppelin IV* was still camped out in the charts) and while in America, they took the opportunity to go into a New York studio to carry out further work.

But it was the sleeve that once again caused the longest delays. This time they were not fighting with Atlantic, who were only too delighted that for the first time in five albums, the band had come up with a 'proper' title. However, the *Houses Of The Holy* title wasn't printed on the sleeve because the band argued it would ruin the integrity of the artwork, but they allowed the label to put a paper wrapper around the record with the title printed on it, a compromise that was the brainchild of Peter Grant. The problem was a technical one of colour registration and trying to match the exact hues of the original artwork with those that came off the printer's press; it took an age. When they got an acceptable match,

The outer sleeve folded out, a spectacular image

The inner gatefold was just as inscrutable

the song 'Houses Of The Holy' then turned up on the next album, *Physical Graffiti*.

After kicking off previous albums with such riff-heavy monsters as 'Whole Lotta Love', 'Immigrant Song' and 'Black Dog', 'The Song Remains The Same' is a disappointingly low-key opener. Not that it's a poor track: there are some fascinating rhythmic twists and turns and lovely shimmering guitar textures, which owe something to the old Yardbirds' number 'Tinker, Tailor, Soldier, Sailor'. At times the track has a jangling, West Coast vibe and Jones plays a lovely, fluid bass part in the upper register, more in the style of Jack Casady or Phil Lesh than his usual bottom-end sound. At other times there's a vaguely Indian influence, presumably imbibed when Page and Plant had stopped in Bombay to do some recording on the way back from an Australian tour in 1972. The piece was originally intended as an instrumental, Page later explained: "It was going to be an overture that led into 'The Rain Song', but I guess Robert had different ideas, You know: 'this is pretty good. Better get some lyrics, quick!'" This doesn't explain why Plant's vocal is irritatingly speeded up in places as he gabbles "all you gotta do now, all you gotta do now", sounding as if he's on helium.

quite what the sleeve was meant to signify was anyone's guess. The outside depicted two naked young children in various poses climbing a mountain (in fact, the Giant's Causeway in Northern Ireland). Inside was an image that suggested some sort of sacrificial worship in a ruined castle (again shot in Northern Ireland). Despite Page's well-known interest in the occult, it seems certain the images were for effect rather than genuinely containing any deep esoteric message.

At first, the album was to be called *Burn That Candle*, as Plant told audiences from the stage on several dates on the 1972 American tour. However, once it had changed to *Houses Of The Holy*, the band ran up against a new problem: when they finally came to select the songs for the album, in early 1973, the newly-anointed title track found itself unceremoniously dropped on the grounds that it was too similar to another song, 'Dancing Days'. Confusingly,

'The Rain Song' is an underrated Zeppelin classic. In some ways it echoes the band's earlier acoustic work. But although the arrangement is serene, it's also considerably more complex than anything they had attempted before, and marks Jones' first use of the mellotron, creating a one-man virtual orchestra which, as Keith Shadwick noted, almost sounds as if The Moody Blues have crashed the party. Plant's love lyric uses what Coleridge described as the "pathetic fallacy", in which human emotions are seen as echoes of the natural elements, and also echoes the Elizabethan poet Ben Jonson's famous line "drink to me only with thine eyes".

'Over The Hills and Far Away' opens with a jangling guitar part in the same key as 'The Rain Song', contributing strongly to the idea that the whole of the first side of the original vinyl LP was conceived as a suite of songs. Then the drums and bass and electric guitar kick in, but it's still clear this isn't the old carnal Led Zeppelin as Plant continues to sing about his wide-eyed wonder at the world ("Mellow is the man who knows what he's been missing, many men can't see the open road"). 'The Crunge' is Led Zeppelin having fun, a jokey number that came out of Bonham and Jones messing around with a Stax rhythm during a jam at Stargroves. Page adds a James Brown guitar riff, Jones contributes some Stevie Wonder-style synthesizer and Plant joins in with a pastiche vocal and lyrics that check the titles of several classic soul songs, including Otis Redding's 'Mr. Pitiful' and Aretha Franklin's

'Respect'. The final exchange between Plant and a studio engineer about looking for the song's bridge (a classic James Brown stunt) is mildly amusing the first time one hears it, but swiftly palls. Is it a parody or an affectionate tribute to 1970s black music? Perhaps the problem is that it tries to be a bit of both at the same time and calling the non-existent "dance" 'The Crunge' – the sort of gag Peter Cook and Dudley Moore might have come up with – was perhaps the wittiest aspect of the entire exercise. At one time, the band even considered putting a spoof diagram of how to dance "The Crunge" on the cover.

'Dancing Days' is one of the album's highlights, a mid-tempo rocker with a snarling guitar motif also with its roots in Page and Plant's recent stopover in Bombay, while Plant's vocal shows admirable restraint on a lyric that combines sly lasciviousness ("I told your mamma I'd get you home but I didn't tell her I had no car") and hippie gibberish ("I got my flower, I got my power"). Engineer Eddie Kramer recalls the band literally dancing with delight on the lawn at Stargroves when they first heard the playback. However, 'D'yer Mak 'er' is just awful, a piece of self-indulgence of the kind that all great bands probably come up with from time to time as a way of letting off steam but few are dumb enough to release. If they got away with the joke on 'The Crunge', they were not capable of pulling it off twice, particularly when the jape was so witless. From its title to everything else about it, 'D'yer Mak 'er' is crap: cod-reggae of the most banal kind, with a totally hopeless thrashing heavy-rock rhythm from Bonham where a Jamaican one-drop rhythm is called for, and a lyric from Plant so totally devoid of content that it sounds as if it was ad-libbed on the spot – which it probably was. "We had just laid down 'The Song Remains The Same' which is a real belter", he told *Zig Zag* shortly after the album's release. "It was about 5 am and I had been hoping for a long time to do something like 'D'Yer Mak 'er'. It was born then and there". Jones and Bonham both hated the song and the bass player candidly admitted that the track made him "cringe". Or was that "crunge"?

Fortunately, the album's final two tracks ensure *Houses Of The Holy* ends strongly. 'No Quarter' is arguably the album's strongest track, a brooding, complex piece on which Jones unusually took the lead compositional credit. His grand piano and synthesizer lend the track a melancholic, jazzy majesty that resembles Emerson, Lake and Palmer (a band who it was rumoured at one point that Peter Grant was going to add to his management stable), but without the bombast. Even Bonham for once plays with restraint (by his standards, at least) and the subdued effect only heightens the song's drama while Plant sings obscurely about some incident from Viking mythology, his voice treated by studio trickery to sound distant and almost disembodied.

'The Ocean' closes the album with a classically brutal Zeppelin riff, as Plant's lyric both pays tribute to the band's "ocean" of fans and tells of his love for his three-year-old daughter,

Carmen. There's a memorable turnaround in the rhythm halfway through, and the track ends on a doo-wop note as an excited Plant spontaneously – and accurately – shouts "So good!"

The reviews that greeted *Houses Of The Holy* were an even more mixed bunch than usual – but there was unanimity that the biggest band in the world had not come up with the masterpiece their status demanded. Even Page himself seemed to recognize the record's faults and failings. "I'm deaf to the album now because we made it such a long time ago", he told *NME* immediately after its release. He sounded almost apologetic in conceding that 'The Crunge' and 'D'yer Mak 'er' were "just a giggle", and even more defensive when he added, "But I know there's some good stuff on there". It was hardly the stoutest defence on behalf of a disappointing album, and it's impossible not to conclude that Page knew full well that they had failed to deliver an album that matched any of its four predecessors.

History has done nothing to salvage the album's reputation and today *Houses Of The Holy* sounds not only like the oddest album in the Led Zeppelin canon, but probably the least satisfying. Had they worked to a deadline and released the album as originally planned in June 1972, it would no doubt have sounded quite different and a lot sharper. For the first time in their career, Led Zeppelin sounded like they could have benefited from an outside producer who might have imposed a little order and discipline. Instead, indecision and drift set in and Page – his growing cocaine consumption possibly clouding his previously impeccable judgement – clearly failed to exert the visionary leadership that had informed and inspired the first four albums.

Yet, if *Houses Of The Holy* is flawed, almost fatally so in places, its strongest asset is that it finds the band still creatively restless and not content simply to repeat past glories. As Dave Lewis put it: "Though devoid of the electricity of *Led Zeppelin I* and *II* or the sheer diversity of *Led Zeppelin III* and lacking the classic status of some of the fourth album, *Houses Of The Holy* took stock of their situation. In doing so, it laid several foundations on which they would expand their future collective musical aspirations".

PHYSICAL GRAFFITI

UK and US, Swan Song, 24 February 1975

CUSTARD PIE/THE ROVER/IN MY TIME OF DYING/HOUSES OF THE HOLY/TRAMPLED UNDERFOOT/KASHMIR//IN THE LIGHT/BRON-YR-AUR/DOWN BY THE SEASIDE/ TEN YEARS GONE/NIGHT FLIGHT/THE WANTON SONG/BOOGIE WITH STU/BLACK COUNTRY WOMAN/SICK AGAIN

Recorded: Stargroves, Berkshire; Headley Grange, Hampshire; Island Studios, London; Olympic Studios, Barnes, London, April–August 1971–74
Produced by Jimmy Page
Engineers: Ron Nevison; Keith Harwood; Eddie Kramer; Andy Johns; George Chkiantz
Cover design/artwork and photography: AGI, Dave Hefferman, Elliott Erwitt, B.P. Fallon and Roy Harper
Highest chart position: UK 1; US 1

After failing to deliver the killer album everyone had expected with *Houses Of The Holy*,

Led Zeppelin knew that if they were to maintain their status as the greatest rock band in the world, their sixth LP needed to be a major statement. They had long talked about a double album and each time rejected the idea as too self-indulgent. The multi-disc excesses of the likes of Yes and Emerson, Lake and Palmer had given a bad name to the notion that an album could contain more than 40 minutes of music and retain a clarity of focus, and so Zeppelin had preferred to eschew such company and cast itself as a lean, mean fighting machine. Yet the "joke" tracks on *Houses Of The Holy* had proved that it was perfectly possible to be just as flabby and wasteful on a single album. What mattered was not the quantity but the tightness of the quality control and so the decision was taken: the band's first release on its own label Swan Song would be a double. Plant even grandiosely told one interviewer: "What we talk about is creating something as notable as Beethoven's Fifth. Not just something that would still be remembered

The Swan Song Apollo/Icarus logo first appeared on *Physical Graffiti*

in 50 years, but something so mammoth that it would last forever". Such hyperbole aside, they were helped by the fact that they had a backlog of already recorded material, some of which was actually superior to several tracks that had made it onto previous albums. Plant recognized as much when in an interview in *Sounds* immediately after the release of *Houses Of The Holy*, he observed: "Yesterday, actually, I was playing some tracks I hadn't heard in years, and sometimes the tracks that haven't gone on are better than the ones that have".

The band reconvened at Headley Grange in November 1973 to see what material, both old and new, was around. After a Christmas break, they got together there again in February, 1974, right in the middle of Britain's three-day week, with compulsory power cuts forced by the OPEC oil-price rise. Not that it worried Zeppelin, who had their own generator installed. It soon became clear that the band was back on a roll as they readied new pieces and resurrected old ones, emerging at the end of the process with a 50–50 split between previously recorded songs and fresh compositions. "At the time of *Physical Graffiti* we were right on top if it", Page recalled later, "there was such freedom and coherence between the players". Plant was similarly enthusiastic and, in an interview in March 1974, dropped the first hint that a double album was in the making. "Our music is more of an excitement thing. It has to be impromptu". He went on: "It just drops out of your mind. It falls out of your head and on to the floor and you pick it up as

it bounces. That's how we work. We hire this recording truck and head off to some cruddy old house in the country. The last thing you'd expect is the music to fall right into place. But it does. We even spent one night sitting around drinking ourselves under the table telling each other how good we were".

The cover art depicted a pair of New York brownstone houses (actually 96 & 98 St. Marks Place in East Greenwich Village). The inner sleeves for the discs were inserted in different orientations, so that various objects and people would appear in the windows of the building. They included not only the obligatory shots of the band (and Peter Grant) but a range of iconic images, including paintings by

The gatefold sleeve referred back to the game-playing of Led Zep III, with hole-punched windows and a variety of images printed on the inner sleeves, allowing the user to customize the characters that appeared in the windows

Leonardo da Vinci and Dante Gabriel Rossetti, Queen Elizabeth II's coronation, and images of Jean Harlow and Lee Harvey Oswald. The effect recalls both the cover of The Beatles' *Sgt. Pepper's Lonely Hearts Club Band* and the artwork of the Rolling Stones' *Exile On Main Street*, again reinforcing the message that, in *Physical Graffiti*, Led Zeppelin were consciously setting out to make a major statement.

Disc One kicks off with 'Custard Pie', one of the new songs which Page described as appearing more or less spontaneously during the sessions at Headley Grange as "great little diamonds just sparkling". The muscular riff is a classic, with a passing nod to Bo Diddley and a lyric that, like 'Hats Off To (Roy) Harper on *Led Zeppelin III*, owes much to Bukka White's 'Shake 'Em On Down'. 'The Rover' is even better. The song had first emerged as an acoustic blues in 1970, but was then worked up during the *Houses Of The Holy* sessions, and its inclusion would have immeasurably improved that album. Bonham and Jones lock into a remorseless groove while Page essays a perfectly constructed solo as Plant sings, with some prescience, "I've all this wonder of earthly plunder; will it leave us anything to show?"

'In My Time Of Dyin'' is one of the band's most intense blues adaptations, this time from a song recorded by Blind Willie Johnson in 1927 and covered by Bob Dylan on his debut album 35 years later. At eleven minutes it's an epic, but the interest is sustained by Page's bottleneck invention, Plant's vocal improvisations and one of Bonham's most monumental performances on the drums. *Houses Of The Holy*, as its title suggests, was originally intended for the previous album and was recorded in 1972. Its jauntiness is appealing enough, but it doesn't really go anywhere and after 'In My Time Of Dyin'' it sounds distinctly like Zeppelin-lite. This impression is reinforced by it being followed by 'Trampled Under Foot', with its irresistible funk rhythm which, unlike 'The Crunge' on the previous album, this time thankfully avoids any hint of parody. Jones contributes a fine clavinet solo and Page

unleashes a barrage of effects including backwards echo and wah-wah as Plant sings a great lyric that is an extended, erotic metaphor about the similarities between a pneumatic woman and a souped-up car ("Trouble-free transmission, helps your oil's flow."). Although the lyric is recessed too far back in the mix, you can even dance to it.

More than 30 years on, 'Kashmir' remains one of the peaks of the band's career. Born of Plant's fascination with Indian and Arabic music, the use of scales not normally found in Western music lends an eeriness and sense of mystery, and yet Page's Moorish riff is also still utterly rock'n'roll. The Pakistani string orchestra (who actually came from Southall in West London) are brilliantly arranged and conducted by Jones, who also joins in on the mellotron. In eight-and-a-half minutes there's actually very little development of the basic theme, yet it doesn't seem to matter. It's a staggering, even awesome, achievement that represented new ground in 1970s rock music, and it's the repetitive, hypnotic effect that gives the track its majestic power.

There's more Eastern promise at the opening of Disc Two on 'In The Light', which opens with a long, two-minute Indian drone over which Jones' keyboards imitate the sound of a shehnai. When Page's R&B tinged guitar comes in the contrast is dramatic, although the riff was invented by Jones, who gets the lead songwriting credit on the track. "You can always tell my riffs from Page's", he says. "Mine have got a lot more notes and are linear. His are chunkier and chordier". Some will find it overlong at almost nine minutes, but there are several changes of tempo, a lovely bridge and the fade-out is a *tour-de-force* of exquisitely overdubbed guitars and Bonham at his very best. After two such epics, Page's acoustic guitar instrumental 'Bron-y-Aur', originally written for the third album, offers a small oasis of tranquillity and then gives way to another old track, 'Down By The Seaside', also written at Bron-y-Aur. It's essentially Plant's homage to the kind of songs Neil Young was writing around the time of *After The Goldrush*, complete with Page on pedal steel and Plant's 1971 vocal finding him sounding appreciably younger than on the Headley Grange recordings from three years later. Its friendly, lazy ramble is lifted halfway though by a dynamic change of tempo into a thrilling instrumental passage in which aficianados of early-1970s British prog-rock might find echoes of Bronco – who were good friends of Plant's and whose line-up included his old Band of Joy colleague, Kevin Gammond and future Honeydripper Robbie Blunt.

'Ten Years Gone' is another highlight, but hardly typical Zeppelin. Those who have detected echoes of The Beatles' 'Dear Prudence' and Wings' 'Band On The Run' in the song are surely right, but it's a brilliantly crafted and constructed piece with a touchingly melancholic vocal by Plant about an old love affair that climaxes dramatically as he pleads, "Did you ever really need somebody?" 'Night Flight' is another 1971 recording that failed to make *Led Zeppelin IV*. Plant is in exuberant form, there's

a chugging raunch that sounds like one of Dave Edmunds' rock'n'roll pastiches and, if it sounds retro, then that's all part of its attraction.

The change in Plant's vocals over three years is again evident when 'Night Flight' is followed by the1974 recording of 'The Wanton Song'. He sounds strained, although the effect is not necessarily a bad one, particularly as his voice seems to reflect the life of sexual exhaustion the lyric describes: "shagged-out" is probably the vernacular phrase. The album takes something of a dip in intensity with 'Boogie With Stu', a 1971 jam based on Richie Valens' 'Ooh! My Head', with Rolling Stones *alumnus* Ian Stewart on piano. For once, the band tried to do the right thing in the songwriting credit, adding the name of the late Valens' mother, although it seems the gesture was not appreciated. "What we tried to do was give Richie's mother credit because we heard she never received any royalties from any of her son's hits and Robert did lean on that lyric a bit", Page says. "So what happens? They tried to sue us for all of the song! We had to say bugger off!"

'Black Country Woman' is in similar vein: an acoustic guitar and mandolin country-blues stomp recorded in the garden at Stargroves in 1972 – the track even opens with the sound of an aircraft overhead and a snatch of conversation about whether to leave the intrusive sound in. Charming but disposable, the song was originally called 'Never Ending Doubting Woman Blues' and Plant's highly stylized vocal suggests he's having great fun pretending he's singing on a Memphis street corner circa 1930.

Fortunately, the album ends on a more dynamic note with 'Sick Again', a classic Zeppelin pile-driver with a Plant lyric about the ever-willing ladies they met in Los Angeles while on the road ("clutching pages from your teenage dream in the lobby of the Hotel Paradise"), some suitably brutal drumming from Bonham, and a Page solo of some considerable flair.

It is always a reasonable question to ask whenever confronted with a double album to ask whether it would actually have made a better single disc with some judicious editing. *Physical Graffiti* isn't a perfect album, but it would surely have been butchery to chop it down to a single LP. True, it is ten or more minutes longer than several other classic double albums, including the Stones' *Exile On Main Street*, The Beatles' "White" album and Dylan's *Blonde On Blonde*, but it still isn't overlong: in this CD age, all but one of the album's 15 tracks could be fitted onto a single silvered four-and-a-half inch compact disc. Had the format been available at the time, perhaps 'Boogie With Stu' or 'Black Country Woman', rather than both, might have made it onto the album and *Physical Graffiti* would then have been a superb single CD.

The first review to appear – an exclusive track-by-track preview by Nick Kent in *NME* some three months before the album's release – set the tone: "The album's tonal density is absolutely the toughest, most downright brutal I've heard on record in well over a year. It

could easily end up in the same pantheon as the band's first and fourth works, a good country mile above the second and third. One thing's for sure – for sheer ferocity, *Physical Graffiti* can eat *Houses Of The Holy* for breakfast".

At the time Page told *Rolling Stone*: "I look at it as a document of a band in a working environment. People might say it's sloppy but I think this album is really honest... [it's] a more personal album, and I think it allows the listener to enter our world". Thirty years later he'd grown even prouder of *Physical Grafitti*, telling *Uncut* magazine that he regarded the album as the band's high watermark.

PRESENCE

UK, Swan Song, 31 March 1976; US, Swan Song, 28 March 1976

ACHILLES' LAST STAND/FOR YOUR LIFE/ROYAL ORLEANS/ NOBODY'S FAULT BUT MINE/CANDY STORE ROCK/HOTS ON FOR NOWHERE/TEA IS FOR ONE

Recorded: Musicland Studios, Munich, Germany, November–December 1975
Produced by Jimmy Page
Engineer: Keith Harwood
Cover art: Hipgnosis
Highest chart position: UK 1; US 1

After Robert Plant's car accident in Greece in August 1975, the band's autumn tour of America, due to start just three weeks later, was cancelled. Unable to receive treatment in Britain due to his tax exile status, the singer was moved first to Jersey and then to Malibu, where in September he met up with Jimmy Page. The two swiftly decided that necessity was the mother of invention: although Plant was too crocked to tour, he was fit enough to work in the studio and the enforced vacation became a working one as they set about preparing and recording the band's seventh studio album.

In fact, the writing process had already started during a trip Page and Plant had made to Morocco in June 1975. More work was done on the material in the adjacent beach houses at Malibu which the pair hired, and Plant was further encouraged by a "Get Well" telegram from Elvis Presley. By October, the entire band had been assembled at Hollywood's SIR rehearsal studios to begin working up their initial song sketches into full-on Zeppelin epics. Perhaps struck by the same notion that rock'n'roll was getting too overblown and fanciful which would soon inspire the punk movement, the band concluded that they wanted to make a no-frills, back-to-the-roots album, built around the basic guitar-bass-drums power-trio format, while Plant mined his passion for the blues for inspiration.

The process was not without its problems. Plant was singing from a wheelchair, there was a blizzard of cocaine and heroin flying around certain band members, and mounting friction between Page and Jones. The guitarist claimed the bass player was never around when he was needed, although the bassist told a different story: "Robert and I seemed to keep a different time sequence to Jimmy", Jones complained, "we couldn't find him…we drove to the studios every night and waited and waited until finally we were all in attendance, by which time it was two in the morning". Bonham, meanwhile, was not coping well with tax exile, and being away from his family, and sought solace in a one-man mission to drink LA dry, his frustrations coming out as he went on the rampage which got him into a series of unseemly fights in various bars around Sunset Strip.

Despite these distractions, the rehearsals were dynamite. It seemed that adversity had once again brought the best out in the band. Within a couple of weeks they felt they had enough material for an album and – needing to get out of America in order not to pay US taxes – at the beginning of November they flew to Germany to record in the Musicland studio, located in the basement of the Arabella Hotel, Munich. On the way, they stopped off for a couple of days in New York where Plant, now out of his wheelchair and supporting himself unsteadily with a walking stick, enthused to Lisa Robinson about the new material: "I've had time to see", he told her. "Before I was always bowled over with the sheer impetuousness of everything we did, of what we are, and what was created around it. That was knocked off course. The fulcrum was tilted a little". He described how he had time to rethink now that the rampaging was over, and the fresh lyrics were a product of this "period of contemplation where I was wondering, 'Christ, is it all through? Is it ended?' And as such the album is full of energy, because of that primal fight within me to get back".

Staying conveniently in the hotel above the studio, things went well in Germany and, despite the heroin that road manager Richard Cole was supplying Page and Bonham on a daily basis, and a tumble in the studio that put Plant back to singing from a wheelchair, the band worked intensely, sometimes putting in 18-hour days in the studio. Within less than two weeks, the album was finished. Working to a tight deadline (the Stones had an imminent booking in the studio to record *Black And Blue*), it was by far the quickest and smoothest recording since the group's debut six years and as many albums earlier. "We didn't go out one night. No riots", Plant later observed, laconically.

Of course, being Led Zeppelin nothing could be quite that simple: a six-month delay ensued between finishing the record and its release due, once again, in large part to problems with the sleeve design. The original plan had been to call the album *Thanksgiving*. It had been completed the day before the American holiday and Plant, who came up with the idea, also felt it reflected his gratitude that none of his family had died in the road accident, and that such a strong album had been miraculously snatched from the jaws of disaster. Page and the designers Hipgnosis had different ideas and came up with a series of prints from *Life* magazine depicting middle-class American life, into which they dropped the image of a mysterious black obelisk. At one point the album was almost called *Obelisk* but, in the end, *Presence* won the day, apparently chosen to reflect the "aura" that Hipgnosis' designers felt surrounded the band.

The title also reflected the power of the music inside. The ten-minute opener 'Achilles Last Stand' is a glorious Zeppelin epic, even if in places it recalls Yes's 'Roundabout' with Page's multi-tracked guitars sounding uncannily like Steve Howe.

Another enigmatic design by Hipgnosis, a composite of a deliberately dated family studio shot, a scene from the Earl's Court Boat Show. The obelisk was painted on later

Bonham's martial attack relentlessly drives the track forward and, although recorded from a wheelchair, there's nothing sedentary about Plant's vocal on a lyric that reflects on his recent visit to Morocco. 'For Your Life' has a grinding, stop-start riff that is not instantly catchy, but buries itself in your brain with repeated listening, while Page adds what he described as "a guitar army". 'Royal Orleans' – at less than three minutes one of the shortest-ever Zeppelin tracks – is the only song on the album to feature the names of all four band members in the songwriting credit (the other six tracks are listed as Page/Plant). Recounting on-the-road antics in the band's favourite hotel in New Orleans, its funky riff recalls 'The Crunge', and it's easily the album's most light-hearted moment.

Like 'In My Time Of Dying' on *Physical Graffiti*, 'Nobody's Fault But Mine' was originally recorded in the 1920s by Blind Willie

Johnson – not that he gets a credit. "The arrangement I came up with had nothing to do with the original", Page insisted defensively in 1998. However, the melody and lyrics certainly do, and it's exactly the sort of piracy that gave Zeppelin a bad name. That said, there's no doubt the band take the song into dramatic new territory with Plant's intense, pleading vocal echoing the song's lyric about a man looking for deliverance from his sins. That doesn't stop him celebrating carnal debauchery on the next track, 'Candy Store Rock', an updated homage to the Sun Records sound *circa* 1954, with Page once again playing homage to one of his first guitar heroes, Scotty Moore.

'Hots On For Nowhere' is a light, frothy piece with another stop-start rhythm and a clever Plant lyric that seems to describe recent events before the album ends with 'Tea For One', the album's second-longest track, opening with a typically frantic heavy riff from Page before cutting dramatically into a slow-burning blues and an anguished vocal from Plant about time hanging heavy on his hands (presumably during his recovery). Ultimately, though, it's overlong and never quite matches the excitement of *Led Zeppelin III*'s 'Since I've Been Loving You', to which it's an obvious cousin.

Despite this slightly disappointing ending, for once the reviews were nearly all good. The band were delighted to have returned to a more spontaneous way of working and felt that the benefits of such an approach showed. "There's a lot of urgency about it.

There's a lot of attack to the music", Page commented. "With this one it came straight up. There's a hell of a lot of spontaneity about it". He went on to call the album "pure anxiety and uninterrupted emotion". Plant was even more enthusiastic. "My only alternative was to turn around and stand against the storm with my teeth gritted and fists clenched and make an album", he told *Rolling Stone* in early 1976, while still hobbling around with a brace on his leg. "All the energy that was smouldering inside us getting ready for a lot of gigs came out in the writing and later in the studio. What we have is an album that is so Zeppelin. It sounds like the hammer of the gods". Thirty years later he had lost none of his enthusiasm for the album, telling this author in *Uncut*: "I think *Presence* has got some of the hottest moments Led Zeppelin ever had – agitated, uncomfortable, druggy, pained".

Yet despite this, and the fact that it went straight to Number One, *Presence* remains an underrated album in the Zeppelin canon. Among the reasons for this was that it was another year before the band went back on the road, and only two of the tracks ('Achilles' Last Stand' and 'Nobody's Fault But Mine') were ever performed by them live. Another factor that soon drowned out the success of *Presence* was now historical: the hullabaloo which surrounded the imminent release of their full-length feature film and its accompanying soundtrack album, giving the band it's second Number One of 1976.

SOUNDTRACK FROM THE FILM *THE SONG REMAINS THE SAME*

UK and US, Swan Song, 22 October 1976

ROCK AND ROLL/CELEBRATION DAY/THE SONG REMAINS THE SAME/RAIN SONG/DAZED AND CONFUSED/NO QUARTER/STAIRWAY TO HEAVEN/MOBY DICK/WHOLE LOTTA LOVE

Recorded Madison Square Garden, New York, 27, 28 and 29 July 1973; mixed at Electric Lady, New York and Trident, London
Produced by Jimmy Page
Engineer: Eddie Kramer
Cover art: Hipgnosis/Hardie
Highest chart position: UK 1; US 2

The story of *The Song Remains The Same* film is told elsewhere in this book, but the soundtrack album stands in its own right as a fine record of the awesome power they were able to summon for their 1973 American tour. Recorded over three nights in New York at the end of a gruelling tour that had kicked off in Florida almost three months earlier, they weren't the best shows they played that year (Plant's voice in particular shows signs of wear and tear) but the music on the soundtrack obviously had to fit the footage in the movie, so they were restricted for choice – although the three filmed concerts totalled almost nine hours in length.

By the time the film and accompanying album appeared, two further Zeppelin studio albums had been written and recorded. Drawing on the first five albums, the material that made the soundtrack included one song apiece from

Led Zeppelin I and *Led Zeppelin III*, two apiece from *Led Zeppelin II* and the fourth album, and three from the then current *Houses Of The Holy*. In the end, much of the material chose itself. 'Rock and Roll' opened every show on the

For a band notoriously careful with album design, this one seems to have slipped through the net

1973 tour, and kicks off Disc One with a suitable thump, although Plant, treating his semi-wrecked voice with caution, sings in an unusually low key. 'Celebration Day' follows, although it was oddly edited out of the film. Why is not clear, for it's one of the best performances on the soundtrack album. 'The Song Remains The Same' is another excellent take and segues into 'The Rain Song', the more delicate passages of which make one regret that they chose not to include any material from the acoustic portion of the set.

At almost 27 minutes, 'Dazed and Confused' is way too long, although there's a great moment when Plant starts singing a snatch of Scott McKenzie's "Summer of Love" Number One 'San Francisco (Be Sure To Wear Some Flowers In Your Hair)'. A 13-minute version of 'Moby Dick' also outstays its welcome. However, 'No Quarter' justifies its twelve-and-a-half minutes, with the band judging the song's dynamics to perfection and Plant sounding less strained than elsewhere on the soundtrack.

Listening to 'Stairway To Heaven' is interesting because, although Plant's introduction in which he describes it as "a song of hope" is greeted with a loud cheer, it's clear that at this stage the song had not quite attained the legendary status it was later to attain. The crowd's reaction is subdued throughout, although that may because Plant also told them, "It's a very quiet song, so shut up!" The album closes strongly with a 14-minute 'Whole Lotta Love' which, despite a few moments of dullness, sustains interest by inserting such oddball elements as the funk chord sequence from 'The Crunge', some Page sorcery with the theremin and Plant's delightful burst of 'Let That Boy Boogie'.

A better live album might have been possible had it been recorded earlier in the tour and, in at least a couple of instances, the choice of material was puzzling – a great version of 'Since I've Been Loving You' was included in the film but not on the soundtrack and decent performances of 'Black Dog' and 'Heartbreaker' were similarly omitted from the album. Although it went to Number One in Britain in November 1976, and Number Two in America (where it was kept from the top spot by Stevie Wonder's *Songs In The Key Of Life*), over the years it has come to be disregarded by Zeppelin fans, who know only too well that much better live performances are available on various bootlegs. Interestingly, *The Song Remains The Same* wasn't even included in the 10-CD Led Zeppelin boxed set issued in 1993.

IN THROUGH THE OUT DOOR

UK and US, Swan Song, 15 August 1979

IN THE EVENING/SOUTH BOUND SUAREZ/ FOOL IN THE RAIN/ HOT DOG/CAROUSELAMBRA/ALL MY LOVE/I'M GONNA CRAWL

Recorded: Polar Studios, Stockholm Sweden; Plumpton Place, Sussex, November–December 1978
Produced by Jimmy Page
Engineer: Leif Mases
Cover art: Hipgnosis
Highest chart position: UK 1; US 1

Following the death of Robert Plant's five-year-old son Karac, and the hiatus in all band activity that the tragedy caused, by the time Led Zeppelin finally reconvened for recording at Abba's Polar Studios in Stockholm at the end of 1978, three years had passed since the dynamic sessions in Munich that had produced Presence. In the world of the modern corporate music industry, that's a standard gap between albums by major acts such as U2, Coldplay or Radiohead. In the 1970s, such an absence was considered a career-destroying lifetime – indeed, Creedence Clearwater Revival, one of the biggest-selling bands of the decade, released seven albums and managed to split up within virtually the same time span.

That Led Zeppelin could disappear for so long and then return with an album that went straight to Number One was testimony to just how completely they had dominated 1970s rock, although the success of their comeback was by no means a foregone conclusion, for the Punk revolution had dramatically altered the musical landscape by 1979. Yet the release of *In Through The Out Door* generated such renewed interest in the band that in October that year Led Zeppelin's entire back catalogue re-entered the American charts. In fact, some have argued that the band, vilified as they were by the Punk spokespeople, retired backstage until the dust settled.

Commendably, neither the band and its management nor Atlantic Records put pressure on Plant to return to work, and he was allowed to take his own time. An exploratory get-together at Clearwell Castle in the Forest of Dean in May 1978 proved abortive when it became clear that the singer was still not in a fit state of mind to resume work and it was almost another six months before he finally agreed to begin serious album rehearsals in London in early November. The band then moved to Stockholm where they took over Abba's studio for three weeks, commuting back to Britain each weekend. "Abba came to us and offered it", Peter Grant revealed, "it was actually a real slog to do it. We used to get the noon flight out on a Monday and then return on the Friday. And it was cold and dark the whole time".

For the first time in eight studio albums, Page, hampered by his heroin addiction, was not the driving musical force. With his songwriting partner Plant so long out of contact, it seemed that he had fewer musical ideas to offer the band than ever before. Faced with this void, Jones stepped into the breach. "For much of the time at those Polar sessions only Robert and I were turning up", he later said. "There were two distinct camps by then and we were in the relatively clean one. We'd turn up first, Bonzo would turn up later and Page might turn up a couple of days after that. When that situation occurs, you either sit around waiting or get down to some playing. So that's what we did in the studio. We made it happen".

Most of the tracks began with Jones and Plant recording keyboards and guide vocals. Then the drums were added and the guitars – often not recorded by Page in Sweden at all, but overdubbed in his studio at Plumpton Place, Sussex when he took the tapes home for the weekend. Jones enjoyed his enhanced role. "When I was playing keyboards I sort of had control of everything tonally", he noted. "If I wanted to change key, it would change key." As a result, most of the songs have a more conventional verse-chorus format than is evident on previous Zeppelin albums and, according to road manager Richard Cole, Page grew increasingly resentful, particularly of Jones' writing credit on almost every track. He also griped that Jones was "trying to take over as producer". In fact, Page takes all the production credits on the record, but so chronic was his heroin addiction, that however much he disliked Jones' enhanced role, he appeared incapable of imposing any better ideas of his own on the record.

The sessions were wrapped up before Christmas and Page, taking charge of the tapes, spent the early part of 1979 sifting the material and creating a running order. Three of the toughest-edged numbers recorded in Stockholm, 'Wearing and Tearing', 'Ozone

Baby' and 'Darlene', were left on one side for a planned souvenir EP which was intended to coincide with the band's return to the live stage. The EP never materialized, but the absence of the three tracks (all of which eventually surfaced on *Coda*) considerably changed the character of the album that was eventually released, and weakened it in the process.

At one time it was rumoured the album was going to be called *Look*. In the end they settled on *In Through The Out Door* in recognition of their long absence because, as Page put it, "that's the hardest way to get back in". The sleeve was shot in a mock New Orleans bar built by Hipgnosis at Shepperton studios in Middlesex, and the album was released in six alternative sleeves, each depicting a different bar-room scene. The LP was then released in shrink-wrapped brown paper so that the buyer did not know which of the six sleeves they were getting. Peter Grant had long joked that you could "stuff a Led Zeppelin album in a paper bag and it would still sell", and took great delight in proving the conceit. He was less pleased when the packaging contributed to missing the deadline to get the album in the shops before the band's comeback concerts at Knebworth in August 1979.

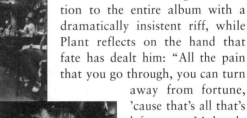

Three of the six variant cover shots for the album, which was sold in a brown paper wrap

When the album appeared two weeks late, the music was certainly a mixed bag reflecting, as Keith Shadwick puts it, "the disunity and confusion in which it was written and recorded". The opener, 'In The Evening', starts with plenty of droning Eastern mystery courtesy of Jones' keyboards before Page makes his most telling contribution to the entire album with a dramatically insistent riff, while Plant reflects on the hand that fate has dealt him: "All the pain that you go through, you can turn away from fortune, 'cause that's all that's left to you. It's lonely at the bottom, man, it's dizzy at the top." 'South Bound Suarez' is a lightweight piece pitched somewhere between Little Feat and the boozy, pub-rock of The Faces. 'Fool In The Rain' is another departure from standard Zeppelin fare, with a Latin-tinged rhythm (inspired by the 1978 soccer World Cup in Argentina) that in its final section ends up sounding rather like 'La Bamba', with Bonham showing an unexpected facility for Afro-Cuban rhythms.

'Hot Dog' – the only song on the album credited solely to the Page/Plant songwriting team – is a throwaway rockabilly number inspired by a girl from Texas called Audrey

Hamilton, with whom Plant was acquainted. Page enjoys bringing out the Scotty Moore impression he had first perfected as a teenager back in the late 1950s, but frankly the track would have been better left in the can. Thinks look up with the ten-minute epic 'Carouselambra', which is one of the album's few high points. Like all of Zeppelin's best marathon pieces, it moves through different movements, in almost symphonic fashion, although today Jones' stabbing keyboards sound somewhat dated and veer dangerously towards Emerson, Lake and Palmer territory in the opening and closing sections. The song also boasts one of Plant's most peotic lyrics, and lines such as "Who cares to dry the cheeks of those who saddened stand adrift upon a sea of futile speech?" suggested he'd been mugging up on Shelley and the Romantics. Unfortunately, the vocal is buried far too deep in the mix. As Plant himself put it: "The whole story of Led Zeppelin in its latter years is in that song – and I can't hear the words!"

'All Of My Love' – the one message of hope and optimism in an album that is otherwise dark and ominous – was a particular bone of contention within the band. With none of the acoustic numbers that populated the early albums, Plant and Jones came up with a pretty, mid-tempo ballad which is sung with great warmth and is underpinned by a semi-classical arrangement of the kind popular at the time with the likes of Genesis and ELO. It's given a loping rhythm inspired by Plant's admira-

tion for Crazy Horse, and Page contributes a vaguely Neil Young-ish guitar part, but he has made no attempt to hide his distaste for the track, which conspicuously lacks his name on the writing credit. "Jonesy started working more closely with Robert and I wasn't that keen on 'All My Love'. It just didn't seem us", he says. He went on to extend his criticism to the entire record: "Bonzo and I both felt it was a little soft, that album. We wanted to make a more hard-driving rock album".

The closing track 'I'm Gonna Crawl' also opens with Jones playing a synthesized string arrangement, but the song then becomes a classy blues ballad with one of Plant's finest vocals and some highly expressive and unusually sensitive drumming from Bonham and a clever use of dynamics.

Predictably, the punk hordes who had taken over the British musical press set about trashing Led Zeppelin: "The manner in which old superfart Led Zeppelin have consistently presented themselves has made the band's name synonymous with gratuitous excess", NME thundered. Paul Simonon, bass player with The Clash was more succinct in his judgement: "Led Zeppelin? I don't need to hear the music. All I have to do is look at one of their album covers and I feel like throwing up". In America, the reaction was far more favourable, and most rock fans were simply delighted to have a major-selling album to rescue them from the endless diet of Disco singles that, by 1979, was swamping Billboard's charts.

Page has seldom talked about the period, but when pressed on the album he is highly defensive. "I couldn't have been in that bad a shape", he protests. "I wouldn't have been able to play and I wouldn't have been able to keep my head together". Some say that he barely did. A quarter of a century later, Plant offered *Uncut* a highly thoughtful analysis of what had gone wrong: "I think the four members had reached a maturity so the music didn't send the same signals of abandon any more", he said. "But it had gone somewhere else and there were some great moments like 'In The Evening'. I'd lost my virginity. My joy of life had been cudgelled and bashed so hard. I became a time-and-motion study man for my own destiny. I was saying 'If I go tomorrow, is this where I want to find myself, in a sex club in Stockholm being silly with Benny and Bjorn from Abba, while Agnetha and Frida are driving round trying to find out to which den of iniquity Led Zep had taken their husbands?' There were some whimsical times. But it was very difficult for me then, and I think the others felt it, too".

CODA

UK, Swan Song, 19 November 1982; US, 22 November 1982

WE'RE GONNA GROOVE/POOR TOM/I CAN'T QUIT YOU BABY/WALTER'S WALK/OZONE BABY/DARLENE/BONZO'S MONTREUX/WEARING AND TEARING

Recorded at various locations 1970–1978
Produced by Jimmy Page

Engineers: Vic Maile; Andy Johns; Eddie Kramer; Leif Mases; John Timperley
Cover art: Hipgnosis/Assorted Images
Highest chart position: UK 4; US 6

Picking up on the previous album's brown paper wrap, this could have not been much plainer

Jimmy Page believed that, despite the unsatisfactory circumstances of *In Through The Out Door*, he could see a way forward for Led Zeppelin – and in Bonham he found a natural ally. "I'd already discussed the next album with him and we said we were going to resort to some really intense riffing", the guitarist told in *Uncut* in 2005. "I don't want necessarily to call it heavy, but you know what I mean by that. That's the way I figured the next album should be, because the music had started to lighten up on *In Through The Out Door* and I wanted to get back to that sort of urgent intensity we managed to evoke".

Bonham's death, of course, meant that it never happened. In December 1980 the band was formally dissolved, but they were still contracted to deliver Atlantic a final album. There were also various large tax demands due on past recordings and so Page agreed to assemble a posthumous album that would represent the band's entire career by rounding up the best leftover tracks from its different phases. Page made the selection during the summer of 1981, working at his studio in Cookham, Berkshire and then called in Plant and Jones to help mix and add a few overdubs to the eight tracks he had selected.

If Bonham had lived, the three tracks set aside from the *In Through The Out Door* sessions for the EP-that-never-was would probably have made it on to the next Zeppelin album anyway. That gave Page a head start, to which he added earlier material to create an enjoyable and respectful elegy to the loudest, heaviest, mightiest rock band of the 1970s. But that it was a new era with a different set of priorities was made symbolically evident when the release of *Coda* was delayed until November 1982, so as not to clash with Plant's solo debut *Pictures At Eleven*, which appeared that summer.

There's some confusion over the provenance of the album's opening track, 'We're Gonna Groove'. The *Coda* sleeve notes claim it was recorded using a mobile truck at the Royal Albert Hall on 9 January, 1970. Certainly the band opened its set that night with the Ben E. King number, but there's nothing to suggest that it was recorded live and Zeppelin expert Dave Lewis is convinced it's the studio version recorded at Morgan Studios, London in June 1969 for possible inclusion on *Led Zeppelin II*. The issue of the Led Zeppelin DVD in 2003 – which includes a film of the Albert Hall performance – suggests Lewis is right, for the live filmed version is considerably longer and slightly different in several respects to the version on *Coda*. However, it's not easy

to tell exactly how Page may have spliced or edited the tapes, particularly as he overdubbed fresh guitar parts using a sub-octivider while putting the album together in 1981–82. Either way, it's a brilliant track that holds its own with much of the best material from the same era that surfaced on *Led Zeppelin II*.

'Poor Tom' is a product of the Page/Plant writing sessions for *Led Zeppelin III* at Bron-yr-aur and was recorded at Olympic Studios in May 1970. A lovely acoustic country-blues played on twelve-string with some highly effective harmonica from Plant, it could have easily replaced 'Bron-y-Aur Stomp' or 'Hats Off To (Roy) Harper' on that album. That it didn't may be down to the fact that its structure and melody owes something to 'That's No Way To Get Along', a 1929 recording by the Rev. Robert Wilkins, which The Rolling Stones had covered as 'Prodigal Son' on *Beggar's Banquet*. 'I Can't Quit You Baby' is a reprise of the Willie Dixon blues song that appeared on *Led Zeppelin I*, again recorded at the Albert Hall. The unreliability of the *Coda* sleeve notes is once more evident for the date of the recording is given as 1 September 1970. In fact, the band was playing several thousand miles way in Seattle that night, and it actually comes from the Albert Hall concert on 9 January 1970. The sleeve further claims it was recorded during an afternoon sound check, but once again this may be further misinformation, for it sounds uncannily like the in-concert version featured on the *Led Zeppelin* DVD. It's followed by 'Walter's Walk', a 1972-recorded leftover from *Houses Of The Holy*, dense and slightly ominous and arguably superior to several of the cuts that actually made that album.

Side Two of the original 1982 vinyl release consists of the three out-takes from *In Through The Out Door*, punctuated only by 'Bonzo's Montreux', a percussion showcase recorded during tax exile in Switzerland in September 1976 and included as a tribute to the late drummer. It's surprisingly inventive, sounding not unlike some of the ethno-percussion initiatives of the Grateful Dead's drummer Mickey Hart but with a definite African vibe that in parts sounds like the heavily distorted rhythms pedalled by the Congolese band Konono No. 1.

That leaves the three *In Though The Out Door* tracks: 'Ozone Baby' is a delight, a classic back-to-basics but tightly-arranged guitar-bass-drums riff without the keyboards that dominated the album that it failed to make. 'Darlene' is a straightforward, rip-this-joint boogie rocker with Jones on piano that tends toward pastiche. But the masterpiece is 'Wearing and Tearing', conceived by the band as its response to punk. "That was our contribution to the whole thing, saying 'yes, you've got it right'", Plant said many years later. Played at a frantic pace over a simple four-chord structure with a yelping Plant vocal, this is surely the direction that Page and Bonham had wanted the next, never-to-be-recorded album to pursue.

Compilations

REMASTERS

UK, Atlantic, 15 October 1990; US, Atlantic, 4 March 1992

COMMUNICATION BREAKDOWN/BABE, I'M GONNA LEAVE YOU / GOOD TIMES BAD TIMES/DAZED AND CONFUSED/ WHOLE LOTTA LOVE/HEARTBREAKER/RAMBLE ON/ IMMIGRANT SONG/CELEBRATION SONG/SINCE I'VE BEEN LOVING YOU/BLACK DOG/ROCK AND ROLL/THE BATTLE OF EVERMORE/MISTY MOUNTAIN HOP/STAIRWAY TO HEAVEN/ THE SONG REMAINS THE SAME/THE RAIN SONG/ D'YER MAK 'ER/NO QUARTER/HOUSES OF THE HOLY/KASHMIR/ TRAMPLED UNDERFOOT/NOBODY'S FAULT BUT MINE/ ACHILLES' LAST STAND/ALL MY LOVE/IN THE EVENING

Produced by Jimmy Page
Engineer: George Marino
Highest chart position: UK 10; US 47

Unhappy with the quality of sound transfer from vinyl to CD engineered by Atlantic Records, in 1990 Jimmy Page and engineer George Marino digitally restored Zeppelin's entire catalogue from the original two-track master tapes. All of the

Crop circles were all the rage in the early '90s, and what better way of creating them than with an airship?

albums were subsequently reissued in sonically upgraded form. Page also compiled a track list for a two-CD "best of" which he submitted to Plant and Jones for their approval. Although fans will argue about individual selections (and four tracks from *Houses Of The Holy* and only three from *Physical Graffiti* surely seems the wrong way around), overall it is a decent introduction. Once again, the surviving band members vetoed proposals to release 'Stairway To Heaven' as a single.

HOW THE WEST WAS WON

UK, Atlantic, 27 May 2003; US, 28 May 2003

*LA DRONE/IMMIGRANT SONG/HEARTBREAKER/BLACK DOG/
OVER THE HILLS AND FAR AWAY/SINCE I'VE BEEN LOVING
YOU/STAIRWAY TO HEAVEN/GOING TO CALIFORNIA/THAT'S
THE WAY/ BRON-YR-AUR STOMP/DAZED AND CONFUSED/
WHAT IS AND WHAT SHOULD NEVER BE/DANCING DAYS/
MOBY DICK/WHOLE LOTTA LOVE (MEDLEY)/ROCK AND
ROLL/THE OCEAN/BRING IT ON HOME*

Recorded: LA Forum 25 June 1972 and Long Beach Arena
27 June 1972
Produced by Jimmy Page
Engineers: Eddie Kramer; Kevin Shirley
Cover art design: Phil Lemon
Highest chart position: US 1

**A memorably dreadful cover
design didn't do justice to a
memorably superb live album**

Searching through the archives for visual and audio material for the *Led Zeppelin* DVD, Jimmy Page came across the master tapes of two concerts from the band's 1972 US tour and merged both shows to create a brilliant two-and-a-half hour, three-CD set that gave Zeppelin fans the official live album they had always craved.

That these were spectacular shows is beyond doubt. "Playing the West Coast was always fantastic, and each member of the band was playing at their best during those 1972 performances", Page said when the live album was released. "When the four of us were playing like that we combined to make it a fifth element. That was the magic – the intangible".

Most of the stage chatter has been cut to leave the music to speak for itself – and probably just as well: to have left in Plant's introduction of 'Black Dog' as "nothing to do with a chick in Detroit" would have won him few friends in these politically-correct times. 'Immigrant Song' is a brutal opener with Bonham sounding like he's got six arms never mind four sticks, while Plant wails at his most primeval. The energy doesn't let up through 'Heartbreaker' and 'Black Dog', but an elegantly graceful 'Stairway To Heaven' is greeted in near silence, not yet having attained its status as lighter-waving anthem. It is followed by a lovely acoustic set that includes 'That's The Way' and 'Going To California', on which after the line about "a girl with love in her eyes and flowers in her hair", Plant ad-libs, "I didn't see too many this time".

The second and third discs offer more scope for the band to stretch out. 'Dazed and Confused' from the Forum show lasts more than 25 minutes, a showcase for Page to produce some astonishing guitar effects with the violin bow while Plant moans and screams in the Arabic semi-tones he'd learned to imitate on his trips to Morocco. The track also incorporates the funk riff from the yet-to-be-released 'The Crunge'. After a fantastic 'Dancing Days' – which the crowd are also hearing for the first time – Plant announces: "John

Henry Bonham – Moby Dick". Almost 20 minutes later, Bonzo is still thrashing about but while you have to admire his energy (and from the reaction of the crowd it sounds like one of the best-received pieces of the night) you also wonder why Page imagined that three decades on anybody would actually want to listen to it.

A 23-minute 'Whole Lotta Love' is far more excusable, for it also inventively takes in John Lee Hooker's 'Boogie Chillun', the Elvis Presley/ Wanda Jackson standard 'Let's Have A Party', Ricky Nelson's 'Hello Mary Lou' and almost nine minutes of the blues classic 'Goin' Down Slow' before returning thrillingly to the original riff. The oddest thing is that apart from *The Song Remains The Same* soundtrack, Led Zeppelin never released a live album when they were in their pomp. Had *How The West Was Won* been released in1972 between *Led Zeppelin IV* and *Houses Of The Holy*, it would surely be revered alongside *The Who Live At Leeds*, the Allman Brothers' *Live At The Fillmore East* and the Stones' *Get Yer Ya-Yas Out* as one of the great live albums of all time.

LED ZEPPELIN BBC SESSIONS

UK, Atlantic, 18 November 1997; US, 19 November 1997

YOU SHOOK ME/I CAN'T QUIT YOU/COMMUNICATION BREAKDOWN/DAZED AND CONFUSED/THE GIRL I LOVE SHE GOT LONG BLACK WAVY HAIR/WHAT IS AND WHAT SHOULD NEVER BE/COMMUNICATION BREAKDOWN/TRAVELLING RIVERSIDE BLUES/ WHOLE LOTTA LOVE/SOMETHIN' ELSE/ COMMUNICATION BREAKDOWN/I CAN'T QUIT YOU BABY/ YOU SHOOK ME/ HOW MANY MORE TIMES/IMMIGRANT SONG /HEARTBREAKER /SINCE I'VE BEEN LOVING YOU/ BLACK DOG /DAZED AND CONFUSED/STAIRWAY TO HEAVEN/

GOING TO CALIFORNIA/THAT'S THE WAY/WHOLE LOTTA LOVE (MEDLEY)/THANK YOU

Recorded: 1969–1971
Highest chart position: UK 23; US 12

Led Zeppelin's early BBC Radio One broadcasts had long circulated among collectors on bootleg but surprisingly did not receive an official release until 1997. The two-disc set makes an essential companion piece to the band's first four

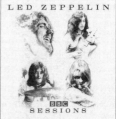

Another strangely inappropriate cover design concealed hidden treasures

albums. The first session, recorded for John Peel's *Top Gear* programme on 1 March 1969, just two weeks after their return from their first US tour, finds them in rip-roaringly earthy form on four songs featured on their debut album. 'You Shook Me' features Jones on organ and a quite different Page guitar solo from the album version. 'I Can't Quit You Baby' is notably different for Plant slipping into Muddy Waters' 'She's 19 Years Old' half way through the track, although 'Dazed and Confused' is presented in very similar style to the way it's heard on *Led Zeppelin I*. A storming 'Communication Breakdown' from the same session is not included here. The session was broadcast on 23 March 1969, a week before Zeppelin's debut album was released in the UK, and so represented the first chance many British listeners had to hear the band. Sessions by The Moody Blues, Free and Deep Purple were also all broadcast on the same programme.

Three months later, after a second American tour, they were back at the Beeb for three more sessions in the space of eleven days. The first, recorded on 16 June 1969 for the long-forgotten *Tasty Pop Sundae* show and broadcast six days later at a rather inappropriate 10am on a Sunday morning, found presenter Chris Grant introducing them by saying, "Alright boys, let's go underground!" (although unfortunately this wonderfully time-warped piece of crassness is not included on the official CD release). What we do get from the session is a powerful 'Communication Breakdown' deemed superior to the version broadcast in March, with a Page solo played at breakneck speed, plus two songs that never featured on an official Zeppelin studio album. The first, 'The Girl I Love She Got Long Black Wavy Hair' is based on a Sleepy John Estes song and its main riff would soon mutate into the intro for Bonham's drum showcase, 'Moby Dick' on the second album. The second is Eddie Cochran's 'Something Else', which was a stage favourite at the time and features Jones on some rollicking Jerry Lee Lewis-style piano and a super-confident Plant ridiculously hamming it up. The fourth track recorded but not included here was a preview of 'What Is And What Should Never Be' from the forthcoming second album.

Just eight days later they were back at the BBC recording their second *Top Gear* session. All four tracks are featured here, including 'What Is and What Should Never Be' and a slightly shorter and crisper 'Communication Breakdown'. Of most interest, however, is the first airing of the song that was to become the band's early anthem, 'Whole Lotta Love'. It already sounds majestic with some great wah-wah effects from Page and Plant ad-libbing at the end about having "those West Bromwich blues". The set is completed by an equally magnificent version of Robert Johnson's 'Travelling Riverside Blues', with some terrific slide guitar from Page and Plant delivering some more Midlands blues. Although a section of the blues lyric was subsequently lifted for 'The Lemon Song' on *Led Zeppelin II*, it's the only known recording by the band of the original Johnson song. The session was broadcast on Sunday 29 June 1969 more or less as the band was taking the stage at the Royal Albert Hall for its biggest London appearance to date.

Two days earlier on 27 June 1969, Zeppelin had recorded their third BBC session of the month when they played a six-song set at London's Playhouse Theatre in a pilot show for what was to become Radio One's long-running *In Concert* series, which the band would return to play two years later. They opened with 'Communication Breakdown', included for the third time in this collection but the inclusion by Plant of lines from the Isley Brothers' 'It's Your Thing' makes it sufficiently different from the previous versions to warrant its presence. They followed with 'I Can't Quit You Baby' and then ten minute-plus versions of 'You Shook Me' (with a long and moody organ solo from Jones) and 'How Many More Times', which includes band introductions and excursions into 'The Hunter' and 'The Lemon Song'. It was the first time the band had been allowed to stretch out on the radio as they did in their live shows, and the session was eventually broadcast on Peel's *Top Gear* on 10 August 1969. Not included here, the session also included Page's acoustic guitar showcase 'White Summer – Black Mountain Side' (which turned up in 1990 on the *Led Zeppelin* boxed set) and a ten-minute 'Dazed and Confused'.

The second disc is taken up with the band's recording for Radio One's *In Concert* programme recorded at the BBC's Paris Theatre on 1 April 1971, some six months before the release of *Led Zeppelin IV* and capturing them in the middle of their British "return to the clubs" tour. They played a dozen tracks, eight of which were broadcast on 4 April and ten of which are included here, the only omissions being 'What Is And What Should Never Be' and 'Communication Breakdown', sensibly not included for what would have been a fourth time. After a Peel introduction in which he notes "this is something we've waited for a long time", the band crash into 'Immigrant Song'. Plant initially sounds uncertain as if he's testing his voice (the recording had been postponed from the week before because he had throat problems) but by the time they're into 'Heartbreaker' his confidence has returned. Highlights include a great 'Black Dog' from the forthcoming album (surprisingly not included in the original radio broadcast), a 19-minute version of 'Dazed and Confused' that finds Page deploying his full range of effects, including violin bow, and the radio premiere of 'Stairway To Heaven', which sounds slightly tentative but builds nicely as Page gives an early try-out to the double-neck guitar.

After the recording, Peel hung out with the band and was impressed enough to record in his diary: "Zeppelin played for 100 minutes. Nice people, too".

Post-Flight: Going Solo

Page and Plant

NO QUARTER: UNLEDDED

UK, Fontana, October 1994; US, Atlantic, October 1994

NOBODY'S FAULT BUT MINE /NO QUARTER/FRIENDS/TRUTH EXPLODES/RAIN SONG/CITY DON'T CRY/ SINCE I'VE BEEN LOVING YOU/BATTLE OF EVERMORE/WONDERFUL ONE/ WAH WAH/THAT'S THE WAY/GALLOWS POLE/FOUR STICKS/ KASHMIR

Recorded: South Bank Television Studios, London 25 and 26 August 1994; Marrakesh, Morocco, 9–10 August 1994
Produced by Jimmy Page and Robert Plant
Engineer: Mike Gregovich
Highest chart position: UK 7; US 4

After resisting huge amounts of money to reform Led Zeppelin for almost a decade and a half, Robert Plant finally agreed to team up again with Jimmy Page in February 1994 for a programme in MTV's popular *Unplugged* series. Rather than simply do straightforward acoustic versions of the band's best-known songs, the pair used the show to reinterpret favourites from the band's classic repertoire in completely fresh and new ways. John Paul Jones was miffed at not being told, let alone invited, but Plant insisted that it was noth-ing personal: he simply wanted to present the show as a new Page and Plant project rath-er than risk the proj-ect being presented as a new incarnation of Led Zeppelin.

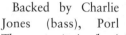
Showing their age, but a return to strong imagery: the boys as windswept Romantics

Backed by Charlie Jones (bass), Porl Thompson (guitar/banjo), Michael Lee (drums), Nigel Eaton on hurdy-gurdy and an Egyptian ensemble and the London Metropolitan Orchestra, two shows were eventually recorded in August 1994 and the resulting film aired on MTV in Europe and America that October. It was followed by a soundtrack album which included 13 Zeppelin classics, many of them quite bril-liantly reinvented. Highlights included 'Battle Of Evermore', with Najma Akhtar singing the Sandy Denny part, and a string-laden 'Since I've Been Loving You'. 'Kashmir' was given a dramatic new twist as the Eastern and Western orchestras inter-twine thrillingly. The performance also included 'Wonderful One', the first joint Page/Plant com-position in 15 years. Drawing on folk, blues, and ethnic or World Music influences, there's a diversity and richness to the arrangements that may not have been what diehard Led Zeppelin fans wanted to hear, but was far more rewarding than the usual reunion of middle-aged men trying to recreate past glories.

Three further tracks, 'Yallah' (subsequently retitled 'The Truth Explodes'), 'Wah Wah' and 'City Don't Cry' were recorded on location in Morocco. Collectors should note that several different versions of the album exist. 'The Rain Song' replaces 'Thank You' on some editions, and 'Wah Wah' was not included on the origi-nal release, but added later as a bonus.

WALKING INTO CLARKSDALE

UK, Mercury, 20 April 1998; US, Atlantic, 21 April 1998

SHINING IN THE LIGHT/WHEN THE WORLD WAS YOUNG/ UPON A GOLDEN HORSE/BLUE TRAIN/PLEASE READ THE LETTER/MOST HIGH/HEART IN YOUR HAND/LISTEN/ WALKING INTO CLARKSDALE/BURNING UP/WHEN I WAS A CHILD/HOUSE OF LOVE/SONS OF FREEDOM

Recorded: Abbey Road Studios, London, autumn 1997
Produced by Jimmy Page and Robert Plant
Engineer: Steve Albini
Highest chart position: UK 3; US 8

Recorded in 35 days and named after the town in Mississippi soaked in blues his-tory, there's a dry and sombre sound to the first (and to date only) full-length studio collaboration by Page and Plant since Zeppelin split up in 1980. Backed

A return to the enigmatic, with little obvious link between the title and the angelic youths – but check out the track titles

by bassist Charlie Jones (no relation) and drummer Michael Lee, highlights include the epic 'Most High' which vaguely hints at the majesty of 'Kashmir' and 'When the World Was Young', which might also have made a decent Zeppelin song. But Page seems unusually restrained and hesitant to cut loose on electric guitar. The solo on 'Sons of Freedom' offers the best example of his lead work, while his acoustic dexterity can be heard to good effect on 'Shining In The Light'. Few of the other songs really stand out, sounding solid and at times even stolid, disappointingly one-dimensional and bereft of the dynamics that Zeppelin always prided themselves on.

Ironically, the album won a Grammy for best hard rock performance in 1999 – something Led Zeppelin never achieved during the band's existence. Despite this recognition, overall it's a dispiriting affair that offers incontrovertible evidence that you can't turn back the clock. With the benefit of hindsight, there was no more chance of the pair of them repeating their triumphs of the 1970s together than there was of John Bonham returning from the grave to join them. Plant's reluctance to team up with Page again suggests that he's all too aware that *Walking Into Clarksdale* did nothing to enhance either of their reputations.

Jimmy Page

DEATH WISH 2 (Soundtrack)

Swan Song, February 1982

WHO'S TO BLAME/CHASE/CITY SIRENS/JAM SANDWICH/ CAROLE'S THEME/RELEASE/HOTEL RATS AND PHOTOSTATS/ SHADOW IN THE CITY/JILL'S THEME/PRELUDE/ BIG BAND, SAX AND VIOLENCE/HYPNOTIZING WAYS (OH MAMMA)

Produced by Jimmy Page
Highest chart position: UK 40; US 50

For his first post-Zeppelin project, Page improbably agreed to score Michael Winner's nasty, sleazy, exploitative junk film *Death Wish 2*, starring Charles Bronson. Some of the music was rescued and remod-

It is what it says on the cover, unfortunately

elled from his aborted soundtrack for Kenneth Anger's notorious 1980 film *Lucifer Rising* and in parts the score is highly listenable. Much of it is standard blues-rock but there's a creepy, chilling and at times genuinely menacing atmosphere to much of it that fitted the film's purpose well. The 1980s synthesizer sounds inevitably lend a somewhat dated quality in places, but Page's guitar-playing on the funky 'Jam Sandwich' and 'Big Band, Sax And Violence' is particularly fine. Much of the album is instrumental and frankly it might have worked better if all of it had been, for the vocals by Chris Farlowe and others are uninspiring.

THE FIRM (with The Firm)

Atlantic, February 1985

CLOSER/MAKE OR BREAK/SOMEONE TO LOVE/TOGETHER/ RADIOACTIVE/YOU'VE LOST THAT LOVIN' FEELING/ MONEY CAN'T BUY/SATISFACTION GARANTEED/MIDNIGHT MOONLIGHT

Produced by Jimmy Page and Paul Rodgers
Highest chart position: UK 15; US 17

By the mid-1980s, Page's lack of action since the break-up of Led Zeppelin suggested that

An interesting and bold typographic solution, but who was The Firm one wondered?

he badly needed someone to provide the creative foil that Plant had offered so effectively. On the surface, former Free/Bad Company singer Paul Rodgers seemed an inspired choice after the two had collaborated on the ARMS benefit tour for Ronnie Lane in 1983. However, joined by veteran drummer Chris Slade and bassist Tony Franklin, The Firm's album received a critical drubbing and sold disappointingly – and it's easy enough to hear why. Slade batters the skins in a decent imitation of Bonham, Rodgers' voice is still in fine shape and Page's layered guitar textures are reminiscent of some of his overdubs on *Coda* – but there is an almost total lack of memorable songs. The opener 'Closer' has a half-decent riff but goes nowhere and the horn section is ineffective. The cover of the Righteous Brothers' 'You've Lost That Loving Feeling' was a bad idea in the first place, and the execution is even more horrible. 'Radioactive', which was a minor hit single, today sounds risibly gimmick-ridden. 'Midnight Moonlight' attempts to recreate the Zeppelin acoustic/electric dynamic but collapses under the banality of the arrangement. 'Someone To Love' is a decent rocker that could almost have been late-period Zeppelin were it not for a plodding rhythm section that makes you realize just how good Jones and Bonham were. The mid-tempo 'Satisfaction Guaranteed' chugs along nicely enough on the back of an insistent Page riff and a snaking solo but the track that is of greatest interest to Zeppelin fans is the album-closer 'Midnight Moonlight', based on an unfinished cut entitled 'Swansong' left over from the *Physical Graffiti* sessions. It's the best song on a disappointing set, and the fact that the best song on the album was a decade old says it all.

MEAN BUSINESS (with The Firm)

Atlantic, April 1986

FORTUNE HUNTER /CADILLAC/ALL THE KING'S HORSES/LIVE IN PEACE/TEAR DOWN THE WALLS/DREAMING/FREE TO LIVE/ SPIRIT OF LOVE

Produced by Jimmy Page, Paul Rodgers and Julian Mendelson

Highest chart position: UK 46; US 22

If The Firm's debut album was a disappointment, the follow-up was no better. That said, it kicks off in dramatic fashion on 'Fortune Hunter', an urgent, turbulent track that for the first time actually sounds exactly as you might imagine a mix of Zeppelin and Free should sound. It ranks as one of Page's better post-Zeppelin moments but sadly and predict-

The second Firm sleeve promised more, but sadly the musical contents delivered less

ably, from there it's mostly downhill all the way. 'Cadillac' finds Page's guitar growling with menace but the song itself is a droning nonentity. 'All The King's Horses' is a keyboard-driven song that sounds like something John Paul Jones might have come up with for *Presence* but then rejected, and 'Tear Down The Walls' has a Page riff that Zeppelin might have turned into a killer but here is thrown away. 'Live In Peace', 'Free To Live' and 'Spirit Of Love' are simply tedious: mid-1980s corporate stadium rockers depressingly free of inspiration and as hollow as their banal song titles would suggest.

WHATEVER HAPPENED TO JUGULA (with Roy Harper)

Beggar's Banquet, March 1985

NINETEEN FORTY-EIGHTISH /BAD SPEECH/ HOPE/HANGMAN/ ELIZABETH/FROZEN MOMENT/TWENTIETH-CENTURY MAN/ ADVERTISEMENT (ANOTHER INTENTIONAL IRRELEVANT SUICIDE)

Produced by Roy Harper
Highest chart position: UK 44

With its cover designed to resemble an orange-coloured packet of Rizla cigarette rolling papers, it's not entirely clear why Page's name gets co-billing on what is essentially a Roy Harper solo album, other than it raised the maverick singer-songwriter's profile and enabled him to make a rare foray into the lower reaches of the album charts. In fact, it was the fifth Harper album that Page had played on and the idea of promoting it as a 'joint' album (a pun which presumably

inspired the cover artwork) came out of an appearance they made as a duo at the Cambridge Folk Festival in 1984, followed by a 15-minute televised slot on *The Old Grey Whistle Test* which featured Harper and Page playing their acoustic

A direct appeal to the ageing hippy audience. How many spliffs were rolled on this album sleeve?

guitars and being interviewed on the side of Scafell Pike in the English Lake District.

Harper produced and wrote all eight of the songs, the only co-writing credit on 'Hope' going not to Page but to Pink Floyd guitarist David Gilmour. Page is credited on the sleeve with "electric and/or acoustic guitar on everything including the snooker table". The interplay of their two acoustic guitars is often quite lovely but it's really an album whose appeal is restricted to Harper's cult following rather than mainstream Led Zeppelin fans.

OUTRIDER

Geffen, June 1988

WASTING MY TIME/WANNA MAKE LOVE/WRITES OF WINTER/ THE ONLY ONE/LIQUID MERCURY/HUMMINGBIRD/EMERALD EYES/PRISON BLUES/BLUES ANTHEM

Produced by Jimmy Page
Highest chart position: US 26; UK 27

And finally – 20 years after forming Led Zeppelin – Jimmy Page gets around to recording his first real solo album. As you would expect, it's a guitar-heavy set of blues-rock tempered with 1980s influences and featuring a variety of sidemen, including John Bonham's son Jason on drums and Robert Plant, who co-wrote and sings on 'The Only One'. The other featured vocalists and

The haircut says it all, the 1980s were a bad time. This time the music was better than the sleeve design suggests

co-writers are John Miles and Chris Farlowe, whose bludgeoning efforts did little to enhance the *Die Hard 2* soundtrack, but whose voice here complements Page's guitar rather well on the blisteringly slow blues of 'Prison Blues', arguably the album's most impressive track. Of the three instrumentals, 'Emerald Eyes' stands out as the most inventive.

There's an impressive diversity to Page's guitar sounds as he switches between a Les Paul, Telecaster, Stratocaster, Roland Synth and Martin and Washburn acoustics, but although some respected Zeppelin-watchers such as Dave Lewis have heralded the set as representing "an almost phoenix-like rebirth", the reality is that *Outrider* merely proved that Page was never really cut out to be a solo artist. It seems that Page himself knew it too.

Despite no end of hints and promises of a new studio album in countless interviews since, to date *Outrider* remains his only solo album.

COVERDALE/PAGE

Geffen, 27 March 1993

SHAKE MY TREE/WAITING ON YOU/TAKE ME FOR A LITTLE WHILE/PRIDE AND JOY/OVER NOW/FEELING HOT/EASY DOES IT/TAKE A LOOK AT YOURSELF/ DON'T LEAVE ME THIS WAY/ ABSOLUTION BLUES/ WHISPER A PRAYER FOR THE DYING

Recorded: Little Mountain Studios Vancouver; Criteria Miami Florida; Abbey Road, London; Highbrow Productions, Hook City NV, autumn 1992
Produced by Jimmy Page and David Coverdale
Highest chart position: UK 4; US 5

It is widely held that Page teamed up with David Coverdale merely to annoy Robert Plant, who believed that the bouffant-haired Whitesnake singer had ripped off his vocal style and was possessed of little or

Signage was all the rage by the 1990s. Enigmatic? No, just uninspired

no original talent. If so, it worked. After rumours that the Plant-Coverdale pairing would be joined by John Paul Jones and Jason Bonham in a reformed Led Zeppelin, Plant was sufficiently irked to agree to team up with Page a year later for *No Quarter*. Plant may also have been spurred into action by the fact that the sole Page-Coverdale album proved to be the guitarist's most commercially successful project since Zeppelin. Listening to the album today, it's hard to understand why, for it's difficult to disagree with the judgement expressed on *Amazon.com* that the record represents "the worst kind of Led Zep mimicry". Page's guitar rocks out with abandon on 'Shake My Tree' and 'Feeling Hot', while 'Take Me For A Little While' and 'Over Now' find him in slower, bluesier mode. But the songs are poor, and if Coverdale is a third-rate Plant copyist as a singer, his lyrics are even more woeful. Ultimately, it's an album of karaoke sub-Zeppelin heavy-metal posturing and unworthy of Page's talents. A further six tracks recorded at the time of the album remain unreleased and should probably remain that way.

LIVE AT THE GREEK (Jimmy Page and The Black Crowes)

TVT, 4 July 2000

CELEBRATION DAY/CUSTARD PIE /SICK AGAIN /WHAT IS AND WHAT SHOULD NEVER BE/ WOKE UP THIS MORNING/SHAPES OF THINGS/SLOPPY DRUNK/TEN YEARS GONE/IN MY TIME OF DYING/YOUR TIME IS GONNA COME/THE LEMON SONG / NOBODY'S FAULT BUT MINE/HEARTBREAKER/HEY HEY WHAT CAN I DO/MELLOW DOWN EASY/OH WELL/SHAKE YOUR MONEY MAKER/YOU SHOOK ME/OUT ON THE TILES/WHOLE LOTTA LOVE

Recorded: Greek Theatre, Los Angeles, 18/19 October 1999
Produced by Jimmy Page
Highest chart position: US 64

Following the 1998 tour with Plant around the *Walking Into Clarksdale* album, Page seemed to rediscover his taste for live appearances. With Plant unprepared to countenance any further projects ("I've been trying to propose scenarios whereby we could do this or that, but Robert didn't want to do anything, and kept postponing and cancelling, so in the end,

I just...lost patience", Page reported at the time), in 1999 the guitarist teamed up with The Black Crowes. After joining the Atlanta rockers at a one-off London charity concert in June, four American dates were then announced for October that year, under the banner "A Rock'N'Roll Evening". Following two shows at New York City's Roseland Ballroom, the remaining two performances at the Greek Theatre, Los Angeles were recorded for a double album. Due to contractual problems with their record company, nothing of the Crowes' own repertoire from the shows (on which Page did not play, in any case) was available for inclusion, leaving an album of classics drawn from Led Zeppelin's illustrious back catalogue and half-a-dozen other blues and rock standards.

Zoso lives, live! An elegant, Moorish-inspired graphic rebus, one suspects that Page probably objected to the type appearing at all

There's nothing adventurous or innovative about the set and Page and the band stick closely to the original arrangements. Unlike David Coverdale, the Crowes' singer Chris Robinson doesn't try to imitate Plant but allows his own personality to shine, lending his pleasing soulful, southern swagger to the Zeppelin covers, which account for no less than 14 of the 20 tracks. Pleasingly, the choices are not always the most obvious, and include 'Out On The Tiles'

The Music

from *Led Zeppelin III* and 'Sick Again' and 'Ten Years Gone' from *Physical Graffiti*. The Black Crowes excel on the more blues-based material and stand-outs include 'In My Time of Dying', sung with aplomb by Robinson, a magisterial 'Nobody's Fault But Mine', a delightfully shuffling take on B.B. King's 'Woke Up This Morning' and a stomping version of the blues standard 'Sloppy Drunk'. The non-Zeppelin covers include songs by Fleetwood Mac and The Yardbirds.

Page was said to have been paid a million dollars for the album, which was initially released only via the Internet. When on-line sales proved disappointing (reportedly less than 50,000 copies), the album was released to record stores in July 2000. The Crowes were also allegedly paid a million dollars, in which case the record company made a heavy loss. Accusations that the record was a cynical money-making exercise were strongly rebutted by the band's Chris Robinson who insisted: "Jimmy Page is a musician who happened to be in a band called Led Zeppelin that we all love. We're musicians who have a band called The Black Crowes, and we got together 'cause we wanted to play music together. You know, it's not really that difficult a concept. There's no marketing strategy".

An enjoyable enough live album that found Page playing with some of his old fire, it was, however, soon eclipsed by the belated release in 2003 of the 1972-recorded live Led Zeppelin set, *How The West Was Won*.

Robert Plant

PICTURES AT ELEVEN

Es Paranza, 28 June 1982

BURNING DOWN ONE/MOONLIGHT IN SAMOSA /PLEDGE PIN/ SLOW DANCER/WORSE THAN DETROIT/FAT LIP/LIKE I'VE NEVER BEEN GONE/ MYSTERY TITLE

Recorded: Rockfield Studios, Monmouth, September 1981–spring 1982
Produced by Robert Plant
Engineer: Pat Moran
Highest chart position: UK 2; US 5

Clapton, Jagger and now Plant all went for vaguely surreal photo-sleeves in the early 1980s. Blame Guinness and B&H

Plant's debut album found him trying hard – possibly too hard – not to sound like Led Zeppelin. Accompanied by guitarist Robbie Blunt (who also co-wrote the songs), Paul Martinez on bass, Jezz Woodruffe and Phil Collins and Cozy Powell on drums, the rhythms are lighter, the tunes more melodic and his vocals contain few of the "mmm, baby, baby" mannerisms he patented with the group. Critics have suggested that where Plant used to rock, here he is content to noodle. Others regard it as his finest solo album. Overall, it's an engaging collection of mature, polished, adult-oriented rock with progressive influences. That is has stood the test of time better than some of his 1980s solo work is down to the fact that the synths heard on some of his later albums are mercifully absent and his clean and crisp production – on the only set he ever produced entirely on his own – sounds remarkably fresh.

Highlights include the lovely 'Like I've Never Been Gone', which owes much to his early West Coast influences, 'Moonlight In Samosa' with its brooding strings and minor keys, and the jazz-rock 'Pledge Pin' with a great sax solo by Raphael Ravenscroft. But he hadn't quite sloughed off his old skin and the bluesy 'Worse Than Detroit' owes something to his Zeppelin past, as does the melodramatic blues-rock ballad 'Slow Dancer' with its eastern Kashmir-style semi-tones and a riff from Blunt that is almost worthy of Page himself. Somewhat surprisingly, Plant did not include anything from *Pictures at Eleven* on *Sixty Six to Timbuktu*, the only solo album not represented on the 37-track, two-disc career retrospective.

THE PRINCIPLE OF MOMENTS

Es Paranza, July 1983

OTHER ARMS/IN THE MOOD/MESSIN' WITH THE MEKON/ WRECKLESS LOVE/THRU' WITH THE TWO STEP/HORIZONTAL/ STRANGER HERE...THAN OVER THERE/BIG LOG

Recorded: Rockfield Studios, Mommouth December 1982–April 1983
Produced by Robert Plant, Pat Moran and Benji Lefeure
Engineer: Pat Moran
Highest chart position: UK 7; US 8

Using the same group of musicians who had performed so well on *Pictures At Eleven*, except for the arrival of Jethro Tull's Barriemore Barlow on drums, Plant

went back into the Rockfield Studios in Wales to record the follow-up less than six months after the release of his solo debut. The style is broadly similar, although certain 1980s techniques style have started to

A tricky title to capture in design, so probably best not to try

creep into the production, particularly in the drum sound and the widespread use of synths as Plant seems even more determined to offer as few echoes of Led Zeppelin as possible. When he supported the album with his first solo US tour, he refused to sing any songs by the band at all. "The times had changed. I was determined to go my own way and start again with no reference to the Zeppelin songbook", he subsequently explained. "I am sure I frustrated many people in so doing. However, that's the way it worked". Indeed, Blunt's smooth, crystalline guitar work could not be further removed from Page's pyrotechnics, and Plant is clearly enjoying the opportunity to sing rather than wail and shout, his voice roaming impressively and at times experimentally across the spectrum.

The album kicks off with 'Other Arms' and Plant screaming "lay down your arms!" on a mid-tempo rocker that might have done service on *In Through The Out Door*. Yet that's as close to Zeppelin as it gets. For the rest it's clever, inventive soft-rock and

The Music

cool atmospherics, climaxing with the closer 'Big Log', with its meandering but brooding sense of mystery enhanced by a mercifully subtle synth arrangement. The song gave Plant his biggest solo hit single, when the track made the Top Twenty on both sides of the Atlantic in July 1983.

THE HONEYDRIPPERS VOLUME 1

Es Paranza, 12 November 1984

I GET A THRILL/SEA OF LOVE/I GOT A WOMAN/YOUNG BOY BLUES/ROCKIN' AT MIDNIGHT

Recorded: Atlantic Studios, New York; London March–April 1984
Produced by the Fabulous Brill Brothers and Ahmet Ertegun (credited as Nugetre)
Highest chart position: UK 56; US 4

Named after the 1945 instrumental 'The Honeydripper' recorded by Joe Liggins and the blues pianist Roosevelt Sykes who revelled in the sexually-charged nickname, Plant first played with an *ad hoc* group he dubbed The Honeydrippers at a Stourbridge wine bar in March 1981. The notion of a semi-anonymous bar band playing old R&B, rockabilly and even doo-wop hits remained with him, and during his 1983 tour of America, Plant took advantage of a day off in Memphis to record a version of Charlie Rich's 'Philadelphia Baby' at the Sun Studios with Phil Collins on drums. Encouraged by Atlantic Records boss Ahmet Ertegun, once the tour was completed, he went back into the label's New York studio in March 1984 with a bunch of

top players including Chic's Nile Rodgers, Jeff Beck, keyboardist Paul Shaffer, bassist Wayne Pedziwiatr and drummer Dave Weckl to record a bunch of vintage numbers under Ertegun's supervision. Back in London, Jimmy Page then added guitar to

A self-conscious and appropriately dated design ensured that customers got the message

a cover of Phil Phillips and The Twilights' 1959 hit 'Sea Of Love' and to 'I Get A Thrill'. Other highlights on the five-track EP include an explosive version of Roy Brown's jump blues tune 'Rockin' At Midnight', a string-laden Spectoresque 'Young Boy Blues' and a lightweight but enjoyable cover of Ray Charles' 'I Got A Woman'.

Although the record sold poorly in Britain, in America it was a major success, providing Plant with a Number Three hit single with 'Sea of Love' – one place better than Led Zeppelin's highest-charting single, 'Whole Lotta Love'. The expanded version of the EP included in the *Nine Lives* boxed set includes a superlative live version of 'Rockin' At Midnight' with a spirited vocal from Plant that actually betters the studio version.

To date, a *Honeydrippers Volume 2* has never appeared, Plant apparently reluctant to align himself too heavily with the Shakin' Stevens rock'n'roll pastiche market.

The Music

SHAKEN 'N' STIRRED

Es Paranza, May 1985

HIP TO HOO/KALLALOU KALLALOU/TOO LOUD/TROUBLE YOUR MONEY/PINK AND BLACK/LITTLE BY LITTLE/DOO DOO A DO DO/EASILY LEAD/SIXES AND SEVENS

Recorded: Swanyard Studios, London and Rockfield Studios, Monmouth, autumn 1984–spring 1985
Produced by Robert Plant, Benji Lefuere and Tim Palmer
Engineers: Benji Lefuere, Tim Palmer
Highest chart placing: UK 19; US 20

When Plant was asked about his 1980s output in an interview in *Uncut* magazine in 2005 and replied "will sorry do?", *Shaken 'n' Stirred* is probably the album he had foremost in his mind. Today it sounds horribly dated with its brash 1980s

Cool abstraction, and something of a departure

production having more in common with a Phil Collins solo album than Led Zeppelin.

The Genesis drummer isn't actually on the album, and Richie Hayward fills the drum stool, but his playing seldom recaptures the effortless funk he once lent to Little Feat. Elsewhere Robbie Blunt, after his sterling work on Plant's first two solo albums, struggles to come to terms with his Roland synth guitar, the backing vocals of former Eurythmics singer Toni Halliday are hopelessly inappropriate and Jezz Woodroffe's synthesized keyboards just sound plain nasty. Even Plant's own vocals seem to have

fallen prey to the 1980s emphasis on trickery rather than emotion.

'Little By Little' and 'Sixes And Sevens' emerge as the most interesting compositions, yet even they are virtually ruined by the dated arrangements and production. It's no wonder that when Plant came to compile his career retrospective *Sixty Six To Timbuktoo*, only 'Little By Little' made the cut – and that only by dint of having been a hit single in America and therefore hard to omit.

NOW AND ZEN

Es Paranza, February 1988

HEAVEN KNOWS /DANCE ON MY OWN/TALL COOL ONE/THE WAY I FEEL/HELEN OF TROY/BILLY'S REVENGE/SHIP OF FOOLS/WHY/WHITE, CLEAN AND NEAT/WALKING TOWARDS PARADISE

Recorded: Swanyard Studios and Marcus Studios, London spring–autumn 1987
Produced by Robert Plant; Tim Palmer and Phil Johnstone
Engineers: Rob Bozas; Martin Russell; Dave Barrett; Michael Gregovich; Tim Burrell; Jonathan Dee
Highest chart position: UK: 10; US: 6

After a two-and-a-half year break, Plant eventually returned in 1988 with a new band and apparently more at ease with his past than at any time since Led Zeppelin had broken up. At the heart of the new project were Dave Barrett and Phil Johnstone, who worked as the production team Act Of War and were dubbed by Plant "the Dangerous Brothers". Impressed by a demo tape by the pair that included their songs 'Heaven Knows' and 'Upside Down', he began working with them in early 1987 on an album that was originally given the working title *Wolves*, a reference to Plant's new tour logo. With additional support from drummer Chris Blackwell (no relation to the Island Records founder), bassist Phil Scragg and guitarist Doug Boyle, this line-up was responsible for eight of the album's ten

Exotic, mythic, inscrutable: this attractive cover pretty much brings together Plant's main interests, and presses all the right buttons

tracks. The other two were the result of an earlier alliance with Robert Crash from the New York post-punk band The Psychotic Tanks, who had been recommended to Plant by Dave Stewart.

Despite some heavily programmed keyboards that today sound a little dated (particularly on 'Why' and 'Dance On My Own', the two electro-pop tracks recorded with Crash), *Now and Zen* was a major improvement after the disappointments of *Shaken 'n' Stirred*. No longer running from the shadow of Led Zeppelin, he even sampled several of the band's greatest moments on 'Tall Cool One', which also features Page in the studio on guitar, as does 'Heaven Knows'.

For the most part it's mid-tempo, radio-friendly adult rock of the highest quality, although it's the album's sole ballad, the lovely 'Ship Of Fools' that is the undoubted stand-out with a wonderfully subtle vocal and lyrical words. The rockabilly tones of 'Tall Cool One' and 'Billy's Revenge' echo The Honeydrippers, but there's nothing retro about their entirely contemporary treatment.

MANIC NIRVANA

Es Paranza, March 1990

HURTING KIND (I'VE GOT MY EYES ON YOU)/BIG LOVE/S S S & Q/I CRIED/SHE SAID/ NIRVANA/TIE DYE ON THE HIGHWAY/ YOUR MA SAID YOU CRIED IN YOUR SLEEP LAST NIGHT/ ANNIVERSARY/LIARS DANCE/WATCHING YOU

Recorded: Olympic Studios, Barnes, London, autumn 1989
Produced by Robert Plant and Phil Johnstone
Engineer: Mark 'Spike' Stent
Highest chart position: UK 15; US 13

Using the same band that recorded *Now And Zen* but with Charlie Jones replacing Phil Scragg on bass, on its release *Manic Nirvana* was the hardest rocking album Plant had made since the demise of

Another sleeve that lets down the title, artist and contents ...

Led Zeppelin a decade earlier. With guitars rather than keyboards taking the front seat again, it's clear this was a conscious decision from the outset as 'Hurting Kind (I've Got My Eyes On You)' and 'Big Love' kick and stomp with more venom than almost anything from the singer's 1980s output. 'S S S & Q' opens with a snarling guitar solo that owes as much to Hendrix as Page. 'Tie Dye On The Highway', with its sampled voices from the Woodstock festival, is a high-energy tribute to the hippie era, while the slashing guitar riffs of 'She Said' and 'Nirvana' also conjure the ghost of Zeppelin's 1970s pomp, revealing Boyle as a highly underrated axeman.

The more reflective material is impressive too, particularly the gorgeous 'I Cried', 'Liar's Dance', which recalls the acousting outings on *Led Zeppelin III* and the haunting 'Anniversary', which refers to his divorce from his wife Maureen but which many fans also believe to be a tribute to John Bonham, occasioned by Plant's feelings upon re-forming Led Zeppelin for a day without the late drummer for Atlantic Records' 40th birthday party in 1988.

FATE OF NATIONS

Fontana, 1 May 1993

CALLING TO YOU/DOWN TO THE SEA/COME INTO MY LIFE/I BELIEVE/29 PALMS/MEMORY SONG (HELLO HELLO/ IF I WERE A CARPENTER/PROMISED LAND/THE GREATEST GIFT/GREAT SPIRIT/NETWORK NEWS

Recorded: RAK Studios, London, autumn 1992–spring 1993
Produced by Robert Plant and Chris Hughes
Engineer: Michael Gregovich
Highest chart position: UK 6; US: 34

More line-up changes saw the introduction of Kevin Scott MacMichael on guitar and Chris Hughes on drums and a host of guests who helped to make *Fate Of Nations* the most adventurous album of Plant's solo career to this point and signposted the way to some of his later work with *Strange Sensation*. 'Calling To You' kicks the album off in crunching fashion with a 'Kashmir'-like riff before Nigel Kennedy's thrilling violin coda takes the track to new heights. The slow-burning 'Come Into My Life' features Nigel Eaton on hurdy-gurdy, Clannad's Marie Brennan on ethereal backing vocals and the unmistakeable guitar of Richard Thompson on a track that recalls the mysterious moods of 'Battle Of Evermore', while 'Colours Of A Shade' is another Celtic folk excursion. 'Greatest Gift' and 'Great Spirit'

...but not as much as this one, which seemed strangely dated and message-driven

are finely crafted ballads, while the Tom Petty-ish '29 Palms' and the lovely, jangling 'I Believe' are object lessons in pop perfection. The tenderly sung cover of Tim Hardin's 'If I Were A Carpenter' is given a beautiful arrangement with mandolin and strings by Lynton Naiff. After such gentle, melodic interludes, the album closes on a tougher-edged note with 'Network News', a protest song about the first Iraq war that makes an alarming companion piece to 'Freedom Fries' on *Mighty Rearranger* more than a decade later.

DREAMLAND

UK, Mercury, 24 June 2002; US, Universal, 16 July 2002

FUNNY IN MY MIND (I BELIEVE I'M FIXIN' TO DIE)/MORNING DEW/ONE MORE CUP OF COFFEE/LAST TIME I SAW HER/ SONG TO THE SIREN/WIN MY TRAIN FARE HOME (IF I EVER GET LUCKY)/DARKNESS, DARKNESS/RED DRESS/HEY JOE/ SKIP'S SONG/DIRT IN A HOLE

Recorded: RAK Recording Studios early 2002
Produced by Robert Plant and Phill Brown
Engineer: Phill Brown
Highest chart position: UK 20; US 40

The Music

The Albums

An elaborate, stylish and intriguing gatefold CD cover and insert, beautifully executed from an original concept by Plant himself

After the 1990s reunion with Page on *No Quarter* and *Walking Into Clarksdale*, Plant retreated into semi-anonymity with his pub band, Priory Of Brion. He eventually re-emerged in 2002, nine years after his last solo album, with *Dreamland*, a collection which mined the covers that formed his repertoire he'd been playing with Priory of Brion. In interviews at the time, he went out of his way to stress that he saw the album very much as a band effort by Strange Sensation, comprising Justin Adams and Porl Thompson on guitars, John Baggott on keyboards, Charlie Jones on bass and Clive Deamer on drums.

The brace of original group compositions, 'Last Time I Saw Her' and 'Dirt In A Hole', are lightweight but there's no doubting the passion of Plant's interpretive skills on some of his favourite songs by West Coast troubadours Tim Buckley and Jesse Colin Young ('Song To The Siren' and 'Darkness, Darkness'), Bob Dylan ('One More Cup Of Coffee') and some of his old blues heroes (including Bukka White on 'Fixin' To Die' and Arthur "Big Bo" Crudup, John Lee Hooker and Robert Johnson, all of whom crop up in the course of the medley, 'Win My Train Fare Home').

MIGHTY REARRANGER

UK, Sanctuary, 2 May 2005; US, 10 May 2005

ANOTHER TRIBE/SHINE IT ALL AROUND/FREEDOM FRIES/ TIN PAN VALLEY/ALL THE KING'S HORSES/ENCHANTER/ TAKAMBA/ DANCING IN HEAVEN/SOMEBODY KNOCKING/LET THE FOUR WINDS BLOW/MIGHTY REARRANGER/BROTHER RAY

Recorded: The Lodge, Bathford autumn 2004–spring 2005
Produced by Robert Plant and Strange Sensation
Engineer: Steve Evans
Highest chart position: UK 4; US 22

There's always a temptation when a significant artist returns with a decent album after a period of low-key activity to talk in overexcited terms of a "comeback". But after easing himself into the new millennium with the Priory

Again, one suspects the hand of Plant: quirky, obscure, successful

of Brion and an enjoyable but unchallenging cover album in *Dreamland*, 2005's *Mighty Rearranger* sounded like an important statement by a man with much to get off his chest. 'Another Tribe', 'Takamba' and the brilliant 'Freedom Fries' ("and burns and scars") seemed to provide a sharp and concerned commentary on the post-9/11 world. 'Tin Pan Valley' was a candid analysis of the dangers of living on former glories and a fairly uncoded attack on those who "flirt with cabaret" (take a tuxedoed bow, Rod Stewart) and continue in old age to "fake the rebel yell" (arise Sir

Robert Plant on the Mighty Rearranger

Despite delight at such a strong album, two-and-a-half decades after Zeppelin last flew, there was some consternation as to what the title meant. Plant attempted to put the record straight:

– Who is the Mighty Rearranger?

RP: "He's an abstract character. He's around all of us. He's fate. He's everything we want and everything we don't want. We're all governed by The Mighty Rearranger. He's right there and he's a pretty powerful dude."

– There's a lot of imagery in the lyrics on the record drawn from the blues...

RP: "Dylan has been a beacon to me as a writer all through my life. He judiciously borrows blues terms and I decided to write an entire song like that, which is 'Somebody Knocking'. There's stuff in there from Blind Willie McTell and Son House and all those references that are buried inside my brain."

– Should we see this album as a great comeback?

RP: "If people will think I've returned and say 'he's regaining his crown', that's very nice of them. But I don't know who had it last. It's a bit like pass the parcel, isn't it?"

Mick). Forays into mysticism ('The Enchanter' and 'Dancing In Heaven'), lyrical nods to old heroes ('Somebody Knocking' and 'Let The Four Winds Blow'), rock riffing ('Shine It All Around'), blues wailing (the title track), burnished West Coast filigree ('Dancing In Heaven'), *Led Zeppelin III*-style acoustics ('All The King's Horses'), and Arabic and North African influences ('Another Tribe' and 'Takamba') all collide in unexpected and often thrilling fashion. Backed again by Strange Sensation, with guitarists Justin Adams and Skin Tyson making a particularly outstanding contribution, Plant reckoned it was the best he'd ever sung, with plenty of subtle shading and nuance and that open-throated, leonine roar unleashed only when strictly necessary.

Compilations

FROM SIXTY SIX TO TIMBUKTU

Mercury, November 2003

TIE DYE ON THE HIGHWAY/UPSIDE DOWN/PROMISED LAND/ TALL COOL ONE/DIRT IN A HOLE/CALLING TO YOU/29 PALMS/IF I WERE A CARPENTER/SEA OF LOVE/DARKNESS, DARKNESS/BIG LOG/SHIP OF FOOLS/I BELIEVE/LITTLE BY LITTLE/HEAVEN KNOWS/SONG TO THE SIREN/DARKNESS, DARKNESS (VIDEO)/YOU'D BETTER RUN/OUR SONG/HEY JOE/FOR WHAT IT'S WORTH/OPERATOR/ROAD TO THE SUN/ PHILADELPHIA BABY/RED FOR DANGER/LET'S HAVE A PARTY/ HEY JAYNE/LOUIE LOUIE/NAKED IF I WANT TO/21 YEARS/IF IT'S REALLY GOT TO BE THIS WAY/RUDE WORLD/LITTLE HANDS/LIFE BEGIN AGAIN/LET THE BOOGIE WOOGIE ROLL/ WIN MY TRAIN FARE HOME (IF I EVER GET LUCKY)/CALLING TO YOU (VIDEO)

Recorded 1966–2002
Highest chart position: UK 27; US 134

A well-chosen two-disc representation of Plant's entire solo career, with tracks from seven of his first eight albums (nothing from his debut *Pictures At Eleven*) plus a generous handful of rarities and previously unreleased tracks.

Disc One contains the highlights of his solo albums plus one out-take, 'Upside Down', which dates from the *Now And Zen* sessions. The buried treasure, however, is to be found on Disc Two.

Plant wears his hippy credentials on his well-travelled sleeve

'You'd Better Run' is his 1966 debut single with the ill-fated Listen, and 'Our Song' his own debut single on CBS a year later. 'Hey Joe' and á frankly awful version of Buffalo Springfield's 'For What It's Worth' come from Band of Joy's 1967 demo, recorded at London's Regent Sound. 'Operator' is a rolling acoustic blues that represents his brief pre-Zeppelin tie-up with Alexis Korner. The rockabilly cover of Charlie Rich's 'Philadelphia Baby' appeared in the 1985 film *Porky's Revenge* and 'Louie Louie' was recorded for 1993's *Wayne's World 2* and finds Plant playing lead guitar on a highly creditable solo. A rollicking cover of Elvis Presley's 'Let's Have A Party' complete with weeping pedal steel was recorded for *NME* in 1990. Other rare covers include Moby Grape's 'Naked If I Want To', only ever released as a B-side on a 1993 single, and 'Little Hands', from 1999's *More Oar – A Tribute To Skip Spence*. 'Hey Jayne' is another 1993 B-side, chiefly notable for the fact that it finds plant playing sitar. 'Red For Danger' is a techno-sounding oddity recorded in 1988 with multi-instrumentalist Robin George, a mate of Plant's from the Midlands.

'21 Years' features the Tucson, Arizona-based guitarist Rainer Ptacek, and appeared as the B-side of Plant's 1993 single, '29 Psalms'. 'Rude World', another Ptacek song, is of particular interest to Zeppelin fans as it teams Page and Plant together again on a song from around the time of 1997's *Walking Into Clarksdale* sessions which appeared on the US-only tribute album to Ptacek, *The Inner Flame*. The countryish 'If It's Really Got To Be This Way' was recorded for the little-heard 1994 album *Adios Amigo: A Tribute To Arthur Alexander*. 'Life Begins Again' finds Plant singing with Welsh folk singer Julie Murphy on a track recorded with the Afro-Celt Sound System in 2001 and 'Let The Boogie Woogie Roll' is a 2003 collaboration with Jools Holland.

NINE LIVES (boxed set)

Rhino, November 2006
Recorded 1982–2005

Coming just two years after *Sixty Six To Timbuktu*, *Nine Lives* brought together all nine of Plant's post-Zeppelin solo albums in a splendidly packaged boxed set, but although each album was offered in an "expanded" version, in

Into the mythical – entirely appropriately in retrospect

truth they contained little that was new. A total of 26 previously unreleased tracks consisted mostly of live versions of album cuts and remixes, with a handful of out-takes of varying interest.

John Paul Jones

SCREAM FOR HELP (Official Soundtrack)

Atlantic, March 1985

SPAGHETTI JUNCTION/BAD CHILD/SILVER TRAIN/ CRACKBACK/ CHILLI SAUCE/TAKE IT OR LEAVE IT/ CHRISTIE/ WHEN YOU FALL IN LOVE/ HERE I AM

Produced by John Paul Jones

A recommendation from Jimmy Page to the film director Michael Winner led to Jones's name appearing on a record as a solo artist for the first time in 20 years, and Led Zeppelin fans have long sought out this hard-to-find soundtrack for the opening and closing

With official soundtracks, you are stuck with the promotional artwork for the film. Another Winner loser

instrumentals, both of which feature the guitar pyrotechnics of Jimmy Page. 'Spaghetti Junction' has a Booker T.-inspired funky, Stax feel and 'Crackback' crunches hard and fast in true Zeppelin style, with a bass part from Jones that recalls the riff on 'Black Dog'. In addition to playing a variety of instruments, Jones' vocals can be heard on 'Bad Child' and 'When You Fall In Love', backed on the latter by the folk guitar of John Renbourne. Other vocalists include Yes's Jon Anderson and Madeline Bell, while

his daughter Jacinda Jones helped out with the lyrics. The film flopped badly, which accounts for the fact that the album is hard to find. With the exception of the splendid 'Crackback', it's probably one for completists only.

ZOOMA

Discipline Us, September 1999

ZOOMA/GRIND/THE SMILE OF YOUR SHADOW/GOOSE/BASS 'N' DRUMS/B. FINGERS/SNAKE EYES/NOSUMI BLUES/TIDAL

Produced by John Paul Jones

Appearing out of the blue in 1999, Jones' first genuine solo album was an all-instrumental affair that found him playing four-, eight- and ten-string bass guitars as well as synthesizer and organ. Stand-outs on the diverse collec-

Elegant, arty, with a frisson of cool: nice one, John

tion include the title track, with its torrents of guitar noise from Paul Leary of Butthole Surfers (whom Jones had produced) and the epic blues-rocker 'Snake Eyes'.

THE THUNDERTHIEF

Discipline Us, February 2001

LEAFY MEADOWS/THUNDERTHIEF/HOEDIDDLE/ICE FISHING AT NIGHT/ DAPHNE/ANGRY ANGRY/DOWN TO THE RIVER TO PRAY/SHIBUYA BOP/FREEDOM SONG

Produced by John Paul Jones

The Music

And who is The Thunderthief? The sinister figure on the cover provides a hint, as does the chorus to the song: he "licks the language off her tongue... while unconscious in our cots, he excavates our deepest thoughts"

The follow-up to the all-instrumental Zooma found Jones adding vocals to his prowess on bass, keyboards, guitars, mandolins, autoharp, koto and ukulele. "I knew I wanted to do something very different than Zooma, and my first inclination was to use some computer voices to add a little bit of personality", he explained at the time. "After a while, I thought, 'This is silly', and I decided to use my own voice." The results are not unpleasing, ranging from 'Angry Angry' which finds Jones adopting the persona of a Cockney-voiced punk to the haunting tones of 'Ice Fishing at Night'. "It ain't Pavarotti and it ain't Plant, but I think it's all right", the reluctant singer modestly observed. Peter Blegvad contributed to the lyrics, but it is still as an inventive musical arranger that Jones' skills are best displayed. King Crimson's Robert Fripp – owner of the Discipline Us label – adds some imaginative guitar to the driving opener 'Leafy Meadows', the seven-minute 'Hoediddle' is an instrumental cornucopia of arresting eclecticism, 'Daphne' and 'Shibuya Bop' riff and rock with some force, whilst 'Freedom Song' incorporates traditional Japanese influences.

Rarities and Bootlegs

You might have thought that the round-up of studio out-takes on the 1982 album *Coda* and the issue of the BBC radio sessions in 1997 would have meant that there's very little Led Zeppelin material left that hasn't been officially released. On the contrary – there's everything from Page and Plant's rehearsals at the cottage at Bron-yr-aur to the sessions they recorded in Bombay on their way back from Australia in 1972, via alternate takes, different mixes and rehearsal tapes from almost all of the studio albums. Then there are the literally dozens of live recordings from every tour between 1969 and 1980.

Peter Grant hated bootleggers with a rare passion and dealt out summary justice and physical violence to those he caught illicitly taping shows on several occasions. He also once visited a London record dealer and personally smashed copies of an early Zep bootleg titled *Blueberry Hill*, recorded live at the LA Forum in September 1970.

Over the years, members of the band have grown more relaxed in their attitude towards the bootleggers. Plant has been known to autograph them and has even been heard to recommend the pirated recording of the Bombay sessions in 1972. Page expressed his gratitude when a fan gave him a 10-CD bootleg boxed set compiling out-takes and soundboard recordings from across their career and declared an amnesty when he invited the pirates to supply material for the Led Zeppelin DVD project.

This relaxed attitude does not extend to pirated copies of official albums. Plant tells the story of a visit with Page during their mid-1990s reunion to a market in Istanbul, where they discovered illegal copies of *Led Zeppelin IV*. Page gathered them up, telling the bemused Turkish stallholder that they were his intellectual property and he had no right to sell them. An embarrassed Plant remonstrated with his colleague and when Page walked away with the CDs, pulled out his wallet to pay for the discs.

There's no space here to offer a comprehensive guide to the hundreds of Zeppelin bootlegs on the market but a note of caution when entering the field of unauthorized recordings: many of the CDs contain a substantial overlap of material and are of varying quality. A detailed guide to them can be found at www.stryder.de. However, here are ten rarities of different provenance that throw fresh light on Led Zeppelin's creative processes and which are more than worth tracking down...

Baby Come On Home (Tribute To Bert Berns)

A slow blues with Jones on Hammond organ from the autumn 1968 sessions which produced Zeppelin's first album, the tape of this track was allegedly lost for 23 years, eventually turning up in a refuse bin outside Olympic Studios in 1991. It was then included in 1992 on the second *Remasters* boxed set. Bert Berns (the reference seems to have been added by an engineer at the time) was the renowned 1960s manager, producer and songwriter who composed 'Twist and Shout' and produced Van Morrison's first solo work after he had left Them. He died in December 1967.

White Summer/Black Mountain Side

A staple of early live shows, Page also recorded a tremendous eight-minute version during the live broadcast from the BBC's Playhouse Theatre in June 1969. The track combines an acoustic number from The Yardbirds days with a tune he worked up on the first Led Zeppelin album, and owes much to the influence of such folk guitarists as Davy Graham and Bert Jansch. The track was not included on the *BBC Sessions* album but can be found on the 1990 first *Remasters* set. Another fine version recorded eleven years later during rehearsals for the *Over Europe* 1980 tour at the Victoria Theatre, London can be found on the bootleg *Last Rehearsal: (Strange Tales from the Road)*.

Sugar Mama

A cover of a Sonny Boy Williamson song recorded in June 1969 at Morgan Studios for *Led Zeppelin II* but not included on the album. "Where you been? Sugar mama! Say you love me sugar mama, I'll never let you go", Plant wails in fine form. The track can be found on the bootleg CD *Alternative Coda*.

Hey Hey What Can I Do

Recorded at Island Studios in July 1970 during the sessions for *Led Zeppelin III*, this mellow, semi-acoustic commercial-sounding song is the only track ever to appear on a single and not on an album. Typical of the material Page and Plant had worked up during their stay in the cottage in Wales, with added mandolin from Jones, it appeared in America as the B-side to 'Immigrant Song' and in Britain on a 1972 bargain-price LP sampler called *The New Age Of Atlantic*, but it's only appearance on an official CD is its inclusion on the four-CD 1990 boxed set.

Jennings Farm Blues

Named after Plant's farmhouse home which he bought following the release of the second album, this number – basically an electrified version of the acoustic song that turned up on *Led Zeppelin III* as 'Bron-y-Aur Stomp' – was recorded at Olympic Studios in November 1969. The bootleg entitled *The Lost Sessions Volume Five* contains no less than eleven takes of the song in varying stages of completion.

Feel So Bad (medley)

Following the release of *Led Zeppelin III*, Page revealed that the 'Hats Off To (Roy) Harper' track had been taken from "a whole tape of us bashing out different blues things". A six-minute track recorded at Hedley Grange in the early summer of 1970 has subsequently materialized on bootlegs, and is probably what he was referring to. It includes Plant singing snippets from 'Feel So Bad', 'Fixin' To Die' and 'That's Alright Mama', with a backing track similar to 'Hats Off'. It can be found on *The Lost Sessions Volume Six*.

Friends/Four Sticks

"In 1972 Jimmy and I stopped in Bombay on the way back from a tour of Australia and we recorded with an Indian orchestra", Plant recalled in 2005. "We recorded some Led Zeppelin songs with them – 'Friends' and 'Four Sticks'. You can hear them on bootlegs and they sounded amazing". The pirated CD, *The Lost Sessions Volume Two: Led Zeppelin in India* includes several takes of 'Friends', which lends itself well to the unconventional instrumentation which includes sitar, tabla and Indian strings, and several more of 'Four Sticks', offering a total of 48 minutes of music.

Swan Song

Before it became the name of the band's record label, 'Swan Song' was the title given to a lengthy instrumental Page worked up with Bonham in 1974 during rehearsals for the *Physical Graffiti* album. The song was later modified to become 'Midnight Moonlight' on The Firm's debut album in 1985. Two versions by Led Zeppelin, one of them a Page solo instrumental, can be heard on the bootleg *Brutal Artistry*. A second unfinished song from the *Physical Grafitti* sessions called 'Take Me Home' can be found on the same bootleg.

Woodstock

Robert Plant was prone to dropping snatches of all kinds of odd songs into Led Zeppelin live performances, from Cliff Richard's 'Bachelor Boy' to 'Down By The Riverside'. Full-length covers were rarer, but on three of the five nights of Led Zeppelin's Earl's Court residency in May 1975, 'Dazed and Confused' included a near-complete version of Joni Mitchell's 'Woodstock' (on the other two nights its place was taken by Scott McKenzie's 'San Francisco'). Pick of the performances came on 24 May, when the song appeared in the middle of a 34-minute version of 'Dazed and Confused'. Available on the *Shenondoah* bootleg.

Fire

Following the death of Robert Plant's young son in 1976 and the cancellation of all Zeppelin activity, the band eventually reconvened at Clearwell Castle in the Forest of Dean in May 1978. The sessions were unproductive and were abandoned when it was clear Plant wasn't yet ready to return. But they did produce a great riffing number called 'Fire', which was never taken further but can be found in unfinished state on the bootleg *The Lost Sessions Volume Four*, along with early takes of 'Carouselambra', which would appear in more developed form on *In Through The Out Door*.

"I can't put a tag to our music. Every one of us has been influenced by the blues, but it's one's interpretation of it and how you utilize it. I wish someone would invent an expression, but the closest I can get is contemporary blues".

Jimmy Page, press release for *Led Zeppelin I*

50 Great Led Zeppelin Tracks

Although Page described Plant as a tentative songwriter in the early days, their collaboration rapidly bore remarkable fruit; a shared interest in blues imagery helped, which in addition to Plant's ability to skilfully improvise within the idiom, meant that by *Led Zeppelin II* there was a distinct originality to their approach, which would only grow over the next decade.

1. Babe I'm Gonna Leave You

Recorded October 1968; available on *Led Zeppelin*

Page and Plant first bonded over a 1962 recording of this folk song on the album *Joan Baez In Concert* during their initial get-together at the guitarist's home on the River Thames in August 1968. It then provided the perfect vehicle for Page's vision of a new kind of rock music built around dynamic contrasts of quiet and loud passages. The version Led Zeppelin recorded for their debut album shifts dramatically from folky verses accompanied by acoustic guitar to pummelling choruses driven by a wonderful descending riff and some unrestrained cymbal crashing from Bonham. Keith Shadwick, whose book *Led Zeppelin: The Story Of A Band And Their Music* is particularly perceptive in its musico-logical analysis, suggests that a model for Zeppelin's arrangement was Big Brother & The Holding Company's 1968 version of George Gershwin's 'Summertime' with its quiet, semi-whispered passages and interludes of screaming guitars and pounding drums. This has the ring of truth, for there are also obvious similarities between Janis Joplin's bravura vocal on the Big Brother track and Plant's performance, right down to the "baby, baby, baby" mannerisms.

The song was initially credited as "traditional, arranged by Jimmy Page". Rumours persist that there is an earlier unreleased version of the song recorded by the guitarist with Steve Winwood on vocals. In the 1980s, the song was re-credited to the American folk singer Anne Bredon who, it transpired, had composed the song in the late 1950s. For once the failure to credit was not Zeppelin's fault:

they genuinely didn't know who had written the song, for Baez's recording contained no composer's credit and the liner note which described it as "a white blues, a form which was created in our century by the meeting of the Southern lyrical lament and the Negro blues" further suggested a composition in the public domain.

2. Dazed And Confused

Recorded October 1968; available on *Led Zeppelin*

Jimmy Page first heard this song one night in the autumn of 1967 at a folk club in New York's Greenwich Village while on tour with The Yardbirds. He and other members of the band had turned up at the Café A-Go-Go to see Janis Ian, whose song 'Society's Child' was a big hit at the time, but arrived early and caught the support act, Jake Holmes, singing a song called 'Dazed And Confused', in which he described a bad acid trip to the accompaniment of droning guitar and a sinister-sounding descending bass scale. Page was impressed enough to seek out the album from which it came, *The Underground Sound Of Jake Holmes*, and adapted the song for The Yardbirds, with Keith Relf reworking the lyrics. The band called their version 'I'm Confused' and worked it into their live set but never recorded the song. Page then put it forward for inclusion on the first Zeppelin album.

The arrangement opens with a superb walking bass line from Jones, Page rings some tortured and menacing effects out of his guitar by attacking it with a violin bow and Plant turns in an open-throated falsetto vocal that perfectly suits the song's anguished lyrics. The performance can now be recognized as a key milestone in the development of so-called "heavy rock" and became a cornerstone of their live show.

3. Communication Breakdown

Recorded October 1968; available on *Led Zeppelin*

One of the all-time great Zeppelin anthems, 'Communication Breakdown' was first developed by the band while touring Scandinavia in September 1968. Like 'Dazed And Confused', the song deals with themes of disorientation and alienation but in contrast to that six-minute-plus epic, everything here is done and dusted inside two and a half minutes. The inspiration for the song may owe something to Eddie Cochran's 'Nervous Breakdown' and has a simple pop structure built around three chords. The track is driven by the insistent, repeated guitar riff from Page and reaches its climax around Plant's cry of "suck it!" as the guitar screeches from one speaker to the other. An example of how brevity could suit Led Zeppelin, 'Communication Breakdown' was the number the band chose to play on their only ever live UK television appearance, in March 1969. The song remained a near constant in their set until the final 1980 tour and was often used over the years as a rabble-rousing encore.

4. Black Mountain Side

Recorded October 1968; available on *Led Zeppelin*

Away from the bludgeoning riffs and screaming electric guitar lines, Jimmy Page was a subtle and sophisticated exponent of acoustic guitar finger-picking, much influenced by the likes of Bert Jansch and Davy Graham. 'Black Mountain Side' was his take on a tune called 'Blackwater Side' which he learned from Jansch's 1966 album, *Jack Orion*, although the tune's origins were more complicated. In fact, Jansch had learned the song from the folk singer Anne Briggs, adapting her vocal performance into a virtuoso guitar piece. Briggs in turn had got it from the noted folk song collector Al Lloyd, and when she discovered Led Zeppelin had adapted the piece she suggested that some of the royalties should be given not to her, but to Lloyd's widow.

Using a twelve-string Gibson guitar, Page adds some frenetic improvisation with an almost sitar-like sound, and the Eastern feel is emphasized by the tabla playing of Viram Jasani, who today runs the Asian Music Circuit, the main body promoting Asian music in the UK. Oddly, Page and Jansch only got to meet for the first time in 1996. "He's a very good acoustic player", Jansch says. "He's always liked the folk thing but he leans a lot on other players apart from me. I don't think there was anything schizophrenic about Led Zeppelin playing acoustic music or using traditional tunes. In those days, everybody was trying to put different sounds together. Davy Graham probably started those fusions. He was very into Eastern music and then he crossed it with the blues. Jimmy Page was doing a similar thing".

5. How Many More Times

Recorded October 1968; available on *Led Zeppelin*

The final track on Led Zeppelin's debut album was also the closing number of the band's early live shows. The song's archetypal, pile-driving blues riff owes something to Albert King's 'The Hunter' and the track also has antecedents in The Yardbirds' version of 'Smokestack Lightnin'' and in the rhythm used in 'Beck's Bolero', written by Page and recorded with Jeff Beck in 1966. It later featured on The Jeff Beck Group's 1968 album *Truth*, a record which rivals Led Zeppelin's debut as one of the foundation stones of heavy rock. 'How Many More Times' is one of Page's finest constructions on the first album, from the dramatic opening and the clever use of wah-wah to the manically eerie effects created by the use of the violin bow. Each change in the tempo and dynamics of the song is driven not by the rhythm section but primarily by the guitar, although this is done with impressive subtlety as Page cleverly avoids the usual axe-hero histrionics. Plant's vocal embellishments which find him dropping in lines from 'Rosie' and 'The Hunter' were apparently ad-libbed in the studio during the session, as was his "Little Robert Anthony wants to come and play" line – although it's hard to imagine him today getting away with "I got a little schoolgirl and she's all mine".

6. Whole Lotta Love

Recorded summer 1969; available on *Led Zeppelin II*

The signature tune that even 'Stairway To Heaven' never wholly displaced. The distinctive three-note opening blues riff played on bass and guitar must be one of the most memorable intros in rock – even if it was closely modelled on Muddy Waters' recording of Willie Dixon's 'You Need Love'. The late Steve Marriott went to his grave believing that Zeppelin had taken the idea from a number he sung with the Small Faces called 'You Need Loving', and which was also derived from Dixon's song. Yet whatever the antecedents and the rights and wrongs over songwriting credits, there's no doubt that Page and Plant take the track into previously uncharted territory. From the opening "you need coolin', baby I ain't foolin'", it's evident this is a supercharged, self-confident Plant who is rapidly overcoming any nerves he may have displayed on the debut album. Bonham plays his part too, with a staggering syncopated pattern that ricochets between snares, tom-toms, hi-hat and bass drum. It's also his hi-hat and cymbals that introduce the track's famously experimental middle section on which Page used a theremin, an early electronic instrument first patented in the 1920s by the Russian inventor after whom it is named and which was used to great effect by the Beach Boys on 'Good Vibrations'. Its spiralling, high-pitched tone careers from speaker to speaker as Plant overlays an orgasmic vocal which then develops into a dialogue with Page's guitar. Many of the effects of the middle section Page later credited to engineer Eddie Kramer: "I told him exactly what I wanted to achieve and he absolutely helped me to get it", he said. "We already had a lot of the sound on tape, including the theremin and slide with backwards echo but his knowledge of low-frequency oscillation helped complete the effect. If he hadn't known how to do that I would have had to try for something else". The track's enduring power is evinced in the fact that eleven years after it was recorded, it was the last track Led Zeppelin ever performed live, when it was given a 17-minute work-out at their final gig in Berlin on 7 July 1980.

7. What Is And What Should Never Be

Recorded summer 1969; available on *Led Zeppelin II*

One of Plant's very first efforts as a lyricist, according to Richard Cole, the song was about a romance the singer apparently had behind his wife's back. He'd like to give up his present life and start a new one ("sail away, leave today") but in his married state that's impossible ("the wind won't blow, you really shouldn't go") – hence 'What Is And What Should Never Be'.

Whatever the inspiration, the lovely, dreamy, semi-whispered verses, which owe a debt to Julie Driscoll's version of Donovan's 'Seasons Of The Witch' are driven by an inventive counter-melody played on the bass by Jones, and are dynamically contrasted with some kicking drums and a crashing guitar riff. However, Page's main solo (which found him using for the first time the Gibson Les Paul with which he would become so associated) has a pleasingly gentle and understated late-night quality. In another production triumph for the Page-Kramer team, the guitars pan thrillingly back and forth between the two channels and Plant's vocals are also impressively phased in places.

8. The Lemon Song

Recorded June 1969; available on Led Zeppelin II

One of the most notorious songs in Zeppelin's canon due to its blatant sexual innuendo, 'The Lemon Song' has its roots in Howlin' Wolf's 'Killing Floor' and, following legal action for breach of copyright, the bluesman's name later had to be added to the writing credit. The name of Robert Johnson also comes to mind, for the infamous line "squeeze my lemon 'til the juice runs down my leg" was taken from his 'Travellin' Riverside Blues', which Zeppelin performed on a BBC Radio One session in 1969. There's also a debt to Albert King's 'Cross-Cut Saw', all of which help to make it one of the band's dirtiest and rawest-sounding blues outings. The song is given a contemporary flavour by Jones' funk-influenced bass line, although some have accused him of over-playing. The track was recorded more or less live in the studio, with Plant once again indulging in some considerable ad-libbing.

9. Thank You

Recorded summer 1969; available on Led Zeppelin II

Another of Plant's early lyric writing efforts, if 'What Is And What Should Never Be' was about an illicit extra-marital love affair, 'Thank You' represents the other side of the coin – a heartfelt love song to wedded bliss and his wife Maureen, which finds him emotionally claiming "you to me are the only one". Movingly sung, and with Plant sounding surprisingly like Rod Stewart in places, it's one of the loveliest moments on the album, with Page's delicate picking on a Rickenbacker acoustic twelve-string strongly underpinned by Jones' haunting Hammond part, which seems to owe something to Chris Stainton's organ playing on Joe Cocker's 'With A Little Help From My Friends'. Often used live in the early days as a showcase for Jones' organ playing, it was regularly used as an encore on the 1972/73 tours and was revived by Page and Plant when they were on tour together in the mid-1990s.

10. Heartbreaker

Recorded summer 1969; available on Led Zeppelin II

Opening with another blues-influenced riff, 'Heartbreaker' contains a typical Plant lyric about an "evil" woman well versed in "the wicked ways of love" but is primarily a platform for Page's guitar virtuosity. The unaccompanied solo he plays some two minutes in is a piece of blatant but glorious showing-off, although critics are divided about its merit. According to Dave Lewis, it's "a breathtaking exercise in string-bending" but Keith Shadwick reckons that it's one of Page's poorest solos, concluding that "he frequently stumbles in execution at speed and repeats time-worn fingerboard patterns rather than attempt anything fresh". It's an excessively harsh critique of a track that is an established and long-standing favourite with most fans. The track also became a live staple, with Page at different times adventurously incorporating into the song's basic structure snippets of everything from Bach's Lute Suite No.1 to Simon and Garfunkel's '59th Street Bridge Song'. At different times it was a show opener and an encore and it was still part of the set in 1980; it had the honour of being one of the five songs chosen for their reunion at Atlantic's 40th birthday gig in New York in 1988.

11. Ramble On

Recorded summer 1969; available on *Led Zeppelin II*

Even more than 'What Is And What Should Never Be' or 'Thank You', 'Ramble On' sign-posted the way to the more ethereal sound that would come to the fore on *Led Zeppelin III*. The folk-rock combination of acoustic and electric guitars is much in the vein of something Fairport Convention might have recorded at the time, while the unusual bongo-like sound of Bonham's drums was reportedly obtained by him hitting a plastic garbage pail. Plant's vocals move effortlessly up the gears as the softly-delivered narrative of the verses gives way to the high-octane punch of the chorus on

a set of lyrics that are a jumble of images and characters from *The Lord Of The Rings*. The track also features a wonderful double-tracked guitar solo from Page, with a tone quite unlike anything else on the album. Oddly, the song was never performed live.

12. Moby Dick

Recorded summer 1969; available on *Led Zeppelin II*

Drum solos have a bad name in rock music and will be forever associated with Spinal Tap banality and macho rock-boorishness. John Bonham's contribution to the genre was 'Moby Dick', on record a relatively crisp four minutes twenty-one seconds of inventive percussion, book-ended by a killer Page guitar riff that he didn't have any other use for (although it became the theme tune of the BBC2 music show, *Disco 2*) and which was allegedly adapted from a blues tune by Sleepy John Estes. Bonham's percussive storm in the middle was assembled by Page and Kramer from a series of edits. "I didn't actually sit there and play a solo especially for the record", the drummer explained. "They just pieced it together".

Live, 'Moby Dick' was a different and far longer story. Originally known in early set lists as 'Pat's Delight' in honour of Bonham's wife, the drum showcase was retitled 'Moby Dick' in mid-1969 and stayed in the set until 1977, when it was renamed 'Over The Top' and reconfigured using the riff of 'Out On The Tiles', rather than the *Disco 2* theme. According to the writer and broadcaster

Andrew Collins, the birth of Punk in 1976 was "fanned by discontent at rising unemployment, industrial unrest and a 30-minute Led Zeppelin drum solo at Earl's Court". Bonham performed 'Moby Dick' at every one of their five nights at the venue the previous year and although the average length was probably nearer 20 minutes than half an hour, you know what Collins means.

13. Immigrant Song

Recorded summer 1970; available on *Led Zeppelin III*

A classic up-tempo rocker to kick off an album that included so many gentler, semi-acoustic flavours, 'Immigrant Song' is one of Zeppelin's most brutal assaults, from Plant's banshee war cry to the sonic assault of Page's martial riff. Keith Shadwick reckons Plant's wail is a repetition of the opening notes of 'Bali Hi' from Rodgers and Hammerstein's *South Pacific* and that the galloping guitar-drums rhythm is a cousin to Jimi Hendrix's 'Little Miss Lover'. The latter seems more probable than the former.

The lyrics were in part inspired by the band's visit in June 1970 to Iceland ("the land of the ice and snow") as part of a cultural exchange sponsored by the British government. They were apparently written by Plant with tongue somewhat in cheek, but few got the humour and the line "The hammer of the gods will drive our ships to new lands" was picked up by fans to give the band an Olympian nickname which was used many years later by the

writer Stephen Davis as the title of his salacious biography. Elsewhere, the imagery of Viking war and invasion dominates, although as an inveterate old hippie, Plant cannot resist ending the song by insisting that after all the rape and pillage, "peace and trust" will win the day. The song opened every Zeppelin concert from 1970–72 and was released as a single in America, where it rose to Number 16 on the *Billboard* chart.

14. Gallows Pole

Recorded summer 1970; available on *Led Zeppelin III*

The American folk-blues singer Huddie Ledbetter – better known as Leadbelly – popularized the traditional folk song 'Gallows Pole' in the 1930s, but the recording that inspired Jimmy Page to record it with Led Zeppelin was a later version by the twelve-string guitarist Fred Gerlach on the Folkways label. "We have completely rearranged it and changed the verse", Plant said at the time of the release of *Led Zeppelin III*. "That's John Paul Jones on mandolin and bass and I'm playing the banjo, six-string acoustic, twelve-string and that's Robert doing the harmonies as well as the lead".

One of the songs worked up by Page and Plant during their stay at the cottage in Bron-yr-aur, the rewrite is less comprehensive than the guitarist has suggested, for the song is still instantly recognizable as the one sung by Leadbelly, and most of the details of the narrative are still in place. Nevertheless, it's a wonderful reinterpretation, brilliantly executed as the tension builds

Love & Theft: Zeppelin's debt to the blues

Fans will tell you that Led Zeppelin took their blues influences and transformed them into something new and unique that was all their own. Detractors argue that they robbed and stole from the blues, and were little more than a bunch of thieving magpies who seldom gave credit to those whose work they plundered. A more objective and neutral judgment would be to state that much of the band's greatest material borrowed from blues idioms, both musically and lyrically – a long-standing practice among the great bluesmen themselves, after all – but that sometimes they were strangely careless about citing the source of their inspiration. The band itself responded to the criticisms by pointing out that much of the blues derived from traditional sources and, in any case, their performances were totally different to the originals. "Bluesmen borrowed from each other constantly and it's the same with jazz; it's even happened to us", Page observed to *Guitar World* in 1998. "As a musician I'm only a product of my influences". Of course, the disputes arise over how carefully those influences are credited, and where the lines are drawn between influence, borrowing and outright theft, especially when it comes to the niceties of writing or arranging credits. That said, even Bob Dylan has fallen foul of the same problem, but regarded himself as working in an ongoing tradition evinced by the likes of Leadbelly, Woody Guthrie and even the Grateful Dead – that is, one of eclectic musical, and lyrical, development.

Zeppelin's blues-drenched debut album included two Willie Dixon songs (both credited), and the traditional 'Babe I'm Gonna Leave You', which they rearranged from a version by Joan Baez. Another track, 'How Many More Time', which was listed as a group compo-

sition, lent heavily on Albert King's 'The Hunter', but the band could reasonably argue that King's song had, in turn, been based on an earlier Howlin' Wolf number.

The controversy over the band's appropriation of blues "originals" really started with *Led Zeppelin II*. The album included their signature tune, 'Whole Lotta Love', which borrowed liberally from the lyrics of Willie Dixon's 'You Need Love'. Yet, unlike the same author's 'You Shook Me' and 'I Can't Quit You Baby' on the first album, this time the song was listed as a band composition, and Dixon failed even to get a mention. He sued, and Led Zeppelin settled out of court. Equally controversial was 'The Lemon Song'. Heavily based on 'Killin' Floor' by Howlin' Wolf, it also drew lyrically upon Robert Johnson with its infamous "squeeze my lemon" sequence, and from Albert King's 'Cross-Cut Saw'. That the songwriting credit was given to Plant, Page, Jones and Bonham, provoked a protest from Jewel Music, the publishers of 'Killin' Floor'; it resulted in another settlement, and a change in the songwriting credit on future copies of the album. A third song on the record, the blues-rocker 'Bring It On Home', can be traced to Sonny

Boy Williamson's track of the same name.

By 1970s, with *Led Zeppelin III*, the blues was still providing a powerful source of inspiration and material. The album included 'Gallows Pole', a trad folk tune that was popularized by Leadbelly, although Page apparently based the group's take on it on a version by Fred Gerlach. Another song on the same album,'Hat's Off To (Roy) Harper', a tribute to the maverick English folk singer, borrowed from the Bukka White tune 'Shake 'Em On Down'. The fourth Zeppelin album, which appeared in 1971, included 'When The Levee Breaks', based on the 1929 recording by Memphis Minnie and Kansas Joe McCoy, and appeared with this hybrid writing credit: Page, Plant, Jones, Bonham – and Minnie.

Even in the middle of their rock'n'roll excess, the blues remained a source for much of Led Zeppelin's work. 1975's *Physical Graffiti* featured a version of 'In My Time Of Dyin'', while *Presence*, released the year after, included 'Nobody's Fault But Mine'. On the record it was credited to Page and Plant, although the latter cheerfully admitted when they played it live that it had been originally written by Blind Willie Johnson.

The posthumously-released album *Coda* featured further blues songs, this time properly credited to B.B. King and Willie Dixon. Since the band broke up, Plant, in particular, has remained a staunch advocate of the blues, and is an enthusiastic collector with an encyclo-pedic knowledge of the most obscure recordings and artists to match.

Even in the middle of their rock'n'roll excess, the blues remained a source for much of Led Zeppelin's work. 1975's *Physical Graffiti* featured a version of 'In My Time Of Dyin'', while *Presence*, released the year after, included 'Nobody's Fault But Mine'. On the record it was credited to Page and Plant, although the latter cheerfully admitted when they played it live that it had been originally written by Blind Willie Johnson.

The posthumously-released album *Coda* featured yet another version of 'I Can't Quit You Baby'.

Recommended listening:

The Early Blues Roots of Led Zeppelin (Catfish)

In the absence of an official compilation of Zeppelin's blues material, this collection of the original source material from which they drew and/or bor-rowed or stole, makes fascinating listening and includes inspi-rational tracks by Memphis Minnie, Sonny Boy Williamson, Blind Willie Johnson, Robert Johnson, Bukka White, Leadbelly and Big Bill Broonzy.

powerfully as the different instruments come in and Page caps it with a fine, understated electric guitar solo towards the end which cleverly mimics the phrasing of a saxophone. Rhythmically, the final section bears a strong resemblance to Traffic's 'You Can All Join In'.

15. Tangerine

Recorded summer 1970; available on Led Zeppelin III

On one level, Tangerine is one of the slighter pieces on *Led Zeppelin III* but it's a lovely song and occupies an interesting place in the band's history. When it began life as a joint Jimmy Page and Keith Relf composition in The Yardbirds, it was called 'Knowing That I'm Losing You'. The song was recorded by the band in New York in early 1968 but never released. When Zeppelin recorded the song as 'Tangerine' two years later it appeared with a sole Jimmy Page writing credit, although according to Yardbirds' historian Greg Russo, the lyrics were little changed from those which Relf had written. The song also points the way to the future, for the mock-Renaissance style acoustic guitar intro can be seen as an early template for 'Stairway To Heaven'. Plant's double-tracked vocal is highly effective and the track is lifted out of its mid-1960s pop feel by the addition of some lovely pedal steel from Page. The song was often performed as part of the band's acoustic set and at Earl's Court in 1975 was unveiled in a revamped version with harmony vocals and Page on the famous double-necked Gibson.

16. That's The Way

Recorded summer 1970; available on Led Zeppelin III

First known when it was written at the cottage in Bron-yr-aur as 'The Boy Next Door', 'That's The Way' is arguably the loveliest of all the gentler numbers on *Led Zeppelin III*. Opening with a simple acoustic guitar, Page soon introduces his newest toy, the pedal steel, while Plant abandons his usual high energy delivery for a simple, conversational style, augmented by Crosby, Stills and Nash-style harmonies at one point. The lyrics, which Dave Lewis rates as among the best Plant ever penned, concern a pair of star-crossed lovers, with the singer at one point philosophically noting that "all that lives is born to die". Page again makes his instrument sound horn-like on a wistful track notable for the total absence of drums. Unsurprisingly, it became a highlight of their acoustic set in the early 1970s.

17. Bron-y-aur Stomp

Recorded summer 1970; available on Led Zeppelin III

As its title suggests, no song on *Led Zeppelin III* evokes the folky, fireside jamming that Page and Plant enjoyed in their Welsh cottage better than this piece of light-hearted acoustic fun. There's an irresistible jubilation to this recording that makes it easy to understand why the band chose to include it on the album rather than 'Jennings Farm Blues', an electric take of the same song recorded around the same time. Page's virtuoso finger-picking at the song's commencement is borrowed from

Bert Jansch's arrangement of the traditional 'The Waggoner's Tale' and it fits perfectly with Plant's lyric about the joys of rural life and walking the country lanes with his dog, Strider. Jones plays a fretless acoustic bass and Bonham joins in the fun on spoons and castanets. Perhaps very few fans would list 'Bron-y-aur Stomp' in their Top Ten Zeppelin tracks and, on its release, those who had hoped for an entire album of head-banging riffs like 'Immigrant Song' must have shaken their bonces in bafflement. Nevertheless, its spirit, humour and *joie de vivre* are unstoppable.

Incidentally, the band consistently misspelt the name of their Welsh bolt-hole, which is correctly called Bron-yr-aur.

18. Since I've Been Loving You

Recorded summer 1970; available on *Led Zeppelin III*

Amid all the mighty riffs, it's often overlooked that Led Zeppelin were also a magnificent straight blues band, particularly in their element on the slower, moodier material. Nowhere is this more evident than on 'Since I've Been Loving You'. Each of the four members is at a peak here, and the interplay between them is extraordinary, with Plant's voice effectively operating as the fourth instrument. Jones' Hammond organ is unbelievably atmospheric (with the bass part played on the organ pedals) and Bonham locks down deep into the groove. Page unleashes one of his most inventive solos, rooted in Chicago blues

but elongated and expanded in a fashion that perhaps only Hendrix and Duane Allman were similarly capable of at the time (and prefaced by an entirely justifiable shout of "watch out!" from Plant, whose vocals scream and plead with awesome power. When it comes to British blues, you can forget about John Mayall, Chicken Shack, Savoy Brown and the rest: this is how it should be done.

19. Black Dog

Recorded January–February 1971; available on *Led Zeppelin IV*

It was obligatory to kick off Zeppelin albums with a mighty surge of power and 'Black Dog' is up there with the best of them. The initial idea for the riff came to John Paul Jones one day after he and Jimmy Page had been listening to Muddy Waters' 1968 album, *Electric Mud*. A complicated series of changing patterns and time signatures were then added by Page so that the only way Plant can fit in one of his most carnal vocals is as a call-and-response with the bass and guitar riff, an idea that he later admitted was copied from Fleetwood Mac's 'Oh Well'. The fact that this means most of his vocals are sung unaccompanied between the instrumental fills only adds to the track's drama. Page layers up to four guitars and Bonham plays a remarkable rhythm that turns around and sounds as if it's likely to implode at any minute under its complexity, but instead explodes out of the speakers with bludgeoning force. In the face of all this musical mayhem and a classic Plant lyric about a mean, mistreating woman, it seems almost banal to add that the beast in the title with the "eyes that shine burning red" belonged to a dog that followed Plant around when they were recording at Headley Grange.

20. Rock And Roll

Recorded January/February 1971; available on *Led Zeppelin IV*

A simple title for one of the most frenzied, swashbuckling tracks Zeppelin ever recorded, the genesis of 'Rock and Roll' lay in Bonham fooling around with the riff played by drummer Earl Palmer on Little Richard's hits 'Good Golly Miss Molly' and 'Keep A Knockin'' during a jam at Headley Grange that include Rolling Stones' alumnus Ian Stewart ("Stu") on piano. Page added the Chuck Berry-influenced guitar riff and within 15 minutes the track was delivered at full tilt. Plant hastily concocted a lyric and 'Rock and Roll' was used either as a set opener or an encore at almost every live show the band played until the end.

21. The Battle Of Evermore

Recorded January–February 1971; available on *Led Zeppelin IV*

Originally conceived by Page as an instrumental after he picked up Jones' mandolin late one night at Headley Grange, the ultimate realization of 'The Battle Of Evermore' owes much to Plant and his admiration for folk-tinged groups such as Pentangle, The Incredible String Band and, of course, Fairport

Convention, whose Sandy Denny duets on the track. The mandolin lends an ethereal quality and the combined voices of Plant and Denny work so well together that one regrets it is the only Zeppelin track to feature an outside voice. The lyric reflects Plant's fascination with the history of the ancient border wars fought between the English and their Scottish neighbours, although his ongoing fascination with *The Lord Of The Rings* is also evident. The only downside is the malign influence the song has exerted on lesser bands; Andy Fyfe in his book *When The Levee Breaks: The Making Of Led Zeppelin IV* blames 'The Battle Of Evermore' for "much of the wizards and demons nonsense that many metal bands felt compelled to record in its wake".

The song was only ever played live by Led Zeppelin on a handful of dates on the 1977 tour where John Paul Jones sang the Sandy Denny part, but it was revived in radically different form in 1994 by Page and Plant for *No Quarter*, with the British-Asian singer Najma Akhtar on vocals.

22. Stairway To Heaven

Recorded January–February 1971; available on *Led Zeppelin IV*

They say familiarity breeds contempt and Robert Plant is among those who have grown to hate 'Stairway To Heaven', damning it with faint praise as a "nice, pleasant, well-meaning naïve little song". Yet overexposure cannot cloud the fact that 'Stairway To Heaven' is not only a benchmark in rock history but a staggering piece of music. Page had been working on the chord progression for some time and, according to Jones, the music was one of only two pieces brought to the Headley Grange sessions in early 1971 in anything like complete form – indeed, an instrumental version had first been essayed at Island Studios in December 1970. The song was swiftly developed: one night sitting around the fire at Headley Grange with Page (Jones and Bonham had taken the night off to attend a party at The Speakeasy in London), Plant found the lyrics pouring out. "I was holding a pencil and paper and for some reason I was in a very bad mood", he recalls. "Then all of a sudden my hand was writing out the words, 'There's a lady who's sure all that glitters is gold and she's buying a stairway to heaven'. I just sat there and looked at the words and then I almost leapt out of my seat". Within a couple of days Jones had added his multi-tracked recorders and the track was lifted to another level with the much-delayed entry of Bonham's drums. Although all of these elements came together very quickly, Page took the track away to add his guitar solo later at the Island Studios.

Atlantic were desperate to put out the track as a single, but Grant and the band dug in their heels and refused to sanction its release. Plant may today be embarrassed by the fey mysticism and inchoate hippie fairy-tale of the lyric, but at the time he was proud enough to have the words printed on the album's inner sleeve, the first time Zeppelin had taken such a step. Since the band's demise, he has consistently refused to sing the song, although Page has been happy to celebrate its legacy in concert as an instrumental piece. Jones has also professed his continued affection for the song. "Everything built nicely", he says. "Both Jimmy and I were quite aware of the way a track should unfold and the various levels that it would go through".

23. Misty Mountain Hop

Recorded January–February 1971; available on *Led Zeppelin IV*

At the time of *Led Zeppelin IV's* release, 'Misty Mountain Hop' tended to get overshadowed by some of the more obviously attention-grabbing songs such as 'Black Dog' and 'Stairway To Heaven'. Over the years, however, it has emerged as a much-loved classic, revived at band reunions and regularly performed by Plant in his solo career. Driven by a bouncing electric piano part from Jones and a swinging drum beat from Bonham, the title again references *The Lord Of The Rings*, although the subject matter is located elsewhere. One of the very few Zeppelin lyrics specifically to mention drugs, the song finds the singer walking through the park and being offered some pot by a bunch of hippies, whereupon the police show up and bust them. Plant once introduced the song on stage in America as "being caught in the park with wrong stuff in your cigarette papers". There has been much speculation that the inspiration came from a pro-cannabis rally in London's Hyde Park in July 1968 and/or an incident in Golden Gate Park, San Francisco.

24. Going To California

Recorded January–February 1971; available on Led Zeppelin IV

Robert Plant's admiration for Joni Mitchell knew no bounds, and it all flowed out on 'Going To California'. With Page contributing some deft acoustic guitar and Jones on mandolin, Plant sings about "a girl out there with love in her eyes and flowers in her hair" and there's no doubt who he had in mind. "When you're in love with Joni Mitchell, you've really got to write about it now and again", he noted. However, the song also references the darker side of West Coast existence, living on a fault line with the constant threat of earthquakes – indeed Page and Peter Grant experienced a minor tremor when mixing the album in LA. Stranded in the drab surroundings of the West Midlands, for Plant the hippie tribes who took over Haight-Ashbury in San Francisco in 1967 were "the children of the sun", and his wistful longing to join them received lyrical recognition here. His romantic attachment to the time never really left him, and four years after the so-called "Summer of Love", he introduced the song at a concert in Berkeley, California in 1971 by saying: "Here's to the days when things were really nice and simple and everything was far out, all the time".

25. When The Levee Breaks

Recorded January–February 1971; available on Led Zeppelin IV

In 1927, the Mississippi River burst its banks and flooded an area of 27,000 square miles. It was the worst flood disaster in American history, and in some places the flood waters were 30 feet deep and the swollen river was 60 miles wide. Two years later, the blues singer Memphis Minnie and her husband Kansas Joe McCoy recorded 'When The Levee Breaks', which described the events in graphic terms. Led Zeppelin's version is one of their most towering achievements. The performance is driven by Bonham's remorseless, bone-crunching backbeat, recorded in the hall at Headley Grange with a single microphone. Page contributes some slashing slide guitar, Plant blows a mean harp and the mixing desk adds phasing, backward loops and echo to create a terrifying maelstrom of sound.

Andy Fyfe, author of a fine book about the making of *Led Zeppelin IV*, credits the track with helping "to give rise to an entire genre of music" when rap DJs began cutting up Bonham's sledgehammer beat and grafting it onto endless hip-hop tracks. One of the most prominent was its use by producer Rick Rubin on 'Rhymin' & Stealin'', the opening track of The Beastie Boys' landmark 1986 album *Licensed To Ill*. 'When The Levee Breaks' has since become one of the two most sampled drum beats in musical history, alongside James Brown's 'Funky

Drummer'. According to Fyfe, "The simple fact is that without Bonham and 'When The Levee Breaks', there would be no hip-hop as we know it". Plant was amused by the track's use, noting: "When Jimmy and I talked about it, we figured nothing was sacred as we'd been nicking old blues stuff since the beginning of time". Certainly, there is a delicious irony that a group so often accused of stealing from the blues should years later be credited with having indirectly helped to toughen up a new genre of black American music.

26. The Song Remains The Same

Recorded summer 1972; available on *Houses of the Holy*

Originally conceived by Jimmy Page as an instrumental piece called simply 'The Overture', after Plant had added a lyric the song was given the working title 'The Campaign' before it eventually emerged as 'The Song Remains The Same'. The instrumental origins of the piece are evident in the fact that it's a minute and a half before Plant's vocal enters, more than a quarter of the way through the track. When his voice does arrive, his singing has been slightly speeded up. The overall effect is rather Beatlesque, with Page's shimmering, multi-tracked guitars displaying a strong Eastern flavour, of the kind often favoured by George Harrison. The lyric also makes the connection between East and West, from "California sunlight" to "sweet Calcutta rain" and from Hare Krishna to the Hoochie Coo.

27. The Rain Song

Recorded summer 1972; available on *Houses Of The Holy*

Despite the acoustic tracks on previous albums, the opening moments of 'The Rain Song' hardly sound like a Led Zeppelin song at all. There's a sweet, minor-key melody that might almost have come from the pen of Burt Bacharach, while the string arrangement (coaxed by Jones out of a mellotron) sounds as Shadwick puts it, "as if The Moody Blues had crashed the party". Some of Page's guitar work sounds tropical-Hawaiian, further emphasizing the easy-listening vibe. Yet at the same time, 'The Rain Song' is also extraordinarily beautiful, and evidence that Led Zeppelin still retained the capacity to surprise.

Whenever 'The Rain Song' was played by the band live, it invariably segued out of 'The Song Remains The Same', the song that also preceded it on the album, reinforcing the notion that Side One of *Houses of The Holy* was conceived as a suite of songs, rather than a series of unconnected individual compositions.

28. Over The Hills And Far Away

Recorded summer 1972; available on *Houses Of The Holy*

The third track on *Houses Of The Holy* also has musical themes and motifs in common with the tracks which precede it. The acoustic guitar opening recalls 'White Summer', the acoustic guitar showcase that Page had worked up in The Yardbirds. Then the song changes direction with a potent guitar and bass riff and Bonham is allowed to unleash his full battery for the first time on the album. The title offers the perfect vehicle for Plant to indulge his romantic fancies and there's a touch of Donovan about his lyrics as he sings of his wanderlust and a quest of discovery. Some fans have taken the line a "pocketful of gold" to refer to Acapulco Gold, a particularly fine strain of cannabis grown in Mexico which the band enjoyed smoking while on tour in America. Pot heads are prone to find unintended references to their drug of choice in all sorts of unintended places, but for once they may be right. Certainly the suggestion that Plant was simply talking about a love of money doesn't quite fit with the romantic yearnings expressed in the rest of the song.

29. Dancing Days

Recorded summer 1972; available on *Houses Of The Holy*

When Zeppelin listened to the playback of this song recorded at Mick Jagger's country home Stargroves, according to engineer Eddie Kramer they danced on the lawn in delight. It's easy to hear why with a joyous, summery tune that may have been inspired by something Page and Plant heard while in Bombay several months earlier. Its high spirits are blissfully unselfconscious with one of Plant's wittiest, most playful lyrics: "I told your mama I'd get you home but I didn't tell her I had no car" might have come from the pen of Chuck Berry himself. Keith Shadwick reckons the melody line is "disappointing" and the piece sounds

"uneasy" but is surely in a minority of one while the rest of us are out there on the grass gleefully dancing with the band to the most enjoyable track on the entire album.

30. No Quarter

Recorded summer 1972; available on *Houses Of The Holy*

John Paul Jones gets a rare, and deserved, lead namecheck in the credits for this atmospheric, keyboard-led piece which had first been tried at Headley Grange while the band were recording *Led Zeppelin IV*. With the tempo slowed down and the addition of synthesized bass, it took on a far more mysterious feel, emphasized by a heavily treated Plant vocal. Jones' piano is stark almost to the point of austere, but it fits the mood perfectly and leads into a superb, jazzy solo from Page – or rather two solos, which offer answering phrases from different channels. The lyrics find Plant at his most oblique. The references to the "winds of Thor" hark back to 'Immigrant Song', while "walking side by side with death, the devil mocks their every step" might have come from some ghastly death metal band. No matter, for it's still one of the album's highlights, and the track became a live favourite and was featured as a marathon Jones showcase at every show from 1973 through to Knebworth in 1979.

You can understand why it rankled with Jones when Page and Plant used the title of one of his finest compositional moments in the band for their 1994 reunion *Unledded* album, without even telling him they were getting back together, let alone inviting him to join them.

31. The Ocean

Recorded summer 1972; available on *Houses Of The Holy*

One of Page's most virile riffs opens the final song on *Houses Of The Holy* after Bonham's voice has introduced the track by saying: "We've done four already but now we're steady, and then they went…one, two, three, four". However, overall the kick feels oddly restrained, as did much of the material recorded at Stargroves, leading some to suggest that Jagger's house was simply not suited to record the band to best effect. Towards the end of the track, the mood and tempo changes completely, with a doo-wop chorus as Plant declares "So good!" Elsewhere, the track alternates effectively between vocal and non-vocal passages, with a lyric that makes an analogy between the ocean and the sea of faces in the audience at a Zeppelin concert. He ends up, however, singing not to the band's fans but to his three-year-old daughter Carmen, "the girl who won my heart". It was another riff that The Beastie Boys chose to sample, this time on 'She's Crafty' also on their *Licensed To Ill* album.

32. Custard Pie

Recorded summer 1974; available on *Physical Graffiti*

The title suggests more knockabout nonsense in the vein of 'D'yer Mak 'er' and 'The Crunge', but the opening track on *Physical Graffiti* might almost have come from Zeppelin's debut album, and after the underachievement of *Houses Of The Holy*, the band could hardly have devised a more forceful way of announcing that it was business as usual once again. A killer Page riff warped

and twisted out of a Bo Diddley beat is swiftly joined by some brutal Bonham drumming and it hardly seems mere coincidence that, as soon as they were back at Headley Grange, Zeppelin suddenly sounded heavier and more like their old selves again. A more contemporary mid-1970s feel comes from Jones' use of a clavinet, as popularized by Stevie Wonder, and Page's delivery of a piercing solo through an ARP synthesizer, while Plant delves back to Bukka White's 'Shake 'Em On Down' for his lyrical inspiration, although his vocals sound more strained than back in '68–'69 and clearly display the wearing and tearing of endless touring and screaming. Yet, the effect is not entirely detrimental, adding a more mature, world-weary tone in keeping with Zeppelin's new-found status as elder statesmen of rock – Plant was now all of 27 years old, after all.

33. In My Time Of Dying

Recorded summer 1974; available on *Physical Graffiti*

Standing alongside 'When The Levee Breaks' as one of Zeppelin's most monumental transformations of a pre-war acoustic blues song into an electric tumult, 'In My Time Of Dying' was first recorded by Blind Willie Johnson in 1927 as 'Jesus Make Up My Dying Bed' and was later popularized by Bob Dylan on his debut album under the title used on *Physical Graffiti*. The performance is Zeppelin at their most intense, Bonham creating a train-like backbeat, Page riffing furiously and articulating some glorious slide guitar and Plant delivering one of his best, beseeching blues vocals with plenty of spontaneous improvisation. At eleven minutes plus, it is arguably overlong and yet it doesn't feel so while listening. When it does finally conclude, Bonham is heard coughing and saying, "That's got to be the one, hasn't it?" The reason for including the studio chatter, according to Page, was to show the world that Zeppelin weren't remote rock gods but a working band.

34. Trampled Under Foot

Recorded summer 1974; available on *Physical Graffiti*

Most agree that Zeppelin's first attempt at a James Brown-style funk riff on 'The Crunge' was a failure, not least because it was conceived as a joke and ended up sounding like a pastiche or, even worse, a piss-take of black music. 'Trampled Under Foot' is a much more serious and successful visitation of similar territory. Jones opens proceedings with the clavinet and Page's guitar riff makes innovative use of backwards echo and wah-wah. Jones returns halfway through with a thrillingly funky keyboard solo that paints Zeppelin as disco dance-floor kings. Page's vocal is slightly too far back in the mix on a lyric that makes a connection familiar in blues poetry between a motor car and the sexual act and for which Robert Johnson's 'Terraplane Blues' may have been the model. Zeppelin at their most urgent and irresistible.

35. Kashmir

Recorded summer 1974; available on *Physical Graffiti*

In addition to their attempt at recording in India in 1972, Page and Plant were regular visitors to Morocco and their fascination with Arabic and Asian music reached its apogee on the mighty 'Kashmir'. "Kashmir from my angle was written on the road to Tan-Tan in southern Morocco, just off the Atlantic coast", Plant revealed almost 30 years later. "It's a place where your mind can really dance and where your imagination is way open. After a while all the stuff you've ever thought about has gone and you've got this whole different view".

Originally titled 'Driving To Kashmir', the music came out of a jam between Page and Bonham in late 1973 which, according to Peter Grant, the band didn't like because it was "a bit of a dirge". As a result, they decided to add the Eastern strings and found the players in a Pakistani orchestra in Southall, West London. With its use of Byzantine signatures and motifs not normally found in standard Western scales, there's a sense of mystery and ominous tension that is sustained throughout its eight-and-a-half minutes. That there is little variety in its orchestration or dynamics is exactly what makes it work, the repetition allowing it to build almost imperceptibly. It's an approach common in Eastern music but quite radical in rock'n'roll, and the result is one of the most startling and majestic tracks Led Zeppelin ever recorded. Unsurprisingly, it was a highlight of every Led Zeppelin live show from 1975 until the band's demise in 1980 and was an obvious candidate for reinvention on 1994's *No Quarter*, the *Unledded* album. In 1998 Puff Daddy sampled the track on 'Come With Me' and performed it on *Saturday Night Live* with Page on guitar via satellite link. "It was a real privilege working with him. He has incredible energy and a great imagination", he reported.

36. In The Light

Recorded summer 1974; available on *Physical Graffiti*

Originally called 'In The Morning', Page at one time cited this as his favourite track on *Physical Graffiti*, whih is some accolade, as he has also said that the album is his favourite in the entire Led Zeppelin canon. Jones takes much of the credit and his drone-like keyboards summon up a similar Eastern vibe to 'Kashmir'. This time, though, the mood of the intro is gentler and more specifically Indian, evoking echoes of some of George Harrison's similarly-styled compositions for The Beatles, such as 'Within You Without You' and 'The Inner Light'. After three minutes, however, the tempo changes, and Page's guitar introduces a blues-tinged riff, for which Jones also takes much of the credit. "You can always tell my riffs from Page's because mine have got a lot more notes and are linear", he reckons. "His are chunkier and chordier. Anything with chromatic movement would be mine". Plant's lyrics also draw inspiration from Harrison's portfolio of Indian mysticism ("in the light you will find the road") and Page essays a ringing, melodic guitar solo over a lovely descending bass line. The entire piece is marginally longer than 'Kashmir', but never outstays its welcome.

37. The Wanton Song

Recorded early 1974; available on *Physical Graffiti*

The Oxford English Dictionary defines wanton as: "licentious; lewd; sexually promiscuous" – all qualities associated in abundance with Led Zeppelin's on-the-road behaviour. Robert Plant has often protested that such stories have been overcooked, but in this lyric he blatantly celebrates wanton sex and the ability to lose one's senses in pure carnality. Musically the track thrusts and grinds suitably with another dynamite Page riff with a machine-gun repeat. The bridge then takes off in another direction completely and a set of unusual chords on which Page's guitar sounds slightly out of tune – an effect that is presumably deliberate.

Oddly, although it was played live on a handful of opening dates on their 1975 American tour, it was swiftly dropped. Was the song not working or had Plant had an earful from his wife for singing lyrics about ladies of the night taking the seed from his shaking frame? Only the singer himself knows.

38. Black Country Woman

Recorded summer 1972; available on *Physical Graffiti*

The "Black Country" is defined as the industrial region to the west of Birmingham in the British Midlands, so named in the mid-nineteenth century for the smoke from its foundries and forges and abundance of coal. Its environs were well known to both Plant and Bonham as the place where they had grown up and, although they moved to its more green and pleasant parts, both continued to live in the region.

Originally, the song was subtitled 'Never Ending Doubting Woman Blues', after a line at the end which was eventually left off the released version. Plant's lyric uses classic Delta blues phraseology ("hey hey mama, why you treat me mean") and transfers them to the West Midlands. Is he addressing his wife, Maureen? If so the line "I know your sisters, too" is playing with fire, given that the singer was also said to be sweet on his wife's younger sibling, Shirley.

The song itself is an enjoyable acoustic stomp in the style of 1930s Delta stars The Mississippi Sheikhs and was recorded in the garden of Mick Jagger's Stargroves home in 1972 during the *Houses Of The Holy* sessions. At the commencement of the track an aircraft flies overhead and the band can be heard debating whether to leave the sound in or not.

39. Sick Again

Recorded summer 1974; available on *Physical Graffiti*

Physical Graffiti ends as it began – with a swagger. 'Sick Again' finds Plant revisiting the subject matter of 'The Wanton Song' but with palpable distaste as he sings about the increasingly juvenile groupies who flung themselves at the band, particularly in Los Angeles, derided here as "the city of lies". That the girls are under age is made clear when Plant sings: "One day soon you're gonna reach sixteen". The singer elaborated in an interview in *Rolling Stone*: "It you listen to 'Sick Again' the words show I feel a bit sorry for them – 'clutching pages from your teenage dream in the lobby of the Hotel Paradise, through the circus of the LA queens, how fast you learn the downhill slide'. One minute she's twelve,

and the next minute she's thirteen and over the top. Such a shame".

The track is given a heavy blues-rock muscularity with some battering percussion from Bonham, and Page laying down a dense mesh of guitars. At the end the drummer can be heard coughing, symbolic, no doubt, of the sicknesses and diseases that can so easily be picked up on the road.

40. Achilles Last Stand

Recorded November–December 1975; available on *Presence*

In Homer's *Iliad*, Achilles was the mightiest of the Greek heroes who fought in the Trojan War. After being dipped in the sacred waters of the River Styx he was meant to be invincible, but his heel remained dry and therefore was his one vulnerable spot. This fatal chink eventually led to his death when an arrow wounded him in the heel. The story had an obvious attraction to Plant following his broken legs and damaged ankle following his car crash in Greece in 1975, hence the song's title. But work had begun on the piece prior to the accident, when Page and Plant visited Morocco together in the summer of 1975 immediately following the Earl's Court shows, and the lyrics reflect upon that trip and their plight as tax exiles.

At more than ten minutes long it's a magnificent epic with which to announce their return after so much adversity and, as a sonic journey, it invites inevitable comparisons with 'Kashmir' on the previous studio album. The opening riff is complex and urgent and, as the piece develops, you're struck by the thought that this is as near as Zeppelin ever got to the "prog-rock" of bands such as Yes and Emerson, Lake and Palmer. Yet there's nothing flabby or indulgent: everything is taut and intense, and the cauldron is kept close to the boil. The track also features some of Page's most inventive guitar playing, which he overdubbed in a single night. "I wanted to give each section its own identity and I think it came off really good", he reported, and suggested that as a personal milestone the track's first guitar showcase was on a par with the solo in 'Stairway To Heaven'.

41. For Your Life

Recorded November–December 1975; available on *Presence*

Built around a grinding stop-start riff, Plant sings of his discontent with the rock-star lifestyle ("a cry for mercy in the city of the damned"), although he has also suggested that lines such as "wanna find myself a crystal, payin' through the nose" were inspired by the plight of a friend mired in the Los Angeles drug scene. The song was worked up by Page and Plant when they convened in Malibu following his accident, and offers eloquent evidence of the unease and disillusionment that would come to characterize his final years in Led Zeppelin. 'For Your Life' was surely one of the tracks he was thinking about when he said that *Presence* contained "some of the hottest moments Led Zeppelin ever had – agitated, uncomfortable, druggy, pained".

42. Royal Orleans

Recorded November–December 1975; available on *Presence*

One of the problems of rock stars is that they can become so cocooned from real life that all they are left to sing about is the artificial life that is a rock star's fate or reward, depending on which way you look at it. Bill Wyman has likened it to living in a fishbowl. Led Zeppelin never fell totally into the trap, but their epic, on-the-road adventures in America inspired several songs and 'Royal Orleans' is one of them.

Named after the hotel in New Orleans where the band habitually stayed when playing in the city, the lyric recounts an incident in which John Paul Jones allegedly took a transvestite up to his room, thinking he was a she. The line "And when the sun peeked through, John Cameron with Suzanna, he kissed the whiskers, left and right" only conceals Jones' identity with the flimsiest of veils: John Cameron was an old studio friend and rival from his pre-Zeppelin days. The song further jokes about waking up with a "New Orleans queen" with a voice as deep as Barry White's.

The only song on *Presence* credited to all four members, Plant allegedly set out to poke fun at his colleague in jovial revenge for an interview in which Jones had suggested the vocals were the least important part of the band's music. Bolstered by a spirited funk rhythm reminiscent of 'The Crunge', it's one of the more light-hearted moments on an album that for the most part was inspired by the band's trials and tribulations.

43. Nobody's Fault But Mine

Recorded November–December 1975; available on *Presence*

Like 'In My Time Of Dyin'' on *Physical Graffiti*,' Nobody's Fault But Mine' was written by Blind Willie Johnson. The original was a stark, gospel-influenced number which depicted a man confessing his sins and looking for deliverance, and it was obvious that Plant in his post-accident plight identified strongly with the song's sentiments. The singer embellished the lyrics with a few lines of his own about "got a monkey on my back" but that hardly excused leaving Johnson's name off the writing credit. Many years later, Page offered this explanation: "The arrangement I came up with had nothing to do with the original. Robert may have wanted to go for the original lyrics but everything else was a total different kettle of fish".

Up to a point. Certainly, Johnson would not have recognized the blistering, *blitzkrieg* of the band's sonic attack, but he would certainly have known the tune as his own. As they had credited Memphis Minnie for 'When The Levee Breaks', it made little sense to deny Johnson's authorship here, a fact Plant seemed to acknowledge when he sometimes credited the song to Johnson on stage. The controversial credits apart, it's another monumental Zeppelin blues performance, with some of Plant's best harmonica playing ever heard on record.

44. In The Evening

Recorded November–December 1978; available on *In Through The Out Door*

After two years away and all the rumours that they were breaking up following the death of Plant's son, Zeppelin announced their return with an opening track of emphatic pedigree. The gentle opening swirl of Eastern sounds produced by Page's violin bow is mere camouflage. After Plant has sung the song's title a minute into the track, Page breaks into a swaggering, cascading riff that is his most impressive contribution on an album otherwise dominated by Jones and Plant – and which the guitarist later complained was too "soft" for his taste.

The lyrics are ostensibly addressed to a woman, but the girl who "don't come" and shows "no pity" could well be the fickle mistress that is fortune, as Plant goes on to bemoan "bad luck and trouble" and notes that although it's lonely at the bottom, it's dizzy at the top – a reality that he had been forced to find out the hardest way of all.

45. Fool In The Rain

Recorded November–December 1978; available on *In Through The Out Door*

One of the most unusual songs in the Zeppelin canon was inspired by a samba tune that caught the fancy of Jones and Plant when used as a TV theme during the 1978 Football World Cup in Argentina. Jones contributes some convincing Latin keyboards and Bonham proves a surprisingly dab hand at some tricky and complex Afro-Cuban poly-rhythms. Page's untypically meandering guitar solo is the track's only weakness, but Plant sounds fresh and optimistic on a lyric that talks of the redemptive power of love, even if – as usual – its course doesn't quite run smoothly.

46. Carouselambra

Recorded November–December 1978; available on *In Through The Out Door*

Conceived as the album's "epic", 'Carouselambra' is an ambitious but less than totally satisfying piece. The main problem lies in Jones's over-dominant keyboards, which sound dangerously close to something Rick Wakeman might have come up with. Page unfurls the famous double-necked Gibson but the jabbing, high-pitched organ riff won't go away and gets increasingly irritating. The second section is far better as Page essays a slow, moody theme marked by heavy guitar effects, but the good work is undone when the third section finds Jones' keyboards back with a new but even more irritating motif. Plant's poetic lyrics are fascinating, telling an allegorical tale that mirrors his recent experience, although his vocals are recessed too far back in the mix.

"The whole story of Led Zeppelin in its later years is in that song and I can't hear the words", he later complained. Most agree that ultimately 'Carouselambra' is an opportunity missed: it could and should have

been the album's highpoint but sadly punches considerably below its weight. Had the drug-ravaged Page been in full control he surely would have checked some of Jones' organ excesses and the track might easily have taken its place alongside the likes of 'Kashmir' and 'Achilles' Last Stand' among Zeppelin's greatest epic achievements.

47. We're Gonna Groove

Recorded June 1969; available on *Coda*

For a posthumous, contract-fulfilling miscellany of odds and sods, there was some remarkably potent material on *Coda* from different stages of the band's career that, far from sounding like inferior out-takes, was in several cases as strong as many of the tracks that were released at the time. Among them was 'We're Gonna Groove'.

Recorded in June 1969, it would in no way have lowered the quality of *Led Zeppelin II* and would surely have improved Side Two of the album had it been included at the expense of 'Livin' Lovin' Maid', 'Moby Dick' or 'Bring It On Home'. The quality of the track is underlined by the fact that the band used the song as a set opener throughout the first half of 1970. Quite why it failed to make the cut at time remains a mystery. The version that surfaced on *Coda* is the original 1969 recording with the addition of some sub-octivider guitar effects added by Page at his Sol studio in early 1982.

48. Poor Tom

Recorded June 1970; available on *Coda*

Another legacy of Page and Plant's productive stay at the cottage in Bron-yr-aur to write the material for *Led Zeppelin III*, the only reason 'Poor Tom' was not included on that album at the time was that it would have been an acoustic track too far. Cut from similar cloth as 'Bron-y-aur Stomp', 'Gallows Pole' and 'Hats Off To (Roy) Harper', the song loses nothing in comparison, with some great Plant harmonica work and a slightly over-booming but insistent shuffle from Bonham. The lyric is based on the *crime passionnel* tradition of American folk ballads, along the lines of 'Delia's Gone' (recorded by Johnny Cash and Bob Dylan among others) or 'Frankie and Johnny'.

49. Walter's Walk

Recorded May 1972; available on *Coda*

Had 'Walter's Walk' appeared on *Houses Of The Holy*, for which it was originally recorded, it would arguably have been the best track on the album, and certainly the heaviest. There's none of the clever crispness here that characterized that album, just urgent and dense guitar riffs from Page, a classic Plant vocal (even if the lyric doesn't seem to go anywhere) and sheer, animal ferocity on the drums even by Bonham's violent standards. Who Walter was is unrecorded: perhaps the band simply liked the alliteration and "Percy's Perambulation" didn't quite fit. Why it didn't make the album at the time is another mys-

tery, for the band clearly had some affection for the song, using it as part of the 'Dazed and Confused' medley during the 1972 tour, in which form it can also be heard on the live album *How The West Was Won*.

50. Wearing And Tearing

Recorded November 1978; available on *Coda*

In which Led Zeppelin play at being The Damned – or something similar, for Plant has often claimed that this track was Zeppelin's direct response to the Punk revolution. "Listen to 'Wearing And Tearing' on *Coda*", he claimed in 2005. "That was our contribution to the whole thing, saying 'yes, you've got it right'". Certainly the breakneck pace could have had them pogoing up and down at the 100 Club, although it's hard to imagine any three-chord punk guitar merchant keeping up with the manic speed and precision of Page's hell-for-leather licks. Plant effects a vibrant Punk shout but never quite masters the crucial sneer.

The track was intended for release as a single or EP aimed at the Knebworth audience in 1979, and there was even talk of issuing it under the name of a fake band so it would not be judged as a Zeppelin track, but could then compete against the Punk bands on a level playing field. In the end, that never happened but it's fascinating to wonder what the reaction might have been had 'Wearing And Tearing' been slipped out clandestinely on an indie label under the name of the Nobs, or some such. Frankly, it makes The Clash sound like Freddie and the Dreamers.

Part Three:
Zeppology

*"How on earth do you follow
Led Zeppelin?"*

Peter Grant, 1995

Zep Co-Conspirators

No band can stand on its own, and if a band becomes as big as Led Zeppelin then, in addition to an infrastructure of expert background fixers, the band also leaves a giant footprint of influence, adulation, imitation and, Sometimes, vilification. Nevertheless, attaching your name to the phenomenon which was Zeppelin in full flight, always had, and still retains, a powerful calling card.

Peter Grant

Top of the list has to be Peter Grant, who is covered in depth in Chapter 1.

Terry Reid

Jimmy Page's first choice as Led Zeppelin's singer, Terry Reid has entered rock history as the man who recommended Robert Plant for the job instead. Yet, if Reid has ever regretted his decision, he's never let it show. "People say I'm the unluckiest man in rock but it doesn't feel like that", he told this writer in 2004. "In fact, I think I've been extraordinarily lucky throughout my career".

Yet it's hard not to see Reid as one of rock'n'roll's most cruelly ill-starred "nearly" men. Born in 1949, he was a teenage prodigy and at the age of 16 his band The Jaywalkers were supporting The Rolling Stones. His first two solo albums were produced by Mickie Most, and although they showcase his soulful voice well enough, the cheap pop production today makes them sound very dated. "I have to say that Mickie Most's conservatism held me back on those albums. He'd made these great records with The Animals and Donovan but then music started to evolve and he didn't move with it. I'd want to try new stuff and he wouldn't go to the next page", Reid recalls. "Then I got friendly with Jimmy Page, who Mickie wanted nothing to do with. Jimmy asked me to be the singer in Led Zeppelin but I'd just done a deal to support the Stones on their first US tour in three years". According to the singer's account, he told Page that he was prepared to join, but that they would have to compensate him for what he would have lost by not doing the Stones tour. Whether this was a serious offer is not clear but, in any case, he also recommended his mate Robert Plant – and that was that. Notably, he was also approached by Deep Purple but turned them down, too.

While Led Zeppelin set about conquering the world, Reid's career stalled and he was silenced for two years by a legal dispute over contracts. By 1971 he had grown fed up with the UK and moved to Los Angeles. Two years later he made the album *River*, a semi-acoustic set on which he came across like a cross between a blue-eyed soul singer and the jazz-folk stylings of John Martyn. Today the album is regarded by the cognoscenti as a five-star classic, but Warner's hated it. "When I handed in *River* they said I'd made a jazz album and they wanted a rock'n'roll record", Reid says. "So they paid me $20,000 to go away and didn't get behind it. But I loved that record. It was the first time I got to do what I wanted to do". Which is, of course, what Van Morrison had done on *Astral Weeks* (which flew, interestingly, on Warner Brothers) and Nick Drake did on *Pink Moon* (which didn't).

A handful of further albums followed at sporadic intervals on different labels, the last studio release being 1991's *The Driver*. Today, Reid spends his time playing bars in LA, his sets regularly enlivened by guest appearances from passing rock legends. "I play every Monday night at The Joint in Beverley Hills", he reported a couple of years ago. "When Robert Plant dropped by we did 'Season Of The Witch', which he said he'd always wanted to sing with me. Keith Richards has been down a couple of times and when Roger Daltrey turned up we did 'Stand By Me'".

Nevertheless, Reid re-entered the Led Zeppelin story around 1971, when Richard Cole was managing a West Coast tour for Reid and The Moody Blues. When in Seattle, Cole was recommended the shark-fishing delights of the Edgewater Inn, which became Led Zeppelin's regular hotel of choice when in the city, and was the scene of one of their most notorious debauches – according to Cole.

After several years in The Jaywalkers, Terry Reid went solo, supoporting several major acts including the Stones, Jethro Tull and Fleetwood Mac

Roy Harper

Famously commemorated on *Led Zeppelin III* in 'Hats Off To (Roy) Harper', the idiosyncratic English singer-songwriter became one of Led Zeppelin's closest friends during the 1970s, both making music with members of the band and raising hell with them too.

Born in Manchester, England in 1941, Harper led a colourful early life that included running away to join the Royal Air Force at 15 and then feigning insanity to earn a discharge, followed by spells in jail, in a mental institution and bumming around Europe as a busker. He released his debut album *The Sophisticated Beggar* in 1966 and followed with a series of albums full of uncompromising songs with titles such as 'I Hate The White Man'.

Jimmy Page says he was first drawn to Harper's work because he stood by his principles and refused to bow to commercial pressures. "As far as I'm concerned, hats off to anybody who does what they think is right and refuses to sell out", he noted – hence the Bukka White blues song 'Shake 'Em On Down' on *Led Zeppelin III* being given the otherwise unconnected title, 'Hats Off To (Roy) Harper'. "They showed me this album sleeve and I said 'very nice' and handed it back", Harper recalls. "'No, go on – look again' they said, and then I saw this song 'Hats Off To Harper'. To be honest, it's been more of a burden than anything. A hell of a thing to live up to".

Credited as "S. Flavius Mercurius", Page played on Harper's critically acclaimed 1971 album *Stormcock*. Harper frequently attended Zeppelin gigs and toured as part of the band's entourage in America in 1973, when he was granted favoured person status by Page and Plant – much to the annoyance of some of Zeppelin's road crew, who found him self-obsessed and too full of his own importance. "Fucked if I know why they loved him so. He was just a pain in the ass to me", road manager Richard Cole later observed. Harper was also a famous hellraiser in his time: Robert Plant recalls the two of them one night in the mid-1970s getting "banned for life" from the London club The Speakeasy, although he cannot remember the exact nature of the bad behaviour that resulted in such extreme punishment.

Surprisingly, Harper did not sign up to Zeppelin's Swan Song label but he did contribute sleeve photography to *Physical Graffiti* and appeared uncredited in the 1976 film, *The Song Remains The Same*. Zeppelin weren't his only admirers in the higher echelons of the rock world, and Pink Floyd asked him to sing

Famously curmudgeonly, Harper was a long-standing friend of the band, and his appearance at practically every British festival of note over the last 40 years provided a direct link to their audience

lead vocals on the song 'Have A Cigar' on their 1975 album, *Wish You Were Here*. The band's guitarist David Gilmour appeared on Harper's next album, *HQ*, which also featured John Paul Jones.

After Led Zeppelin broke up, Page toured with Harper in 1984, playing acoustic sets at folk festivals under various guises such as The MacGregors, and Themselves. The following year they released the joint album *Whatever Happened To Jugula?* The live album, *In Between Every Line*, also contained recordings from their joint performance at the 1984 Cambridge Folk Festival. Harper has continued to record and enjoy a cult status and Page and Plant, who remain close friends, both performed at his 60th birthday concert at London's Albert Hall in June 2001.

Richard Cole

A handful of rock managers, such as Brian Epstein and Peter Grant, become famous in their own right but it's almost unprecedented for a humble roadie to become a celebrity (although the Grateful Dead's "Ramrod" earned an obituary in *The Times* in 2006). Not that there was much that was humble about Richard Cole, whose notoriety as Led Zeppelin's road manager is due to his central role in organizing the sex and drugs to accompany the rock'n'roll on the band's infamously debauched tours of America, though much of this was due to the salacious book he wrote describing those experiences when he was

short of cash in the early 1990s. Cole's eventual downfall was due to the fact that he not only organized the debauchery for his employers to enjoy; he was frequently its most enthusiastic participant, and he ended up with an out-of-control heroin habit which forced Grant to sack him in 1980.

Born in North London on 2 January 1946, after a spell as a teenage boxer Cole got his first job in the music industry in 1965 road-managing the pop band Unit 4 Plus 2. He went on to run tours of America for The Who and The New Vaudeville Band (who were managed by Peter Grant) and, in 1967, moved to America to work for Vanilla Fudge as a sound engineer. He continued his association with Grant when he road-managed The Yardbirds' tour of America in 1968, during which time he got to know Jimmy Page well. This put him in poll position when Led Zeppelin formed later that year, and he remained the band's road manager almost until the end, working with them on every tour bar their final 1980 European jaunt.

Cole's name is littered throughout this book for he was ubiquitous as the band's ultimate "gofer" and there's no doubt that he was brilliant at his job – at least when he was (relatively) straight and sober. When Plant and his wife had their car crash in Greece, it was Cole who organized their evacuation. When the singer received the news on tour in New Orleans that his five-year-old son Karac had died, Cole was the first person he told and who then took charge of all the arrangements. Such close bonds transcended a mere employer-staff relationship. On the other hand, his influence had its malign side, for there are those who blame him for encouraging Bonham's alcohol-fuelled rampages and for introducing Jimmy Page to heroin. Arguably, both would have happened anyway, but instead of seeking to curb such destructiveness, Cole was there egging them on.

After he was sacked from Zeppelin's 1980 tour, Grant sent him to a rehabilitation clinic in Italy. The day after he had arrived, Cole was arrested as a terrorist on suspicion of blowing up Bologna railway station and spent long weeks in prison before the Italian police accepted his innocence. He was still in prison when he was given the news that John Bonham had died.

Cole stopped using drugs in the early 1980s and in his book, *Stairway To Heaven,* he wrote that he had given up alcohol in 1986 ,too. He continued to work in the music industry, serving as the tour manager for Eric Clapton, Black Sabbath, Lita Ford, Ozzy Osborne and Three Dog Night, The Gipsy Kings, Crazy Town and Fu Manchu.

The former members of Led Zeppelin undoubtedly felt betrayed when he sold his story to the author Stephen Davis in the sensationalist *Hammer Of The Gods,* although Cole claimed he was paid just $1,250 for his revelations, and so rejects charges of "cashing in". But he then wrote his own book, *Stairway to Heaven: Led Zeppelin Uncensored,* ghosted by Richard Trubo. Today he is said to be a sta-ble family man who divides his time between homes in California and London, grateful to have been there to witness the Zeppelin maelstrom up close and personal – but even more grateful to have survived it.

The Zep Road Crew

In addition to Richard Cole, Led Zeppelin were served by a loyal and tight-knit road crew over the years who tended to the band's every need – on stage and off. They were also often credited with having been the instigators of much of the riotous behaviour associated with the band on tour.

Clive Coulson had sung in a band called Mecca in the 1960s and was part of Zeppelin's road crew from the outset. He was one of the roadies who went with Page and Plant to Bron-yr-aur when they wrote *Led Zeppelin III* in the Welsh cottage. He later road-managed Bad Company and died in January 2006.

Kenny Pickett was a member of cult-1960s band The Creation, whose Eddie Phillips played the guitar with a violin bow before Jimmy Page took up the trick; Pickett was a member of Zeppelin's road crew on their early American tours but left for a career in writing jingles and novelty pop songs, penning the 1971 children's favourite 'Grandad' for Clive Dunn. He died in 1997.

Other early road crew members included Joe Jammer, who was Page's guitar tech and went on to form his own band, Henry "The Horse" Smith and Sandy MacGregor.

Into the 1970s, the crew included Raymond Thomas and Tim Marten, who both worked as guitar technicians for Page; Brian Condliffe, who looked after John Paul Jones' instrumental requirements; Benji Le Fevre who was Plant's assistant; and Mick Hinton, who was not so much Bonham's drum technician as his partner in all manner of crimes.

Other notable staff included Rex King, Bonham's assistant from 1977-80 who later road-managed Page and Plant's reunion tour in the mid-1990s, and the notorious John Bindon who, controversially, went on the road as the band's head of security in 1977. A former actor, whose bit parts in various films including Nic Roeg and Douglas Cammell's *Performance* (1970), Mike Hodges' *Get Carter* (1971), and Franc Roddam's *Quadrophenia* (1979) usually found him playing violent gangsters, his on-screen casting was not too far removed from his other existence as a heavy in the London underworld and a (self-confessed) associate of the Kray Brothers. He was responsible for much backstage violence during Zeppelin's tour and was one of those given a suspended prison sentence for the beating of a security man working for promoter Bill Graham during the band's final American appearance at the Oakland Coliseum in 1977. He was subsequently sacked by Peter Grant, who admitted that hiring him had been the biggest mistake he ever made as manager. This judgement was confirmed when Bindon stabbed someone to death during a knife fight in London in 1978. He fled to Ireland and was acquitted at the Old Bailey after pleading self-defence, claiming he was in fear of his life and was being blackmailed over a drug deal that had gone wrong. During the 1980s, he fell into heroin addiction and he died from AIDS in 1993. For reasons best known only to Morrissey, the former Smiths singer chose to commemorate him on the sleeve of his album *Maladjusted* with the dedication: "John Bindon 1943–1993".

Jason Bonham

Jason Bonham's first public appearance can be seen in the Led Zeppelin movie, *The Song Remains The Same*, playing a mini drum kit while his father, John Bonham, looks on proudly. Born on 13 July 1966, he later recalled how he would be asked as a boy to perform for famous house guests: "Sometimes I would be woken up at two o'clock in the morning to come down and play that scaled-down kit. Robert Plant, Jimmy Page, Jeff Beck, members of Yes, Bad Company, and Emerson, Lake and Palmer would often drop by our house after shows in the area and a major party would follow. After being woken up for a few of these nocturnal performances, I was able to negotiate my first fee, a much needed day off school".

He joined his first band when he was 17, and in 1985 joined Virginia Wolf, recording two albums with them and touring America supporting The Firm. In 1987, he joined Jimmy Page for his *Outrider* album and tour the following year, and drummed with the three surviving members of Led Zeppelin at the reunion for Atlantic Records' 40th anniversary concert in New York. The band were highly self-critical of their performance but all concurred that Bonham had acquitted himself with great credit. The next time Page, Plant and Jones played together was at Bonham's wedding reception in 1990.

Jason Bonham followed in his father's footsteps as an accomplished drummer and *bon viveur* – although that's only toothpaste

His first solo album, *The Disregard Of Timekeeping* appeared in 1989 and included the minor hit single 'Wait For You'. A second solo album, *Mad Hatter,* followed in 1992, before he formed the band Motherland, releasing the 1994 album, *Peace 4 Me.*

In 1995, he again played with Page, Plant and Jones when he represented his father at Led Zeppelin's induction into the Rock and Roll Hall of Fame. His next project was an album called *In The Name Of My Father: The Zepset*, which found him playing Zeppelin songs such as 'Communication Breakdown', 'The Song Remains The Same', 'Ten Years Gone' and 'Since I've Been Loving You'. He later drummed with the band Healing Sixes and recorded and toured with Debbie Bonham, his father's younger sister.

Tony Thompson

After John Bonham's death Led Zeppelin have only ever once seriously contemplated reforming – and when they did, the man they asked to replace their deceased drummer was Tony Thompson. Born in 1954 of Antiguan descent, Thompson began his career on the New York session scene before becoming a founder member of disco pioneers Chic, playing on hits such as 'Le Freak' and 'Good Times'. After Chic disbanded in 1983, Thompson was much in demand as a session drummer, playing on records by Madonna, Rod Stewart, Mick Jagger and David Bowie.

He also became a member of Power Station, along with Robert Palmer and John and Andy Taylor from Duran Duran. Power Station played the American leg of *Live Aid* in 1985, and he was drafted in alongside Phil Collins to provide a double drum attack during Led Zeppelin's performance. The following year, Page, Plant and Jones invited Thompson to join them in a putative full-scale Led Zeppelin reunion. However, after the first rehearsal, he was seriously injured in a car accident and his unavailability effectively put an end to the reunion plan. He died of cancer in November 2003.

Bill Curbishley

As the manager of both Robert Plant and Jimmy Page, Bill Curbishley played a key role in bringing the two former Zeppelin giants back together in the mid-1990s. Curbishley started his career in the music business at Track Records in the late 1960s, working with bands such as The Crazy World of Arthur Brown, Thunderclap Newman and The Who. When Track dissolved in 1974, he set up his own company, Trinifold, and took over The Who's management.

With Peter Grant having retired, in 1986 Curbishley took on Robert Plant's solo management. In 1994 he added Jimmy Page to his roster of clients and set about effecting their reunion. "I encouraged it because I really felt it was a tragedy that these two guys who had written one of the best catalogues of songs in rock'n'roll history weren't together", he later said. "Robert wasn't unwilling to work with Page; he was unwilling to work with Led Zeppelin, because he didn't want to take a backwards step. Every time he worked with a band or a unit, it became quite apparent to me that he was trying to turn the guitarist into another Jimmy Page. In the end I said to him: 'Look, you can work with Jimmy without being Led Zeppelin. Besides, you two write all the songs, so there's no reason why you can't play them'".

His pride in bringing them back together was evident in an interview he gave in 1999: "On a personal level, I think they both walk with a lighter step now", he said. "The fact that they got back together and started playing again unloaded a lot of shit and that's been very important to them. I think they came out of it with a wealth that was way beyond materialistic. It has equally benefited

them spiritually and they are both better people for it". However, Curbishley's professional relationship with Page did not survive when the singer and the guitarist fell out again after Plant pulled the plug on further joint touring at the end of 1998. He no longer manages Page, although he still manages Plant and was instrumental in coaxing him back from his late-1990s pub rock anonymity with the Priory Of Brion and into the studio with Strange Sensation. Trinifold's other clients at the time of writing included Judas Priest and UB40, and the company has also branched out into film production.

Curbishley's younger brother Alan is the manager of West Ham United football club and among all the photographs of Trinifold's famous rock star clients in his office in Camden, pride of place is given to a photograph of him at a football function with his brother and Manchester United supremo Sir Alex Ferguson.

Frank Zappa

Not the most obvious choice of "co-conspirator" maybe; but, in addition to a telling tribute to 'Stairway to Heaven' (see Tributes) which, musically at least, seems not too ironic (despite rendering Page's guitar chords through the brass section, which formed part of his last live band touring set), Zappa earlier managed to inadvertently boost Zeppelin's notoriety into the stratosphere. While, as so often, casting his jaded eye over the contemporary "pop

Frank Zappa, gifted muscian and *agent provocateur*, targetted not only the Establishment but his rock and roll peers

Indications of trouble to come first appear on a song/sketch concerning the Edgewater Inn, Seattle, in which the band Zeppelin were backing on the 1970 tour are actually named: "Let's say you're a big rock band...called the Vanilla Fudge..." The oft-told story ensues, building up to 'The Mudshark', a majestic piece of pseudo pomp-rock ("I'm a steamer baby, goin' to ream right up your slit") variously seen by aficionados as a three-pronged attack on Vanilla Fudge, The Doors and, of course, Led Zeppelin. The business soon segues into the similar "What Kind Of Girl Do You Think We Are?", a song/sketch about groupies, when Volman, being pestered for weird sex by rock'n'roll star Kaylan, announces: "We are NOT groupies! I told Jeff Beck that, I told Robert Plant it...I told all those big guys". Its appearance in Zappa's show evidenced that Cole's story was pretty common knowledge by that point.

To what extent Zappa felt his own considerable virtuosity as a guitarist, his often unabashed liking for "heavy" guitar effects, and his aspirations towards the orchestral in rock, were threatened in any way by Jimmy Page and the boys can now only be a matter for speculation.

music" landscape, in 1971 Zappa's steely gaze focussed on the exponents of the new "heavy" sound. *The Mothers [Live At The] Fillmore East June 1971* captured much of the content of that year's tour, which featured extensive semi-improvised scatalogical verbal exchanges between ex-Turtles Howard Kaylan and Mark Volman ("The Florescent Leech and Eddie").

Ten Tales of Zep Excess

There are, of course, many more than ten tales of Led Zeppelin's more colourful adventures, many of which have been covered in The Story chapters earlier in this book. Some approach such a level of mythic legend that one is tempted to disbelieve them, and there is no doubt that, over the years, the stories have become increasingly elaborated and exaggerated in the telling. It would verge on the criminal, however, not to list their most notorious exploits as a matter for posterity.

1. THE SHARK EPISODE

Edgewater Inn, Seattle, May 1969

When the British tabloid newspaper *The Sun* broke a story about "a young lady who is said to have been whipped by [with] a live octopus", a matter-of-fact John Paul Jones remarked: "I don't think that's entirely true. As far as I can remember it was a dead shark". Thus was one of the most notorious tales of Zeppelin rock'n'roll Babylon first revealed. The incident took place at the Edgewater Inn, Seattle where it was possible to catch fish from the hotel room balconies out of the ocean below. One night, road manager Richard Cole and John Bonham tied a 17-year-old redhead from Portland to the bed and proceeded to insert the shark-like fish they had caught earlier into her vagina and rectum. The proceedings were allegedly filmed by Mark Stein of Vanilla Fudge (whom Zeppelin were backing on this tour). Cole later claimed the fish were not sharks but "red snappers". The alleged incident was both seized upon and immortalized by Frank Zappa and friends on *The Mothers Fillmore East June 1971*.

2. OCTOPUSSY

Pasadena, May 1969

Despite Jones' protestations, there may be some truth in the octopus story. After playing two dates at the Rose Palace in Pasadena, for some bizarre reason Zeppelin were given four live octopuses by promoter Barry Imhoff. Back at the hotel, Page persuaded two young groupies to take a bath, threw the creatures in with them, and settled back to enjoy the show.

3. BONZO BARED

Flushing Meadows, New York, July 1969

Having already wrecked Ten Years After's set by dousing guitarist Alvin Lee mid-solo, an extremely drunk Bonham then hi-jacked Jeff Beck's set by running on stage and stripping completely naked. The police arrived on stage to arrest him but Bonham was rugby-tackled and dragged off by Grant, who locked him in a dressing room before an arrest could be made.

4. THE ART OF VANDALISM

Copenhagen, February 1970

Having had to play a gig as The Nobs after a descendant of the von Zeppelin family had threatened legal action over the use of the name, the band were taken to a Danish art gallery where the record company had organized a reception. Former art student Jimmy Page announced that the modernist abstractions hanging on the gallery walls were "bullshit" and took out his magic marker and added his own embellishments to three of the offending paintings. Allegedly, the gallery owner failed to notice the full extent of the vandalism and the band were only asked to pay for one redesigned "masterpiece".

5. THE MEN GET THEIR MOUNTIE

Vancouver, March 1970

Spotting someone holding a microphone in the audience, Peter Grant and a couple of Zeppelin roadies decided to teach the bootlegger a lesson. Dragging him backstage, Grant smashed his equipment and gave the miscreant a good kicking. Except that he wasn't a tape pirate at all, but a Canadian local government official checking decibel levels. Grant was charged

with assault and was unable to return to Canada for several years. Naturally enough, Bonham's response to his manager's arrest was to smash up his hotel room in protest.

6. THE SAMURAI SLASHERS

Tokyo, September 1971

After buying two Samurai swords from the gift shop in the Tokyo Hilton, Bonham and Cole then used them to chop down the door of John Paul Jones' room. The bass player was comatose and didn't even wake when they carried him out into the corridor and proceeded to chop everything in his room into splinters with their new blades. As a result the entire band was banned from the Hilton chain for life (not that it worried them overmuch). Further mayhem followed when the band got into a fight on an overnight ride on the famous "bullet train", which was then plastered all over the front pages of the Japanese papers.

7. GROUPIE CENTRAL

Los Angeles, June 1972

It was always said that Jimmy Page liked younger girls – and they didn't come much younger than the 14-year-old child model Lori Maddox. After meeting Richard Cole one night at the Rainbow Bar & Grill in LA, she was taken to Continental Hyatt House on Sunset Strip (affectionately known by Zeppelin and other touring rock bands as the "Riot House"), apparently for a secret assignation with the guitarist. No question of sending her "back-to-schoolin'": Lori would stay with Page on-and-off on the band's US tours for the next 18 months. Grant insisted that she was kept locked in a hotel room with a security guard on the door, fearing that if Page was caught with her, he may have difficulty gaining any further US work permits.

8. TVS A GO-GO (AND THE SNOOKER TABLE,TOO)

Seattle, June 1972

By their eighth American tour, throwing colour TV sets out of hotel windows was routine, but when Zeppelin were around it became infectious. When Grant came to settle the bill for their usual mayhem at the long-suffering Edgewater Inn, the hotel manager confessed to a secret desire to join in the TV-hurling. Grant promptly peeled off $500 dollars in crisp bank notes and told him: "Have one on us". The manager allegedly went upstairs and heaved one off the balcony. In LA the following year, Bonham was to go one better by somehow launching a snooker table off the eleventh floor after those below had the audacity to complain about glasses being thrown.

9. MOTORCYCLE MADNESS

Los Angeles, June 1973

After the band had once again taken the entire ninth floor of the Continental Hyatt House hotel on Sunset, Page decided he wanted to try out a new Japanese motorcycle. Tour manager Richard Cole went out to buy one and then rode it through the hotel lobby and into the elevator. Page and other members of the band's entourage then spent all night racing it up and down the corridors. By this time, Jones had had enough of such shenanigans and his hotel bookings wisely specified that his room had to be two floors away from the rest of the band.

10. BEATING UP THE PROMOTER

San Francisco, June 1977

Playing the first of two nights at the Oakland Stadium, Bonham attacked one of promoter Bill Graham's security men after seeing him push Peter Grant's son, Warren. Grant and John Bindon, head of Zeppelin's personal security, then took the guard to an empty trailer and beat him so badly that he required hospitalization. An uneasy truce prevailed the following night, but the next morning Bonham, Bindon and Grant were arrested – Graham had delayed filing charges so as not to risk losing income from a cancelled second show. All three were found guilty of assault and given suspended sentences.

Zeppelin Stopovers: Ten Key Sites

The four members of Led Zeppelin came from radically different backgrounds in Greater London and the West Midlands and their formative years and the circumstances in which they grew up are dealt with in the first section of this book. The ten sites listed here are all associated with the band after they came together as Led Zeppelin in 1968...

The Thames Boathouse, Pangbourne, Berkshire

The boathouse once owned by Jimmy Page on the River Thames at Pangbourne was put on the market in 2007. Listed by estate agents as The Thames Boathouse, it was here that Robert Plant was staying in the summer of 1968, when Page formally invited him to join the "new Yardbirds" – or Led Zeppelin, as they were soon to become known.

As its name suggests, the property was originally a boathouse built over a wet dock. Owned since Victorian times by Hobbs of Henley, its sole purpose was the hiring and maintaining of river craft until 1959, when the property was converted into a private dwelling with a 40-foot river mooring. Page bought the boathouse in 1967 and sold the property in 1973. In 2000, the owners converted the base-ment, where the wet dock had once been, into a heated indoor swimming pool and undertook other substantial improvements.

Bron-yr-aur, Gwynned, Wales

Read the small print of the liner notes to *Led Zeppelin III* and you will find the following dedication: "Credit must be given to BRON-Y-AUR, a small derelict cottage in South Snowdonia for painting a somewhat forgotten picture of true completeness which acted as an incentive to some of these musical statements".

The cottage is on a hilltop looking south over the Dyfi Valley towards the town of Machynlleth in Powys, Wales, (although the cottage lies in the neighbouring county of Gwynned). It is the most visited site on any Zeppelin pilgrimage, and hundreds of fans seek it out every year. Plant had known the place from his boyhood, when his family rented it for summer holidays, and it was here that he and Page stayed in May 1970 to write material for Zeppelin's third album. At the time the cottage had no electricity, gas or running water and the Zep men had to trek to the Glyndwr Hotel in Machynlleth for a weekly bath.

Commemorated in the song 'Bron-y-aur Stomp' (sic) on *Led Zeppelin III* and 'Bron-yr-aur' on *Physical Graffiti*, the cottage was renovated some years ago and is reportedly now owned by Plant – which would explain why he and Page were able to return in 1994 to write material for their *No Quarter/Unledded* project. Plant also wrote material there for his 2005 album, *The Mighty Rearranger*.

The Welsh name Bron-yr-aur translates as "breast of gold" or "hill of gold".

Headley Grange, Hampshire

Headley Grange in the village of Headley, east Hampshire is where Led Zeppelin recorded regularly during the early 1970s and, most famously, where one night sitting around a log fire, Robert Plant wrote the lyrics to 'Stairway To Heaven'.

The place has a fascinating history. Built as a workhouse in 1795 at an estimated cost of £1,500 to shelter the infirm, aged paupers, orphan and illegitimate children of the parish, it was originally known as the "House of Industry". On 23 November 1830, a mob of rioters estimated at around 1,000 strong, sacked the place. Seven men were sentenced to transportation for their part in the riot. After the building had been repaired, it continued to be used as a

workhouse, until it was sold in 1870 for £420 to a builder, who converted it into a private house and renamed it Headley Grange.

After the conversion, the house was sold in 1872 for £490 and was occupied by just three owners over the next 90 years. Theophilus Sigismund Hahn lived there from 1872 until his death in 1907, aged 83. The Grange was then transferred to Colonel Francis Frederic Perry, who lived there until his death in 1939, aged 85. After the Second World War, the house was bought by Lieutenant-Colonel Michael Smith, whose family lived there until his death in 1961. His widow then let the house and it was used for a number of years as a hostel for students from Farnham School of Art, before being let out.

During the 1970s, Led Zeppelin were not the only rock band to take up residence and Genesis and Bad Company also worked there using a mobile recording truck. The drawing room was used as the main recording room, due to its perfect acoustics, although Bonham's drums on 'When The Levee Breaks' were famously recorded in the stairwell. The house is now a private residence but reportedly still contains the piano that was in the house when Zeppelin rented it.

Boleskine House, Highland, Scotland

Once the home of pseudo-occultist and hedonist Aleister "The Beast" Crowley, who infamously used the property to practise magical ceremonies, Jimmy Page bought Boleskine House in 1971. Set amid rugged Highland scenery a mile north-east of the Scottish village of Foyers close to the southern shores of Loch Ness, the house was built in the late 18th century by Archibald Fraser. According to local legend, a church once stood on the site, but this was burnt to the ground with the entire congregation trapped inside. Other macabre stories are also attached to the house, which was owned by Crowley in the early decades of the 20th century. It was Page's interest in the magician that led him to purchase the house and the grounds of the house were the location for some of the fantasy scenes in the film *The Song Remains The Same*. Page seems to have revelled in the place's ill-repute, regaling visitors with ghoulish stories of its history. Crowley's taste for narcotics may have also played a part in Page's interest. After he sold Boleskine in 1992, it was run for a while as a guest house offering bed and breakfast, but is now a private residence.

Plumpton Place, East Sussex

For many years, Robert Plant has lived contentedly on his farm in the Midlands and maintains only a modest London town house in Camden. Jimmy Page, however, has enjoyed the rock star country mansion trip to the hilt. He purchased the Elizabethan manor house Plumpton Place near Lewes in East Sussex in the early 1970s, and immediately installed a recording studio there. *In Through The Out Door* was mixed at Plumpton and the property

can also be seen briefly in the film *The Song Remains The Same* in the scene in which Page plays a hurdy-gurdy.

The grounds contain a water mill built by the Earl of Chichester in 1802, which remained operational until 1916. The Earl is also said to have placed the first carp introduced into England into Plumpton Place moat. The manor house and gardens were remodelled in 1927 by Sir Edwin Lutyens for the then owner Edward Hudson, the founder of the magazine *Country Life*. The Sussex Gardens Trust occasionally organizes visits to the gardens.

Tower House, Kensington, London

Jimmy Page's London home since 1974 has been Tower House in Melbury Road, Kensington. The late-Victorian building was built (for himself) in medieval Gothic Revival style by the Victorian architect William Burges in the 1870s. Burges completed the building by 1878 and then took charge of the interior design. Many of the original features are still preserved in the house, but Burges had little time to enjoy his home as he died in 1881. Page purchased the house from the actor Richard Harris. The property is now estimated to be worth around £10 million.

Stargroves, Hampshire

Led Zeppelin recorded *Houses Of The Holy* and parts of *Physical Graffiti* at Stargroves, renting the country house at East End, Hampshire, a few miles south-west of Newbury, Berkshire, from Mick Jagger. The Rolling Stones also recorded much of *Sticky Fingers* at the house and The Who cut the classic 'Won't Get Fooled Again' there. Jagger bought Stargroves complete with 37 acres of gardens and parkland for £25,000 in 1970, his interest allegedly aroused by an estate agent's claim that Oliver Cromwell had used the house as a Civil War field headquarters, although there is no historical evidence for this. The house was in need of improvement but Jagger never spent a great deal of time there, although Marianne Faithfull for a brief while took some interest in the gardens. Jagger subsequently sold the property and the current owners recently undertook a major programme of renovations, which won a conservation award for best restoration of an historic building in 2005. The house was also used for filming episodes of the BBC series *Doctor Who*, featuring the actor Tom Baker.

Rushock, Worcestershire

The final resting place of Led Zeppelin's drummer lies in a small cemetery at Rushock church, near Kidderminster. It is not easy to find, but driving south from Kidderminster towards Droitwich on the A442 you turn left into a narrow country lane that is marked with a sign saying "Rushock Church". At the top of the lane turn right, then almost immediately left and follow the curving, single-track road for two-thirds of a mile until you see the church. The grave is easily located and the stone bears an inscription from his wife Pat which reads:

"He will always be remembered in our hearts. Goodnight, my love. God bless". The stone is often scattered with drumsticks left in tribute by Zeppelin fans.

The Hyatt Hotel, West Hollywood

On their first trip to Los Angeles over Christmas 1968, Led Zeppelin stayed at the Chateau Marmont, but on all their subsequent visits to the city they stayed at The Hyatt West Hollywood, half a mile further west down Sunset Boulevard. It was here that many of the most legendary tales of Zep-excess took place, the management taking a lenient view of their behaviour, since Peter Grant was always ready to pay up for any damage and destruction in cash.

When on tour, Zeppelin rented as many as six floors of the hotel in the mid-to-late 1970s for the band members and entourage. Scenes in Cameron Crowe's 2000 film *Almost Famous*, based loosely on the antics of Led Zeppelin, were filmed at the hotel, refurbished for the occasion with original 1970s decor. The end-of-tour party scene in Rob Reiner's 1983 film *This Is Spinal Tap* was filmed on the roof of the hotel and in Stephen Herek's 2002 film *Rock Star*, the character played by John Bonham's son Jason is seen throwing a TV out of one of one of the Hyatt's windows. In real life, in addition to Led Zeppelin, Keith Richards and Keith Moon are also reported at different times to have indulged in acts of TV-hurling.

The Hyatt Hotel, West Hollywood, or "Riot House", perches over Sunset Boulevard between, to the east, the Chateau Marmont, and to the west the Whisky a Go Go

Originally called the Gene Autry Hotel a when it opened in 1958, it was renamed the Continental Hyatt House in the mid-1960s. Its popularity with touring rock bands was based on its close proximity to popular clubs on Sunset Strip such as the Whisky a Go Go, and its *laissez-faire* attitude towards its clients' unconventional behaviour led to the hotel becoming known among the rock'n'roll fraternity as the "Riot House". It was here that Richard Cole once drove a motorcycle around the hotel corridors one night.

Despite advertising itself as "the rock'n'roll hotel", today the Hyatt exudes a somewhat bland corporatism, although until recently the building housed a restaurant called Chi, which was part-owned by the singer Justin Timberlake.

The Edgewater (Inn), Seattle

Second only to the "Riot House" on Sunset Strip in Zeppelin mythology as a scene of on-the-road debauchery is The Edgewater Inn, Seattle. Its reputation is largely due to being the location of the infamous shark/red snapper episode, but it was used by the band on every tour of America after Richard Cole had discovered it whilst on a tour with Terry Reid and The Moody Blues. Situated on a pier at the north end of the waterfront, its attraction as the only hotel situated directly on the bay is obvious and it was designed to resemble a deluxe fishing lodge. On a clear day, the Olympic Mountains can be seen across Puget Sound, while the best rooms are done out as mountain lodges with rustic fireplaces and pine furniture. The hotel doesn't advertise a "shark room" in commemoration of Zeppelin's most notoriously debauched on-the-road episode, but it does offer the chance to stay in the suites occupied by The Beatles in 1964.

Zeppology

Zeppelin Across The Media

A phenomenon as huge as Led Zeppelin naturally provokes millions of words of history, hagiography and criticism. Nevertheless, as they disbanded over a quarter of a century ago, they are now probably best approached as a subject worthy of social and cultural history. The DVD age has made this increasingly possible, by providing access to more footage of them performing live.

In Print

While none of the band members have committed themselves to print in memoirs or autobiographies, ghost-written or otherwise (and indeed even the lyrics of their songs, with one honourable exception, were not printed on album sleeves), their many interviews with this author among others have provided grist to a veritable publishing mill. Not to mention the abundance of stories, myths and legends that the twelve-year Zeppelin flight left in its wake.

LED ZEPPELIN: THE DEFINITIVE BIOGRAPHY

Ritchie Yorke (1974, revised 1993)

The first into hard covers to chronicle the Led Zeppelin phenomenon was Canadian writer and broadcaster Ritchie Yorke. With the distinct advantage of knowing the band and enjoying their confidence (he introduced them on stage at every one of their five Toronto performances over the years), Yorke's book has provided the platform for all subsequent Zep-scholarship. There's rather too much of the "buddy-to-the-stars" school of journalism, but he was genuinely there and his judgements remain largely objective, although he's perhaps guilty of being a little too veiled over the excesses of the road, which are alluded to but not described. Nevertheless, when the book was substantially updated and revised in 1993, its common sense and sobriety seemed oddly welcome after the salaciousness of Stephen Davis and Richard Cole's books (see below).

LED ZEPPELIN IN THEIR OWN WORDS

Ed. Paul Kendall and Dave Lewis (1981, updated 1995)

For a band who were famously suspicious of the Press, Zeppelin's four members were actually quite loquacious – and were certainly far more accessible to the Press than bands of similar stature today. Through direct quotes without any commentary, the story is told chronologically and subject-by-subject, with Plant by far the most eloquent of the four. The one drawback is that none of the quotes are dated, so it's not always clear if band members are speaking at the time or with the benefit of hindsight.

HAMMER OF THE GODS

Stephen Davis (1985; updated 1995)

Most of Davis's biographies, which include books on the Stones and Jim Morrison, have deliberately courted controversy by concentrating on the sordid, sleazy side of rock'n'roll. But with the band's former tour manager Richard Cole as his "deep throat", in *Hammer Of The Gods* Davis hit an all-time high – or low, depending on how you look at it. Most of the more notorious stories of Zep's debauchery began here, and if band members can pick holes in the accuracy of some of the more salacious detail, nobody has denied the broad thrust, if you will forgive the phrase.

LED ZEPPELIN: A CELEBRATION

Dave Lewis (1991)

Editor of the Zeppelin fanzine *Tight But Loose* for many years, Dave Lewis's enthusiasm and knowledge is legendary and his *Celebration* is a must-have compendium of fact and analysis. Profiles, album-by-album, chronology, discography and much more besides are all here, lovingly assembled by the music's Number One fan. With so much of what is written about Led Zeppelin indulging in cheap sensationalism, the band are lucky to have such an assiduous, dedicated and constructive chronicler. Respect.

STAIRWAY TO HEAVEN

Richard Cole (1992)

Having spilled all his best stories to Stephen Davis in *Hammer Of The Gods*, Richard Cole came back seven years later with a semi-ghost written account of much the same material under his own name. Nobody knows where the bodies are buried better than Cole, and he tells his tale with relish. How much of it is true, who knows? If those who were there with him at the time consumed even a fraction of the drink and drugs that he says they did, then none of them could have been in a fit condition to remember. Yet Cole himself claims perfect recall, recounting alleged conversations at two decades distance and reporting them in direct speech. Even if much of it is questionable, it all makes for a great read.

IN THE HOUSES OF THE HOLY: LED ZEPPELIN AND THE POWER OF ROCK MUSIC

Susan Fast (2001)

Not a biography but, rather, a musicological dissertation in deconstructing rock'n'roll riffs. Fast isn't interested in how many groupies Led Zeppelin laid; she's far keener in telling us how many diminished sevenths they laid down. At times the acuteness of her analysis disappears in impenetrable jargon ("Just under the surface of the melodic and rhythmic squareness is a harmonic and formal openness and irregularity that is highly significant in terms of the semiotics of the piece"). Fortunately it's not all as dense as that and although her approach is rigorously academic, many of her insights on subjects such as the creation of myth and the use of ritual in rock music, and the band's appropriation of Eastern music and the blues, are informative and rewarding.

WHEN THE LEVEE BREAKS: THE MAKING OF *LED ZEPPELIN IV*

Andy Fyfe (2003)

As the fourth biggest-selling album of all time it's unsurprising that authors have tended to concentrate on Led Zeppelin's fourth album. Former *NME* writer Andy Fyfe's book is a workmanlike affair that not only tells the story of the fourth album, but offers plenty of before and after context. There's a tendency to unsupportable overwrought phrases ("…with its fourth album Led Zeppelin helped to give rock music immortality…") and you have to wonder about the judgement of a writer who reckons that "the most obvious parallel acts to Led Zeppelin were Black Sabbath and Deep Purple", which is akin to comparing a *premier cru* from Bordeaux with a cheap merlot from Bulgaria. Even more bizarre is his claim that, in the 1980s, Kiss "…advanced heavy rock nearly as much as Led Zeppelin had before them." Such *faux-pas* aside, however, the book marshals the obvious sources well and presents them attractively.

LED ZEPPELIN: THE CONCERT FILE

Dave Lewis with Simon Pallett (2005)

The estimable Dave Lewis strikes again with a splendid gig-by-gig account with set-lists where available. Yet it's far more than just the concert file suggested in the title: in chronicling their tour and stage performances, Lewis in many ways gives a more comprehensive picture of the band and their development than an analysis of the snapshots that are their ten albums could do. He also takes the story on into 2005 with details of the solo appearances of all three surviving members. Invaluable.

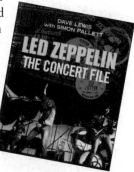

LED ZEPPELIN: DAZED AND CONFUSED: THE STORIES BEHIND EVERY SONG

Chris Welch (2005)

Part of a successful series published by Carlton that now covers most of rock's major figures, when it came to turning the spotlight on the songs on Zeppelin's ten albums, there was no better choice than Welch. Writing for *Melody Maker* in the late 1960s, he championed the band from the outset, when Zeppelin were being derided or just plain ignored by the rest of the British music press. Welch reviewed most of the albums at the time of their release and, bringing to bear all of his long personal history with the band, his analysis is revealing and his judgement sound, although the format of the series of which the book is part has its limitations.

LED ZEPPELIN: THE STORY OF A BAND AND THEIR MUSIC 1968–80

Keith Shadwick (2005)

Shadwick is a musician himself, and writes widely about jazz and classical music as well as rock, so his breadth of musical knowledge gives this book a distinct advantage over many of its competitors. He tells the story of the band's twelve-year existence in highly readable style, but the best aspect of this rather good coffee-table volume is his detailed analysis of the band's music. The approach is musically literate without becoming

academic and fussy: the bridge section after the first two verses of 'Stairway To Heaven', he tells us, is made up of "luminescent A minor sevenths in banks of 12-string guitars and organ pedal tones." It's just enough information without becoming laboured. Sometimes his conclusions are surprising and perhaps far-fetched, such as his comparison between Plant's wail at the start of 'Immigrant Song' and 'Bali Hi' from the musical *South Pacific*. Yet whether he's right or wrong, such observations are never less than fascinating, and his readiness to offer firm opinions that sometimes swim against the tide rather than simply repeating received Zep-wisdom is refreshing.

IF WE ALL CALL THE TUNE: THE STORY OF *LED ZEPPELIN IV*, THE GREATEST HARD ROCK ALBUM OF ALL TIME

Barney Hoskyns (2006)

You can argue with the second half of this book's title (the album was surely so much *more* than that), but not with the quality of Hoskyns' lucid writing or the thoroughness of his research. Like Andy Fyfe's book on the same subject, Hoskyns does far more than tell the story of one album, setting it in the wider context of Zeppelin's career. All the key quotes are assembled and the facts are marshalled superbly, supported by the writer's own astute assessments. If you only want one of the two books about *Led Zeppelin IV* reviewed here, Hoskyns wins over Fyfe by some distance.

THE ORIGIN OF THE SPECIES: LED ZEPPELIN, HOW, WHY AND WHERE IT ALL BEGAN

Alan Clayson (2006)

The prolific Clayson recounts the pre-1968 tale of the four musicians who would become Led Zeppelin with great gusto, combining a prose style full of verve with an encyclopaedic knowledge of 1960s British pop, a subject on which he could probably win a round of TV's *Mastermind*. Not only do we learn about the formative events and influences that made the band, but Clayson also gives us a terrific insight into the era and how British pop music moved from Cliff Richard to Led Zeppelin in the space of one tumultuous decade. His style is a sheer joy, too: where else can you read a discussion of the influence of Bert Weedon on British rock guitar that quotes Baudelaire?

PETER GRANT: THE MAN WHO LED ZEPPELIN

Chris Welch (2006)

The back story of Peter Grant is a fascinating sub-text to the Zeppelin narrative and, as ever, Welch tells it with great professionalism. There are plenty of stories about the band, of course. But the book offers far more than simply the same old Zep tales refracted through the experiences of their manager, with lots of little-known background to topics that tend to merit just a paragraph in the standard band biographies, such as the suspended prison sentence, Grant's retirement from the music industry, and his heroin addiction. An insider who knew him well, Welch paints a compelling picture of an extraordinarily complex man, although by the end the enigma in many ways remains intact.

JOHN BONHAM

Mick Bonham (2006)

"By the man who knew him best – his brother", is the boast of this soft-hearted portrait. That means there isn't much about "the beast", the wild man whose behaviour on tour with Led Zeppelin grew increasingly out-of-control and frequently crossed the line from the merely loutish to the unacceptably abusive. Instead, his brother concentrates on a man  who away from the band was by all accounts warm and generous, and there are plenty of appealing anecdotes from his childhood told not only with obvious affection but with considerable wit and humour as well.

On Screen

There is remarkably little footage readily available today of the band in full flight. Early TV appearances have often been lost (or more appallingly, destroyed along with mountains of other "popular culture" material deemed unworthy of archiving by the likes of the BBC).

THE SONG REMAINS THE SAME (1976)

Pretentious self-indulgence or one of the best concert films of the1970s? Led Zeppelin fans still argue over the matter, but it really requires a blinkered loyalty above and beyond the call of duty to find anything worthwhile to say about *The Song Remains The Same*. The initial idea to film Led Zeppelin in full tilt over three nights at Madison Square Garden in New York in July 1973 was a sound one, although insufficient planning went into the logistics and as a result, some of the on-stage scenes later had to be recreated at Shepperton studios. The band were exhausted at the end of a long and gruelling tour and, by Jimmy Page's own admission, they did not play anything like their best. In particular, Plant's voice was in poor shape. But they were still good enough: they were Led Zeppelin, the greatest rock'n'roll band in the world, after all. But unfortunately, rather than a straight in-concert film, rock star narcissism then took over with the decision to add fantasy sequences, an idea based on the improbable role model of the 1972 T. Rex film, *Born To Boogie*.

Each member was allowed to "script" their own segment. Bonham had the good sense to be filmed more or less as he was – a down-to-earth working-class lad who is seen driving his Harley Davidson motor bike, drag racing at Santa Pod and beaming contentedly with his family and on his farm. The rest frankly made utter fools of themselves. John Paul Jones' scene involved him dressing as a masked highwayman in a pantomine Phantom of the Opera costume. Plant indulged his Knights of the Round Table fantasies as he stormed a castle single-handedly to rescue a witless damsel is distress and Page went in for some very un-magical wizardry and sorcery, rooted in his Aleister Crowley obsession. The scenes are lent even more of a silent movies/Keystone cops comicality by the absence of dialogue as the band woodenly act out these lame vignettes to music from the Madison Square Garden performances. Even manager Peter Grant insisted on getting in on the act, and the film's opening sequence portrays him and tour manager Richard Cole dressed as 1920s gangsters.

Flawed doesn't even begin to describe it. The non-musical sequences were slated by critics at the time and historical perspective has done nothing to redeem them. The best parts of the film are all at Madison Square Garden, but even the onstage performances are marred by being mixed with some uncomfortable looking re-shoots from Shepperton. Best forgotten.

LED ZEPPELIN: THE DVD (2003)

After the disappointments of *The Song Remains The Same*, a visual record that did justice to the power and the glory that was Led Zeppelin live finally appeared 23 years after the band had split. Over two discs with a total running time of five hours and twenty minutes, the Led Zeppelin DVD showcases the band across a ten-year period and it is quite fascinating to track their development from the Albert Hall in 1970 to Knebworth in 1979. In between, we also get film of Earl's Court 1975, including the acoustic segment of the show, and four tracks from Madison Square Garden in 1973, originally filmed by for *The Song Remains The Same*. Intriguing extras include a New York press conference, Plant being interviewed by Bob Harris on BBC 2's latenight *The Old Grey Whistle Test*, some rare early television performances, and grainy bootleg footage sent in by fans.

Culled from thousands of yards of previously unseen film and audio tape, both sound and vision are excellent due to some painstaking restoration and remastering by Jimmy Page and co-producer Dick Carruthers working hand-in-glove with Page. On its release, it broke all sales records for a music DVD – and deservedly so.

Websites

Conveniently, many of the numerous Led Zeppelin websites can now be connected via the homepage at The Ring of Zeppelin (www.crickrock.com/cgi-bin/webring/list.pl?ringid=zepring). The Ring lists 84 different sites which can be accessed by a single click, although a number of them are not devoted to Led Zeppelin, but to tribute bands. Here, however, are ten of the best Zeppelin-related sites, all of which we referred to during the course of researching and writing this book.

ACHILLES' LAST STAND

www.led-zeppelin.org
News, biographies, discographies, song tablatures, "this month in Zeppelin history" and a photo archive.

ELECTRIC MAGIC

www.led-zeppelin.com/home.html
Good-looking, officially-endorsed site with the best up-to-the-minute news coverage, discography, lyrics, biographies and photo galleries.

ROBERT PLANT OFFICAL SITE

www.robertplant.com
The official site, concentrating on Plant today rather than his history. A photo gallery with shots from recent shows and guest appearances, a file of press reports and news of forthcoming activity are all updated regularly.

BUCKEYE'S LED ZEPPELIN PAGE

www.oldbuckeye.com
Reputedly the oldest Zeppelin website, established in 1994. A host of useful stuff, including pictures, interviews and a discussion group.

HOUSES OF THE HOLY

http://trublukris.tripod.com/cristopolo/lz.html
More than 60 archived interviews, album reviews and lists of live tapes, with an invitation to trade.

LED ZEPPELIN LIVE

www.stryder.de
News and all the usual features, but most useful for the most comprehensive listings of bootlegs anywhere to be found.

NOW AND ZEN

www.users.globalnet.co.uk/~liden/plant.html
Excellent unofficial site dedicated to all aspects of Robert Plant's solo career.

MANIC NIRVANA

www.manicnirvana.com
Another good Plant solo site, nicely presented.

JIMMY PAGE ONLINE

www.jimmypageonline.com
Jimmy Page doesn't have an official site but this unofficial version fills the vacuum well enough. At the time of writing, its lead new item was that Page is yet again promising that 2007 will be the year when he finally gets around to recording his next solo album.

JOHN PAUL JONES

www.johnpauljones.com
A well-maintained offical site that covers his entire career, complete with a personal blog updated by JPJ himself, on an irregular basis.

Legacy: Zep Cover Versions

GOOD TIMES: 10 OF THE BEST

Great songs attract great covers, as no doubt Led Zeppelin themselves would have admitted (*pace* Willie Dixon, Sonny Boy Williamson, Howlin' Wolf *et al*). Talking of which, British punk/R&B crossover band Nine Below Zero's version of 'I Can't Quit You Baby' (available on 1980's *Live At The Marquee*) is also worth checking out.

1. Yat-Kha

When The Levee Breaks

Available on *Recovers* (2005)
Zep-blues done Tuvan throat-singing style.

2. Tina Turner

Whole Lotta Love

Available on *The Collected Recordings – Sixties To Nineties* (1994).

3. Jeff Buckley

Kashmir

Available on *Live At l'Olympia* (2001).

4. Tori Amos

Thank You

Available on the EP *Crucify* (1992).

5. Jerry Lee Lewis

Rock And Roll

Available on *Last Man Standing* (2006). With Jimmy Page guesting on guitar.

6. 4 Non Blondes

Misty Mountain Hop

Available on *Encomium: A Tribute To Led Zeppelin* (1995).

7. Ofra Haza

Kashmir

Available on *Ofra Haza Greatest Hits Vol. 2* (2004). The late, great Israeli singer's cover, which first appeared on a single in 1994.

8. Stone Temple Pilots

Dancing Days

Available on *Encomium: A Tribute To Led Zeppelin* (1995).

9. Frank Zappa

Stairway to Heaven

Available on *The Best Band You Never Heard In Your Life* (1991). A live version featuring a note-for-note copy of Page's guitar solo played by the horn section.

10. Ramble On

Iron Horse

Available on *Whole Lotta Bluegrass: A Bluegrass Tribute to Led Zeppelin* (2005).

BAD TIMES: 10 OF THE WORST

Most of these are really dreadful, despite Dread Zeppelin's astonishingly surreal contribution, which is/was available on their eponymous album, that it is better that we don't tell you where they are available… hopefully, most aren't.

1. Rolf Harris

Stairway To Heaven

Harris first performed the song on the TV show *The Money Or The Gun* in 1993 (one of 28 versions of the song by different artists). Since his appearances at the Glastonbury festival, this has become something of a cult hit. Whether Rolf gets the joke is a different matter.

2. Dread Zeppelin

Heartbreaker (Heartbreak Hotel)

The best (or worst) track on a truly bizarre album of Zep/Elvis covers.

3. Sandie Shaw

Your Time Is Gonna Come

It did, and fortunately it went.

Tribute Bands

There are numerous Led Zeppelin tribute bands out there with such daft names as Led Zepplica, Fred Zeppelin, Whole Lotta Led, Stairway To Zeppelin and even a reggae band called Dread Zeppelin fronted by an Elvis Presley imitator (see 'Heartbreaker/ Heartbreak Hotel' above). But our favourite has to be the preposterously pun-tastic Lez Zeppelin, an all-lesbian Zep tribute act whose proud boast is that they "gleefully invert the band's original sexual essence". At the time of writing they were reported to be recording an album of gender-bending Zep covers with the band's former engineer Eddie Kramer. Like just about everything else in the Led Zeppelin story, you couldn't make it up.

4. The Bobs

Whole Lotta Love

The *a capella* version...

5. CCS

Whole Lotta Love

...and the instrumental version, used as the theme for the BBC's chart show *Top of the Pops*.

6. Heart

Rock And Roll

A bandwagon rider, simply horribly done.

7. Sheryl Crow

D'yer Mak 'er

Of course, she should know better but, as so often, her yearning to seem tom-boyishly raunchy outstripped her judgement.

8. London Philharmonic Orchestra

Kashmir

Unfortunately, Page's ambitious arrangements made certain Zeppelin tracks sitting ducks for orchestral pops...

9. Classic Rock String Quartet

Dazed And Confused

...as again here. Although not an obvious choice, it has to be said.

10. Dolly Parton

Stairway To Heaven

'Nuff said.

And finally, some useful advice from Atlantic Records, which appeared on the back of the first Led Zeppelin album: "This stereo record can be played on mono gramophones without loss of musical quality provided a stereo cartridge wired for mono sound is fitted...Your dealer will be able to advise you further if necessary". But, of course, the Stones had pipped Zeppelin to the post with some much more succinct advice which appeared on the sleeve of *Let It Bleed*: "To be played loud".

Index

Index

Index

Index

Available from all good bookstores

D: Rough Guide
DIRECTIONS for
short breaks

ROUGH
GUIDE

Rough Guides presents...

"Achieves the perfect balance between learned recommendation and needless trivia"
Uncut Magazine reviewing Cult Movies

Other Rough Guide Film & TV titles include:

American Independent Film • British Cult Comedy • Chick Flicks • Comedy Movies
Cult Movies • Film • Film Musicals • Film Noir • Gangster Movies • Horror Movies
Kids' Movies • Sci-Fi Movies • Westerns

BROADEN YOUR HORIZONS